S0-BJG-984

907.204
F53s
68648

DATE DUE

GAYLORD M-2   PRINTED IN U.S.A.

STUDIES

in

HISTORY and POLITICS

STUDIES

in

HISTORY and POLITICS

By

The Right Honourable

HERBERT FISHER

Essay Index Reprint Series

BOOKS FOR LIBRARIES PRESS, INC.
FREEPORT, NEW YORK

First Published 1920
Reprinted 1967

LIBRARY OF CONGRESS CATALOG CARD NUMBER: 67-26740

PRINTED IN THE UNITED STATES OF AMERICA

PREFACE

IF within the modest circle of my readers there be those who surmise that these essays have been composed during the ample leisure of official life, let me hasten to disabuse their innocence. No such golden moments of lettered ease sweeten the austere labours of a member of His Majesty's administration, for though in the present crisis of the public nerves it would be unfashionable to assume that he (or any one else) earns his salary, it remains a sombre fact that for a Minister of the Crown an eight-hour day is a luxury beyond the wildest dreams of avarice. The papers, then, which have been here gathered together, belong to a previous, and more tranquil, stage of my existence, albeit one has been published and others have received some fresh critical touches since I was called upon to address myself to public affairs. The first, third, fifth, and sixth papers were brought out in the *Quarterly Review*, the second in the *Edinburgh Review*, the fourth in the *Contemporary Review*, the eighth in the *Hibbert Journal*. The paper on ' Imperial Administration ' was read at King's College and has been published by Messrs. Macmillan in a volume entitled *The Empire and the Future*. The ninth paper on the ' Value of Small States ' was contributed to the valuable series of war pamphlets issued by the Delegates of the Clarendon Press. Only the last two pieces in the volume have so far escaped the scrutiny of the printer, the proof-reader, and the public. For their substance I am indebted to a course of lectures delivered by me at Oxford in my capacity as Chichele Lecturer on Foreign History three years before the outbreak of the Great War.

To the publishers of the pieces which are here reprinted I owe sincere acknowledgements for their generous courtesy.

H. F.

Sept. 1919.

CONTENTS

The Last of the Latin Historians[1]

A STERN and melancholy interest, hardly to be matched in any other epoch, attaches to the records of the Roman Empire in the fourth century of our era. The old world was passing away in storm and agony, its frontiers assailed, its creeds challenged and perplexed, its social tissue suffering a slow and steady process of degeneration, which the political science of that time might note but was impotent to analyse or to cure. It was an age of bitter factions, when the demise of an emperor gave the signal for turmoil, intrigue, or civil war ; when, even within the Christian circle, sect contended with sect in savage and unrelenting animosity, and great political interests were often sacrificed to the vile machinations of the palace. And meanwhile the Empire was assaulted on all sides, by the Persians in Mesopotamia, by the Goths in Thrace, by the Germans on the Gaulish frontier—a contest waged with varying fortunes and exhibiting abundant proof that the legions of Rome had lost neither the discipline nor the coolness of their ancient renown, but nevertheless revealing to the

---

[1] 1. *Ammiani Marcellini Rerum Gestarum libros qui supersunt recensuit rhythmiceque distinxit Carolus U. Clark.* Vol. I, libri xiv-xxv. Berlin : Weidmann, 1910.

2. *Die verlorenen Bücher des Ammianus Marcellinus.* By Hugo Michael. Breslau : Maruschke, 1880.

3. *Ammien Marcellin, sa vie et son œuvre.* By Jean Gimazane. Toulouse : Chauvin, 1889.

4. *Die geschichtliche Litteratur über die römische Kaiserzeit.* By H. Peter. Leipzig : Teubner, 1897.

5. *The Text Traditions of Ammianus Marcellinus.* By C. U. Clark. New Haven, 1904.

6. *Ammien Marcellin.* By L. Dautremer. Lille, 1899.

7. *Studien zu Ammianus Marcellinus.* By W. Klein. Leipzig : Weicher, 1914.

understanding eye the ominous spectacle of a weakening defence against an ever-growing momentum of attack.

This, too, is the century which witnessed the codification of the orthodox creed of the Western Church and the expiring effort of paganism to maintain itself as the official religion of the Western world. In the brief reign of Julian, which occupies a disproportionate space in Gibbon's majestic work and is therefore to Englishmen the most familiar episode of later Roman history, the contest between the Christian religion and a sublimated form of the older beliefs is shown against the sombre background of the German and the Persian wars. The pagan Emperor, fighting against overwhelming spiritual and material forces, dies after a reign of less than two years; and the wheel of fortune swings suddenly round. The worship of the Sun-god is discarded; the Nicene Creed expels the brief and enlightened catechism of the pagan Sallustius; and by the end of the century the official triumph of Christianity is secure.

For twenty-five years of this tormented age we may follow the guidance of a writer who, though standing outside the Christian fold, was so temperate in spirit and so honourably distinguished for judgement and impartiality that critics have been divided as to the exact shade of his religious opinions. The History of Ammianus Marcellinus begins for us (for the earlier books have been lost) in 353 and ends with the defeat and death of Valens at Adrianople in 378, recounting in whole or in part the reigns of seven Emperors, Constantius, Julian, Jovian, Valens, Valentinian I, Gratian, and the child Valentinian II. But the original work, which was designed as a continuation of the histories of Tacitus, went back to the death of Nerva (A.D. 96), so that the accident of literary survival has preserved to us, perhaps fortunately for his reputation, only so much of the history as concerns the period of the author's active participation in the public affairs of the Empire. We have no external evidence as to the character of the lost books of Ammianus. Probably Gibbon is right in assuming that the first thirteen books were but 'a superficial epitome of two hundred and fifty-seven years'. It has, however, been argued, from references to the earlier books contained in the surviving fragments and seeming to imply a full treatment of certain topics, that the history was written upon a uniform scale, and that it contained some eighty books, thirty-one of which were devoted to the period with respect to which Ammianus was able to employ ocular and oral testimony. This, however, is an hypothesis entirely unsupported by literary tradition; and, since Ammianus exhibits scant regard to proportion in those parts of his work which we are enabled to test, we need not be at pains to defend the symmetry of his general design.

The last of the Latin historians was a soldier of Greek speech and lineage who was born about A.D. 332 in the half-Greek, half-Syrian city of Antioch. That Ammianus spoke Greek as his native tongue would be a natural inference from his birthplace, even if Greek modes of speech and thought were not plentifully illustrated in his writings. And it may give matter for surprise that, having been suckled in the speech of Herodotus and Thucydides, Ammianus should have staked his literary reputation upon a work written in a foreign language, over which he never succeeded in obtaining an easy and graceful mastery. Language is a delicate and intricate thing, so delicate and so intricate that only a man with a rare genius for style can hope to win complete purity of expression in a foreign tongue; and, though the gifts of Ammianus were numerous and solid, a sense of style in writing was not among them. He wrote Latin, then, not out of an artistic impulse to practise himself in a new and difficult mode, but because Latin was the official language of the Empire, because it was spoken in the armies and the public offices, because it was the instrument of a public career, and because, through the use of a long line of poets, historians, philosophers, and legists, Latin might be regarded as the authentic voice of Roman patriotism itself.

Indeed it is curious to reflect upon the singular power and magnetism which the name and tradition of Rome were still able to exert over the mind of a provincial and critical Greek, some of whose most famous pages are devoted to a delineation of the vices of the Roman capital, to the defeat of Roman armies in Persia and in Thrace, and to the acceptance of an ignominious peace at the hands of victorious Orientals. Ammianus paints the decadence of Rome with every hue of elaborate contempt; he shows us Roman society eaten to the core by the vermin of sloth, luxury, and vice. He notes the shameful rule of the eunuch and the parasite, the break-down of criminal justice, the perennial curse of calumny and terrorism, with its melancholy tale of innocent victims, which has been the inseparable accompaniment of an uneasy and revolutionary age. All this he describes with rude and insistent emphasis, and yet it never occurs to him to question the claims of the sacred city to the eternal veneration of mankind, or to challenge its supreme place in the Divine ordering of the Universe. That the architectural splendours of the Imperial capital—its amphitheatres, temples, baths, and palaces,—contributed in some measure to counterbalance the impression left upon his mind by the degraded habits of its population is probable enough; for, though Antioch was sumptuous and famed for luxury, Rome was in respect of material magnificence far superior to any city in the Empire. But, in his many allusions to Rome, Ammianus was not chiefly inspired by the emotions of the architectural connoisseur or the retired veteran from the provinces, dazzled by the glittering marbles and huge structures of the capital. If we read his mind aright, he thought of Rome chiefly as the mother-city of a great and enduring Empire, rich in sublime associations, celebrated by a long line of famous authors as the shrine of ancient hardihood and virtue, and still in her old age the legitimate object of sentimental reverence. Nothing will enable us more fully to understand the feeling of the devout Catholic for the city of St. Peter than the spell which the grandeur of Rome cast upon the mind of an Antiochene pagan in the last decades of the Empire of the West. In the time of Ammianus it was impossible to discern the future destinies of the Roman Episcopate, but it is clear from his narrative that the city of Romulus still worked its old enchantments, and .conferred upon its officials and upon the members of its aristocracy a special renown throughout the Empire.

It has, indeed, been objected against Ammianus that,

living under a sky black with storm-cloud, he appears to be insensible to the direction of the wind. A philosophic historian, considering the happenings of that time, would at least, one would think, have noted, as likely to change the very warp and woof of Mediterranean civilization, two great tendencies— the impending victory of the Christian religion and the declining power of the Roman Empire. Ammianus did not argue thus. He belonged to that large class of men who feel little interest in theological speculations and possess no gift for the mystical *ascesis* of the spirit. The Christian religion did not attract him. As a soldier he admired the fortitude of the martyrs ; and a well-known passage, contrasting the pomp and luxury of the Roman Bishop with the poverty and self-denial of the poor country priest, shows that he was not insensible to the milder virtues of the pastoral life. But of Christianity as a system of belief or conduct he has little knowledge and less curiosity. To the political mind the religious zealot principally presents himself as an administrative nuisance; and Ammianus condemns the synods of the Christian Fathers on the practical ground that they disorganized the postal transport of the Empire. It is not, therefore, to him that we must look for an appreciation of the strength and promise of the Christian life. A cold and somewhat scornful spectator of ecclesiastical events, he appears to be unversed in the literature and only remotely conversant with the ceremonies of the Christians. So far as he could judge the general outcome of that Oriental movement, it led to barbaric chaos, sect wrangling with sect, and every episcopal vacancy furnishing matter for intrigue or bloodshed. In one disputed election to the Bishopric of Rome a hundred and thirty-seven corpses were counted in a Christian church.

The most impressive feature, on the contrary, of this honest and impartial writer's outlook upon his own age is a robust faith in the permanence and power of the Roman Empire. This Greek from Antioch is in spirit more Roman than the Romans, so Roman that it is difficult to believe that no Latin blood ran in his veins. His masters in literature are the classical authors of Rome—Cicero, Livy, Virgil, Sallust,

Tacitus; and he draws his ideal of human conduct from that older and more simple Roman life which was canonized in the retrospective affection of a luxurious age. Indeed, as we read Ammianus, we are made sensible, at every turn, of the span and impetus of that great body politic which, despite furious batteries from without and more subtle maladies gnawing at the heart, still remained the most impressive monument in the world of force, fortune, and prudence. How could a soldier historian fail to feel the miracle of an Empire which sent its legions to fight on the Tees and the Euphrates, and included within its orbit all the peoples of the Mediterranean world? To a contemporary, the crushing defeat of Julian at Ctesiphon, the immense disaster of the Gothic victory at Adrianople, might well have seemed to be unfavourable episodes, carrying with them no sinister omen of ruin nor seed of mischief beyond repair. For centuries the Romans had fought and absorbed the barbarians; and Ammianus saw little reason to doubt that Rome would continue to fight and absorb barbarians to the end of time.[1]

One other circumstance may help to explain the survival, despite much cause for despondency, of a firm Imperial faith in the spirit of Ammianus. The last and most impressive book of the history is devoted to an account of the Gothic invasion of Thrace, which culminated in the rout of a Roman army and the death of the Emperor Valens. The story of this great calamity is told with sombre force, and loses none of its tragical quality in the hands of Ammianus, who, after working steadily up to the great climax of the battle, ends with two minor but startlingly significant episodes—a Gothic attack upon Constantinople, which was repulsed by a sally of Saracen mercenaries, and the treacherous massacre by order of a Roman governor of a large body of Gothic youths who had been distributed through the cities of Asia Minor. In the light of our later knowledge these ominous passages

---

[1] Fifty years later the Greek historian, Sozomen, started a philosophy of the Decline and Fall; but Rutilius Namatianus, writing shortly after the sack of Rome by Alaric, was still of opinion that the Empire would last for ever.

might seem to be inspired by a profound valedictory emotion, but there is nothing consciously valedictory in the attitude of Ammianus. The history was not composed under the immediate impulse of the disaster of Adrianople, but was begun some ten years later, when the military vigour of Theodosius was asserting itself; so that, writing in a brief oasis of calm when the sky was blue and the sunshine again golden, Ammianus could recount the perils of the past, gravely indeed, but yet without a note of weakness or despair.

Almost all the little that we know of the life of Ammianus is derived from allusions in his own writings. Sprung of noble lineage, he passed early into the ranks of the ' Protectores Domestici ', a *corps d'élite* which may be compared to our Guards Brigade, and was soon attached to the person of Ursicinus, a distinguished and experienced soldier who inspired the confidence and admiration of his youthful aide-de-camp. A better opening for an ambitious and enterprising young man, fond of travel, adventure, and conpanionship, could not have been contrived ; and, before Ammianus had reached the age of thirty, he had voyaged on military and official errands from Mesopotamia to Gaul and from Gaul to Mesopotamia, and had tasted the excitements of a siege, a reconnaissance, and a campaign. It is one of our misfortunes that, with a few rare exceptions, he refrains from recounting his personal experiences, and that his impressions of travel, which must have been various and diverting, are sacrificed to the austere tradition of classical history. Nevertheless here and there we descry traces of his activity. He was at Cologne with Ursicinus in 355, and witnessed the downfall of the rebel Silvanus and the beginnings of Julian's work in Gaul. Two years later he returned to the East, when Roman rule was once more exposed to grave peril from the energy and ambitions of Shapur the Great, the most formidable of the Sassanian kings of Persia. As he recounts this period of his career, Ammianus drops for a moment the impersonal tone which generally marks his history. He describes with some vividness of feeling his own part in the Persian campaign—how he was sent on a mission to the Emir of Corduene, how he took part in the famous defence of Amida (the modern Diarbekr), and joined in that expedition to the Tigris which resulted in Julian's death and the repulse of the Roman legions at Ctesiphon. After that catastrophe he returned to Antioch and for many years vanishes from history. When he emerges, it is as the spectator of the high-treason trials at Antioch in 371, as the tourist visiting the plain of Adrianople that he may inspect the site still strewn with the whitened bones of Goth and Roman, or finally as the man of letters, recently established in Rome and receiving the compliments of his friend, Libanius, upon a successful course of historical lectures. The sun-browned veteran was, in fact, reading instalments of his *magnum opus* to the intellectuals of the capital and tasting the sweets of literary fame. We may guess that his last reading was not later than 392.

It has been conjectured, on the ground of his interest in legal affairs, that, after the death of Julian, Ammianus abandoned a military for a civil career, and that the later part of his life was divided between judicial and literary pursuits. Such a development is not impossible, for the 'Protectores Domestici' constituted a school of training for civil as well as for military duties. Nor is it easy to suppose that a man of so active a temperament would have retired altogether from public life at so early a point in his course. But there is no direct evidence, and we must be content with surmises. We only know that, resembling the Father of History in curiosity and love of movement, Ammianus travelled widely, visiting Egypt and Greece as well as Thrace, and carrying, as we may conjecture, in his head the exciting design of the great book, the Tacitus brought up to date, which was to be recited before an exacting and distinguished audience in the marble capital of the Empire.

The circumstance that the history was intended for recitation was unfavourable to its quality as a work of art. It is a common experience that lectures, effective enough on first delivery, fail through some lack of subtlety and finish to preserve their power when issued to the world in cold print; and the historical lectures of the Syrian veteran were probably injured for posterity by too close an attention to the recondite tastes of an affected public. Ammianus had a rough but powerful mind, and, what is even more important in an historian, and priceless by reason of its rarity in that age, an essential sincerity and justness of judgement. Unfortunately he thought it necessary to conform himself to a literary fashion which we suspect to have been foreign to his real nature. His narrative is stuffed with turgid declamation and interrupted by long stretches of encyclopaedic learning which a modern author would omit or at least consign to foot-notes or appendices. He breaks off to describe a prodigy, an omen, a *cause célèbre*, in order that out of the studied variety of his matter he may provide a stimulus appropriate to the varying appetites of his audience. Probably, if he had taken literature less seriously, he would have written better, for he is capable, when off his guard, of a simple and soldierly narrative. But, though modest as to his own attainments, he cherished a secret flame of literary ambition. He read furiously. He soaked himself in Livy and Cicero and Virgil, in geographical and scientific handbooks, as well as in the proper and authentic sources for an historical narrative; and he succeeded in manufacturing a declamatory style of which we can say nothing more charitable than that accurate statements and moderate judgements have seldom been presented in a vesture so artificial and inappropriate.

If we had to single out the special excellence which marks Ammianus as a writer of history, we should find it in his distinct gift for life-like portraiture. He has provided us with a series of personal sketches than which of their kind there is nothing better in ancient literature ; for the 'Lives' of Plutarch, incomparably more beautiful and attractive, do not come up for comparison, belonging as they do to the category of idealistic literature, whereas the work of Ammianus is founded upon a close and dispassionate study of mixed character. Historians are largely creatures of tradition ; and the portraits of Ammianus may have owed something to a gossipy book, then greatly in vogue but now only surviving in a few scanty fragments, the satirical 'Lives of the Emperors' by Marius

Maximus.[1] In any case, it is reasonable to infer from the success which Ammianus achieves in a most difficult branch of the historian's art that the study of human character was one of the few departments of intellectual inquiry in which considerable progress had been made in the later years of the Roman Empire. Unfortunately the faculty of discerning portraiture was lost as soon as it had reached a point of distinguished excellence in the careful workmanship of Ammianus. The great calamities of the succeeding generation afforded no leisure for that habit of minute and engaging causticity which flourishes in sheltered and critical communities and is nourished by the drama, the satire, and the novel. For eight centuries no greater actor in the stage of European history is so well depicted for posterity as are the Constantius, the Julian, and the Valentinian of Ammianus. Nor was the full spirit of penetrating psychology recaptured for Europe until the Renaissance of the sixteenth century.

History having to do with the business of the State, it is certainly no disqualification in a writer of history that he should have some real working knowledge of one of the great public callings. Ammianus approached history from the angle of a soldier, and his work is a repository of military information. He is, indeed, our principal authority upon the art of war in the fourth century, and has left us some careful descriptions, more appropriate to a dictionary than to an historical narrative, of the poliorcetic engines of his time. Nevertheless we cannot regard him as a good, military historian, and that for a reason which may seem curious, in view of the large space which he allots to geographical surveys. He never seems to understand, or rather he never enables his reader to understand, the strategy of a campaign. He seems to put his geography in one department and his military history in another, and never to bring them into fruitful connexion. A siege he will often describe with intelligent particularity, but his battle-pieces are confused, his campaigns sketchy and imperfectly grounded ; and it is curious to note that, though he records failure after failure, his work is not greatly distinguished for strategical commentary

[1] *Historicorum Romanorum Fragmenta*, ed. H. Peter, pp. 331-9.

or criticism. Poliorcetics, however, he thoroughly understands ; and the serious interest in practical things, which makes him a master of this branch of military science and betrays itself in a great range and variety of technical disquisitions in other spheres of knowledge, is only part of that masculine sanity of character which constitutes his principal force and attraction.

It is not to be claimed for Ammianus that he never talks nonsense. He talks a deal of nonsense. He believes in omens and prodigies, and delights in describing them to an audience which did not think the worse of a popular lecture for an admixture of the sensational and the ghostly. But the general balance of his judgement was undisturbed by such concessions to vulgar superstition. His mind was essentially strong and secular, averse from all religious extravagance and as far removed from the exalted temper of the sects as the first Lord Shaftesbury from the Cameronians. In one passage he condemns his master, Julian, for the intemperance of his paganism, in another he applauds Valentinian for his policy of religious toleration—verdicts not to be explained on Epicurean grounds, but as the considered expression of that moderate and reasonable spirit which formed part of the Greek ideal of virtue. It is therefore possible from a study of Ammianus to derive a notion of the best secular moral standard which prevailed among cultivated pagans of the Roman Empire in the later part of the fourth century.

That standard was by no means low. The conscience of the soldier-historian was revolted by idleness and profligacy, cruelty and intemperance, trickery and injustice. In the main, our virtues and vices were his virtues and vices also. He had sources of moral sustenance which are not ours, but which may not have been inferior in potency to any that modern civilization brings to bear on a character analogous to his. He was inspired by the great classical authors of Greece and Rome, and especially by Cicero, whose writings formed the Bible of humane wisdom as long as the humanities retained their value in the Western world. He had the strong Roman respect for the reign of law, coupled with a hearty detestation of that capricious Asiatic cruelty which, in his own time, had begun to debase the administration of Justice. Life in the army had given him a code of honour which is certainly not inferior to that which now regulates the conduct of some modern armies professedly Christian. Finally, he was moved by a deep sentiment of devotion to the Empire as a providential system for the governance of the world.

War is the supreme touchstone of ethical principle. Ammianus recounts, without adverse comment, the pitiless massacre of women and children in the barbarous fighting of the frontier wars. When a Roman general, after making a truce with a marauding band of Saxons, contrives for them an ambush so that they perish to a man, he observes that a just judge would condemn the act as perfidious and disgraceful, but that reflection would show that it was not improper to destroy a dangerous band of robbers when occasion offered. To assign such sentiments to paganism is to ignore some very recent passages in the history of European morals. A Berlin pastor recently wrote in the *Vossische Zeitung*: ' Do you think it contrary to Christianity for our soldiers to shoot down these vermin, the Belgian and French assassins, men, women and children, and to lay their houses in dust and ashes?' and answered his question in the negative.[1] Ammianus was ignorant enough to suppose that Christianity exhorted men to eschew all courses save the straight way of justice and clemency; but then he did not pretend to be a Christian. His philosophy of war was that of the German War Book, tempered by an honourable dislike for treachery of all sorts; and, if he thought that extreme danger might justify anything, he is no worse than the great majority of men have always been.

A true estimate of our historian's moral quality can be more certainly reached through a consideration of his attitude upon the great topic of civil justice. War is at best a barbarous thing; and the wars of the fourth century, being conducted by barbarous armies on both sides, were not calculated to foster a code of clemency. If Ammianus, living through an age during which the Empire was fighting for its life, is not always too scrupulous, we may make allowances for any

[1] *Times, Lit. Supp.*, Jan. 20, 1916.

hardness of tone which we detect in him. But the break-down in the administration of Imperial Justice moves him to righteous passion. His own city of Antioch was the scene of two frightful persecutions, one under the beautiful young tyrant Gallus, and the other under the insanely cruel and suspicious Valens. Innocent men were tortured to death by the score. Delation flourished ; the forms of justice were flouted ; no one felt secure. The later of these two persecutions touched Ammianus very nearly. He was himself witness of many of the terrible scenes which were enacted in the law-court, the prison, or the amphitheatre. He heard the creaking of the instruments of torture, the cries of the victims, the hoarse and cruel ejaculations of the executioner. Some of his own friends were among the innocents who perished. One particular case branded itself upon his memory as, above all others, calling for vengeance. The young philosopher, Simonides, whose grave and stoical reticence had exasperated the savage mind of the Emperor, was burned alive. ' He quitted life as if it were a mad mistress, smiled at the sudden ruin of the passing moments and died without a quiver.' Simonides was executed in private. The mass of innocent conspirators were murdered in the amphitheatre at Antioch amid the loud wails of the spectators. And so far did the campaign of incrimination proceed that in the eastern province people burnt their libraries for fear that the possession of some treatise or other might furnish ground for a criminal charge.

The sombre story of these judicial murders closes with an eloquent apostrophe to the spirit of humane wisdom which shines through the classical literature of Greece and Rome :

' O glorious wisdom, gift of heaven to happy mortals, who hast often refined their corrupt natures, how many evils wouldst thou have corrected in these dark times, had it been vouchsafed to Valens to learn through thee that Empire is nothing else, in the opinion of the wise, but care for the well-being of others ! If only he had learnt that it was the part of a good governor to restrain his power, to resist insatiate cupidity and implacable passions, and to know that, in the words of Cicero, the recollection of cruelty makes a miserable old age ! Therefore it behoves every one who is about to pass sentence upon the life and spirit of man, who is a part of the world and makes up the complement of living things, to deliberate long and carefully and to resist headlong impulses, for the deed once done cannot be recalled.'

The stress laid upon the sanctity of human life as part of the animate universe is very remarkable.

We suspect, though we cannot bring our suspicions to the proof, that the example of his master, Julian, exercised a deep and enduring influence over the character of Ammianus. Julian was just the kind of man to inspire enthusiasm in a young soldier of sound moral instincts and intellectual aspirations. His frame was strong and athletic, his eyes remarkable for beauty and intelligence, his temperament of that sanguine and impetuous type which specially appeals to young men. When in later life Ammianus comes to compose the full-length portrait of the 'Apostate', the first trait which strikes him is the heroic air of the sitter. The Emperor was no ordinary man. He was to be classed with the heroes—'vir profecto heroicis connumerandus ingeniis'—having that indifference for the comforts and luxuries of life which, combined with high courage, brilliant energy, and moral ardour, strikes the mind with an ineffaceable impression of greatness. The pursuit of philosophy, though it may give lustre to the soul, does not always improve the manners of the student. But it is very clear that Julian was attractive. His retentive memory, his eager excitable interest in the great things of literature and philosophy, his copious and fluent gift of conversation, must have made him a stimulating and perhaps even a fatiguing companion. The philosopher Julian was very unlike the philosopher Kant or the philosopher Frederick the Great. Of that patient, plodding, exploring faculty which goes to the making of metaphysical systems, he was completely innocent. He was, in fact, no more of a philosopher than Napoleon, and no more of a cynic than Carlyle. The principal characteristic of his temperament was a glowing impetuosity. He did everything with a rush and practically nothing on system. He would neglect food or sleep for an interesting book or a metaphysical disquisition, and in disputation would be as careless of his dignity as in battle he was reckless of his life.

If we are to judge from his writings, most of them dashed off at white heat, he possessed that rare power of giving complete expression to mind and temperament which is the sure mark of literary genius. Now a man of this rushing quality, without reticence or reserve, makes mistakes and easily exposes himself to ridicule, but he is apt to be attractive, as the secretive, cunning, balancing intellect can never hope to be. What is singular, however, is to find this kind of temperament united to a very high measure of practical competence, for Julian was an excellent soldier, expert in every branch of the military art. Ammianus, who speaks with authority upon such points, commends his command of the principles of siege warfare, his skill in the selection of healthy spots for camps, his tactical versatility in battle, his signal power over his troops, and the sage principles on which his outposts and defences were managed. And there can be no doubt that these soldierly aptitudes secured an additional measure of respect for qualities which are not commonly met with in the camp.

Among these qualities, Ammianus must have been principally affected by Julian's passionate enthusiasm for the ancient culture. An official patronage of letters is one of the most depressing stocks-in-trade of monarchs; but Julian's attitude towards literature was neither official nor patronizing. It is indeed one of the charms of this singular character, that he preserved upon the throne all the disinterested reverence for learning of the genuine student. His court and camp were thronged by philosophers; and he spent the last moments of his life discussing the mysteries of the soul with two learned experts—father-confessors they may perhaps be called—who had been drawn in his train to the distant waters of the Tigris. Such enthusiasm, coming from so exalted a quarter, can hardly have failed to kindle a flame of emulation among minds susceptible of culture, the more so when we try to conjure up the quality of Julian's talk (and this may be naturally inferred from his writings), with its rich and easy command of literary allusion, its speed and vehemence, and above all its perpetual concern with the loftiest interests of mankind.

On the first contact with a remarkable man we often

exaggerate both his positive and relative magnitude. We feel the enchantment of genius. We are excited by the glow of a strong character, and we do not stop to measure or compare. But, if this was so with Ammianus in his original estimate of Julian, it cannot be said that a cool and true perspective is lacking to the deliberate judgement of his later life. The truth is that an important side of Julian's character was alien, if not unsympathetic, to the lay intelligence of Ammianus. Though the Emperor had abandoned Christianity, religion was still the primary interest of his life. He conceived it to be his mission to oppose to Christianity a State religion compounded of the old creeds of the pagan world but animated by a new and more fervent spirit. In this campaign, which was conducted with desperate energy, Julian received inspiration with equal impartiality from the poets and thinkers of ancient Greece, from the mystical doctors of Neo-platonic philosophy as well as from vulgar quacks and thaumaturgists; and his theology was a vessel into which every liquid, good, bad, and indifferent, had been indiscriminately poured. The centre of his system was the worship of the sun-god, who was regarded as the supreme embodiment of the energy, spirit, and intellect by which the Universe is ruled. Monotheism was in the air; and Julian, who was sensitive to the spiritual currents of his time, acknowledges the force of its appeal. But the gods of the ancient mythology were not to be dispossessed by an Oriental intruder; and place was found in the new system for the traditional polytheism of Greece, Rome, and the Nearer East.

All this religious side of Julian's activity was indifferent, if not distasteful, to Ammianus. He was by nature a *politique*, with an ingrained distrust of ecstasy and enthusiasm; and it is like his Roman love of reserve to single out among the defects of Julian's character his volubility and not infrequent converse with persons of low degree, and to comment with some asperity upon the extremes of his sacrificial zeal. So, although he makes a hero of Julian, he is discriminating in praise and does not try to slur over defects. He comments, for instance, unfavourably upon his habit of asking litigants to what religion they belonged, and denounces in the strongest terms the cruel edict which forbade Christian masters of rhetoric and grammar to teach in the schools. In general it may be said that his portrait is fully substantiated by Julian's written remains, and that this singular body of literature affords the best proof of the discernment which Ammianus brought to bear upon the characters of his history. We read the letters, the orations, and the satires, and then return to Ammianus to find that the strength and weakness of the writer's curious and attractive temperament have been duly noted. Perhaps a modern historian would see more to admire in the religious nature of this Crusader against the Cross and less in his military achievements. But in essential points, there will be no disagreement from this, one of the most remarkable studies of character in the whole range of history.

But, however highly we may be disposed to rate the gift of personal portraiture, it is not the principal treasure of the historical mind. A series of cameos, be they as delicate and true as you will, does not, of itself, constitute a history. We ask for more—for nothing less than the intelligent interpretation of a vanished age, so that we may understand not only the motives of the leading actors on the stage, but the general tendencies of the time, the essential springs of change, the elements of strength and weakness, of progress, recuperation or decay, which may be inferred from the recital of political transactions or from the analysis of the social and economic fabric, and above all so that we may form a just view of the political and social problems of the age. In the highest sense of the term, Ammianus is no philosophic historian. He has neither the moral depth nor the intellectual grasp which is necessary to the grand style in history ; and, if we were compelled solely to rely upon his evidence for our knowledge of the life of the Romans during the later half of the fourth century, some essential elements would be wanting to the picture. But at least it may be said that he enables us to realize, through his own vivid feeling of their importance, two contrasted and portentous facts, the power of the barbarian world and the decay of Roman society. His graphic and vigorous sketches of the Isaurians, the Persians, the Saracens, and the Huns, his admirable story of the Gothic invasion of Thrace and of the terrific fighting at Adrianople—where Rome experienced a defeat more crushing than any since Cannae—the care with which he enumerates and characterizes the barbarian tribes who were pressing everywhere upon the Roman defences, and more particularly the attention which he devotes to the various manifestations of the military art to be found among the antagonists of the Empire—all this side of his work was not only relevant to immediate political needs, but has an enduring importance as throwing light upon one of the greatest changes in recorded history.

We are always a little distrustful of the critic who denounces the decadence of his contemporaries, for every generation can be shown to be corrupt on a careful selection of the facts, and every society takes a morbid pleasure in the recital of its own manifest degeneracy. It is not surprising that a veteran from the provinces, trained at the ascetic court of Julian, should have found much to reprehend in Roman society. And, as Juvenal was still one of the most popular authors of the day, we may well imagine that a lecture on contemporary history would gain vogue through a spice of moral denunciation. But the real strength of the indictment of Ammianus does not consist so much in his portrayal of the profligate manners of the Roman people as in the crushing evidence which he adduces of a general infection of cruelty, incompetence, and disorder, poisoning the whole body politic of the Empire. The strongest Roman fortress on the Tigris was sacrificed through a palace intrigue directed against Ursicinus, the ablest commander in the East. And such an incident does not stand alone. When the armies of the Goths were pouring over the Balkan Peninsula 'like the lava of Mount Etna', the generals selected to oppose them were not only ignorant and rash, but actually sacrificed an important military advantage in order that they might traffic in slaves with the enemy. But perhaps the most signal evidence of the disease in the body politic is supplied by the conduct of the emperors themselves. Constantius was in some ways above the average level of conduct. He was chaste, temperate, laborious, a diligent cultivator of

learning and scrupulous in his distribution of patronage.   But
his tyranny was terrific.   The faintest suspicion—and the
atmosphere of his Court was poisoned by the breath of traducers
—was enough to set in motion the machinery of the most
awful persecution.   The same evil mania, resulting in the same
wild orgy of Asiatic cruelty, afflicted the sluggish and illiterate
Valens.   Even the better emperors interfered with the course
of justice, and were assailed by the voices of intriguers who
wished to use the machinery of government for plunder or
revenge.   And the most sinister feature in this sombre story
of panic and savage violence is that the voice of protest is
silent.   There are epigrams, there are bread-riots and wine-
riots and military revolts, but there are no organs of liberty.
The Senate of Rome is a powerless shadow.   There are no
parties formed on a common basis of political principles.   The
civilized world is governed by an Oriental tyranny.

'We might censure the vices of his style, the disorder and
perplexity of his narrative ; but we must now take leave of this
impartial historian, and reproach is silenced by our regret for
such an irreparable loss.'   So does Gibbon wave his stately
adieu to 'the accurate and faithful guide', whose steps he has
followed with punctuality, sarcasm, and profit.   The records of
the Roman Empire are lamentably imperfect ; and one of the
most curious features in literary history is the complete disappearance of a series of autobiographies written by some of
the most famous of the emperors.   What would we not give for
the memoirs of Augustus and Vespasian, for the autobiographies
of Hadrian and Severus, or the Commentaries of Constantine ?
They have perished ; and no fragment has been quoted
sufficiently substantial to enable us to estimate our loss.   For
centuries, too, the work of Ammianus was lost to Europe ;
and it was not until Poggio's discovery of the Hersfeld
manuscript that this invaluable writer was restored to European
scholarship.

The fifteenth century was a Ciceronian age ; and in the
circle of Italian purists the solecisms of the Syrian veteran
were felt to stand in need of apology.   The *editio princeps*
by Sabinus (Rome, 1494) is prefaced by a letter to the Bishop

of Bergamo, in which the editor craves that his author may not be entirely condemned for his use of the Latin word for 'deacon'. We do not know whether the Bishop was able to condone so grave a departure from classical usage. But to the modern eye it is one of the chief merits of this honest writer that his Latinity is not too pure, that it bears traces of the mingling of Greek, Latin, and Christian elements, and that it reflects with care and fidelity the conditions and transactions of the age in which he lived.

The Political Writings of Rousseau[1]

THE English opinion of Rousseau, whether as man or publicist, has never been very flattering, and a long series of excellent writers, representing the conservative traditions of the country, have denounced him as the source of most of the unsound political sophistries which vex the sages of mankind. Years before the *Confessions* had shocked the world with their pitiable revelations of baseness, Dr. Johnson expressed his opinion with characteristic vehemence: 'Rousseau, sir, is a very bad man. I would sooner sign a sentence for his transportation than that of any felon who has gone from the Old Bailey these many years. Yes, I should like to have him work in the plantations.' And though we do not say these refreshingly one-sided things now, most normal Englishmen and not a few distinguished Frenchmen do in substance agree with Dr. Johnson and think that Rousseau was a bad man who exercised a bad influence, and that it would have been better for the world if he had never been born. Quite apart from all questions of personal character and temperament, we are apt to think of him as a man of genius who, without any real knowledge of life or history, founded a political philosophy in the clouds. It is not an uncommon view that his teaching

---

[1] *The Political Writings of Jean Jacques Rousseau.* Edited by C. E. Vaughan. 2 vols. Cambridge University Press, 1915.

was responsible for some of the worst excesses of the French Revolution, that he represents that dangerous compound of romantic sentiment and abstract logic which has been for more than a century the bane of French political life, and that in him are to be found the first lineaments of that disastrous theory of the Absolute State 'beyond good and evil' which governs the German conduct of the present war.

We are an historical people, and we live in an age in which all studies have been brought to the historical test. The revulsion from Rousseau, caused by the fact that he was regarded as the intellectual parent of the French Revolution, has been intensified by the nature of his procedure. We think of him, principally, as the author of the *Contrat Social*, a treatise of striking merits and commanding influence, founded, as we know, upon imaginary history and false psychology. And we contrast him unfavourably with the judicious Montesquieu, in whose methods of comparative jurisprudence we discover that blessed principle of relativity in which modern political prudence finds a welcome refuge.

To all this kind of depreciation Dr. Vaughan's elaborate edition of the Political Works of Rousseau does in some measure furnish a very necessary modification. It is well, in the first place, to be reminded that the *Contrat Social*, itself the fragment of a larger project, is only one of many political treatises composed by Rousseau, and that apart from this famous manifesto there are other tracts, less abstract in form and shaped with more immediate reference to historical circumstance, notably the *Considérations sur le Gouvernement de Pologne*, which the late Lord Acton picked out from among the writings of Rousseau as the most valuable of all his works. And even from the *Contrat Social* itself there are, as Dr. Vaughan points out, opposite impressions to be gathered. The earlier chapters which principally arrest the attention of the reader are individualist and abstract. But the later part of the book develops a collectivist theory of the State and is distinguished by some sense of those climatic and historical influences which Rousseau, in this country at least, is commonly reputed to have ignored.

But, quite apart from this call to revise traditional verdicts, Dr. Vaughan's edition is a distinguished contribution to scholarship, providing us, as it does, for the first time with a pure text founded upon a careful examination of the manuscripts, and adding to the existing stock of published material some scattered pieces of reflection which have never previously seen the light. These fragments do not in themselves constitute a substantial addition to the body of Rousseau's philosophy, for they contain no ideas which cannot be found in writings previously published. They do, however, shed light upon Rousseau's laboured method of throwing detached reflections upon paper, to be subsequently woven together into a continuous tissue, and so prepare the mind to expect that, in a system of thought built up so painfully, there will be some insoluble and contradictory elements.

There are few subjects less worthy of discussion and more often discussed than the inconsistencies of great authors. In proportion as a man feels deeply and is capable of expressing his feeling with point and eloquence, he is likely, if his sympathies be wide and various, to be betrayed into propositions which are not easily combined in the same philosophical system. Not that Rousseau was defective in tenacity of principle, or to be dismissed as a mere rhetorical writer sacrificing everything to effect. There is a very hard kernel of business in Rousseau, despite his vagaries and sentimentalities, and one proof of it is that he has managed to engrave indelibly certain very practical conclusions about law and politics upon so keen-witted a people as the French. But he undoubtedly was a great artist, and we do not expect artists to speak as if they were on oath in a witness-box, least of all when they clearly take delight in affronting the conventional prejudices of mankind. Besides, it was Rousseau's method to make a clear-cut incisive effect with every stroke. He does not blur the salient outline of his phrase with adverb, parenthesis, or participial clause. If qualifications be needed, they will appear later on in the work, shining in their own substantive right, brightly burnished and acute. So in the *Contrat Social* the Republic is declared to be the only legitimate form of government. Yet all the objections and drawbacks to Democracy are clearly apprehended and etched in high relief.

Political philosophers have generally been persons of the tabulating order of mind, but the distinction of Rousseau is that, like Plato and Coleridge, he was a poet. In a fragment written in old age and printed for the first time by Dr. Vaughan, he says of himself: ' My whole life has been nothing but one long reverie, divided into chapters by my daily walks.' A dreamer, but with forked lightnings in the cloud, a confirmed melancholy, yet cherishing sublime illusions of hope, lyrical and romantic, yet with the strange capacity of putting everything which he writes into the most exciting and startling form, he is clearly not one of those logical people who repay a dry mechanical analysis. It is, of course, easy to trace a genealogy for Rousseau's theories. We may say, if we please, that he got his ' Social Contract ' from Locke and his ' General Will ' from Diderot, his division of legislative and executive functions from Montesquieu, and his political economy from the Physiocrats; and, with very little exercise of ingenuity, it would be possible to contend that he had nothing new to announce at all. But all this will tell us nothing as to the sources of his power. The secret of Rousseau was not purely intellectual: it consisted in the fact that, while endowed with fine intellectual penetration, he felt certain simple things about the rights and wrongs of human life very deeply, things of which there was already a confused and general consciousness in the society of his age, and which his language of matchless ardour and perspicuity first rendered articulate to the world.

One of these feelings was a romantic enthusiasm for nature, and, as connected with nature, for simplicity. It was part of that exquisiteness of sense which made him so delicate a judge of the voices of birds, so passionate in the presence of mountain scenes and flaming sunsets, that he should view the life of the city, with its hard pavements and jarring noises and not easily intelligible conventions of society, as an offence against the natural reason of man. But there is more than one way of admiring the simplicities of nature, and Rousseau's way was not altogether simple. Mingled with the genuine passion of the poet was the acid consciousness of the vagabond and the outcast, sensuous, restless, ill at ease, tormented with suspicions and humiliating memories, and, even in the midst of fame and flattery, feeling himself singular and estranged from the human kind. So that it was not altogether out of a youthful love of paradox that, in his first essay, the 'Discours sur les Sciences' (omitted, by the way, in Dr. Vaughan's edition), he championed the extravagant thesis that the human soul was corrupted in proportion as Science and Art approached perfection, that astronomy was born of superstition, eloquence of flattery and lies, geometry of avarice, physical science of vain curiosity, even morality itself of human pride, for the apostle of the civic virtues was in some moods himself more than half a misanthrope.

And yet, when we have said this, we are at once arrested by the recollection of his quick and loving sympathy for the poor, and by his faith in the value of ordinary men. 'One of the great causes of the sterility of our modern historians', he would say, 'is their lack of interest : they have nothing for the people.' The proposition is true also of the political philosophers : of Hobbes, whose genius he so warmly admired ; of Locke, from whom he drew much of his formulated opinion ; of Montesquieu, whose influence on his speculations is clearly apparent to the unprejudiced reader. They, too, have nothing for the people. And part of the originality of Rousseau consisted in the fact that he drew attention to the claims of undistinguished, uncultivated humanity. 'Je parle des mœurs, des coutumes, et surtout de l'opinion, partie inconnue à nos politiques, mais de laquelle dépend le succès de toutes les autres.' That the guidance of opinion was the true secret of statesmanship was a startling revelation, indicating a displacement of all the established political values. 'There was a time', wrote Kant, 'when I despised the people because they did not care for intellectual progress. Rousseau brought me to a truer state of mind. My foolish vanity has disappeared. I have learnt to honour men.' It all seems very simple and elementary now ; it is in all our text-books ; but it needs either a great war or a great genius to make us really feel this sentiment of human fraternity which Rousseau's eloquence made popular in Europe.

A third influence, leading to a view of the State sometimes difficult to reconcile with the individualist outcome of these romantic sympathies, was the enthusiasm for civic virtue which he derived in part from the traditions of his native Geneva, but chiefly from a study of classical antiquity. Not that Rousseau can be numbered among the scholars. He had no Greek and very little Latin, and for him the living residue of the ancient world was principally enshrined in the ' Lives' of Plutarch, read in a French translation, and so ravenously devoured that they could be repeated from memory. So it came about that, while he would not willingly allude to contemporary politics, the examples of Hellenic and Roman patriotism were never far from his mind. He would say that he was more familiar with the streets of Athens than with his native Geneva ; and from this pertinacious Classicism, in which he was not indeed peculiar, but only more intense and one-sided than his contemporaries, there arose in him that passionate restoration of the civic ideal which is his main contribution to the history of European morals.

Indeed, although he wrote on many topics, such as religion, music, botany, love, war, his principal concern was public virtue. Contemporaries spoke of him as 'the virtuous Jean Jacques' because he specialized on virtue and talked about it constantly in a feeling, eloquent, arresting way, so that ladies wept tears of sensibility as they listened to the little man's beautiful voice and watched the play of his black and flashing eyes. It was virtue in the grand old classical style which had taken his heart captive—the virtue of Lycurgus framing laws for Sparta, of Cato dying for the Republic, not the laborious humdrum sacrifice of the modern parliamentary voter who sits upon countless committees and endures a hundred painful speeches to cure the civic drains or to oust the Tory at the next election. And, given the character of French society at that time, the large passionate way in which Rousseau felt about public virtue, about the call of the State and the utter devotion of the true citizen, was the most effective means which could have been devised for diffusing very widely among men and women who had ceased to be interested in public things something of that elevated and heroic conception of political life which is found in the writers of antiquity.

It is this paramount concern for the being and authority of the State which lies behind the theory of the 'Social Contract'. In a passage in the 'Letters from the Mountain' Rousseau allows us to see what meaning the doctrine held for him and why he believed in it. The problem before him was to find some sure, indisputable, rational ground for political obligation, some authority for the State other than brute force, and, for this purpose, what could equal mutual agreement? He did not pledge himself to the historical character of the contract. The important point for him was that the State should be legitimate, and he could see no source of legitimacy other than the rational consent of consciously directed wills. The doctrine of the general will, always omnipotent and always right, followed as a natural sequel, but was vitiated by a fatal confusion between the will of the majority and the will for good. It was a doctrine of extreme collectivism, wholesome as an antidote to the more material and fashionable forms of individualism, but carrying with it as a logical consequence the red spectre of persecution. In a famous chapter of the *Contrat Social* Rousseau advances with habitual courage to the grim conclusion of his premisses. After contending that it is important for the State that every citizen should have a religion which makes him love his duty, he continues thus :

'Il y a donc une profession de foi purement civile, dont il appartient au souverain de fixer les articles, non pas précisément comme dogmes de religion, mais comme sentiments de socialité, sans lesquels il est impossible d'être bon citoyen ni sujet fidèle. Sans pouvoir obliger personne à les croire, il peut bannir de l'État quiconque ne les croit pas. Il peut le bannir, non comme impie, mais comme insociable, comme incapable d'aimer sincèrement les lois, la justice, et d'immoler au besoin sa vie son devoir. Car si quelqu'un, après avoir reconnu publiquement ces mêmes dogmes, se conduit comme ne les croyant pas, qu'il soit puni de mort ; il a commis le plus grand des crimes : il a menti devant les lois.'

It is true, as Dr. Vaughan reminds us, that Rousseau is not always consistent, and that, in a note to *La Nouvelle Héloïse*, published at the beginning of the year in which this passage was written, a position is taken up entirely at variance with this advocacy of political persecution. Nevertheless it may be noted that Marat publicly commented upon the *Contrat Social* in the streets of Paris, and that the worst excesses of the Committee of Public Safety may find theoretical justification in its keen and brilliant argument.

The doctrine of the State as an end in itself has received so much attention of late, through the hold which it has obtained over the German mind, that it is worth while to consider how far the Prussian theory is contained in the philosophy of Rousseau. In certain very material points the standpoint of ' the virtuous Jean Jacques ' is very different from the pitiless theory which is the foundation of modern German political thinking. Rousseau hated war. So far from regarding war as the medicine of the State, as a great purifying agency, or as an essential condition of human progress, he declared it to be one of the two worst scourges of mankind, and, ' in spite of the horrible theory of Hobbes ', contrary to nature.

' L'homme est naturellement pacifique et craintif: au moindre danger son premier mouvement est de fuir : il ne s'aguerrit qu'à force d'habitude et d'expérience.'

So, in the introduction to St. Pierre's *Projet de Paix perpétuelle*, he states with truth and eloquence the tragic contrast between the professions and the practice of Europe :

' À voir d'un côté les dissensions perpétuelles, les brigandages, les usurpations, les révoltes, les guerres, les meurtres qui désolent journalement ce respectable séjour des sages, ce brillant asile des sciences et des arts : à considérer nos beaux discours et nos procédés horribles, tant d'humanité dans les maximes et de cruauté dans les actions, une religion si douce et une sanguinaire intolérance, une politique si sage dans les livres et si dure dans la pratique, des chefs si bienfaisants et des peuples si misérables, des gouvernements si modérés et des guerres si cruelles, on sait à peine comment concilier ces étranges contrastes ; et cette fraternité prétendue des peuples de l'Europe ne semble être qu'un nom de dérision pour exprimer avec ironie leur mutuelle animosité.'

C

And after noting the various seeds of war in the European organism, he points out how impossible it is to derange the equilibrium of Europe; how neither one Power nor a league of two or three Powers could hope to establish a universal dominion; and how, whatever suppositions may be made, it is improbable that either a prince or a league could henceforth hope to make any considerable change in distribution of territory and political force. The solution which suggested itself was, accordingly, a federation of Europe, a scheme of which a partial outline already existed in the German Federation—'a body redoubtable to foreigners by the extent and by the number and valour of its people; but useful to all by reason of its institution, which, by depriving it of the means and will to conquer, makes it the stumbling-block of conquerors'. It is curious to reflect that, to the thinker of the eighteenth century, the German Federation offered the chief guarantee for the preservation of the balance of power in Europe, and furnished to pacifist thinkers the principal hope for a realization of their dream. So, too, a wise professor at Göttingen, whose lectures the youthful Bismarck may sometimes have attended, sharing in some measure this older opinion, ventured to predict that, if ever the German peoples were united in a single State, they would constitute a menace to the liberties of Europe.

The speculations of Rousseau about war and peace, his view that no aggressive war can be just, and that wars should only be waged to maintain the equality between peoples, would be dismissed as fantastic by the modern professors of 'Realpolitik'. He lived before the age of fierce nationalism, and conceived of Europe as 'a real society, with its religion, morals, customs, and even laws', as, indeed, in a sense it truly is, and may again be conceived to be. He anticipates also some of the modern arguments directed against the supposed economic advantages of conquest. He speaks of the destruction of lives in battle as the most apparent and sensible, but at the same time the least grave, of the losses incurred in war. There are other losses, less easy to repair—the children who are not born, the fields which are left untilled, the grinding taxes and the interrupted commerce. The true power of a State consists in its men, and every subject who is born is as good as an enemy slain.

It would be easy also to collect from the body of Rousseau's political writings a series of passages expressly directed against the doctrine of the omnipotence of the State. Indeed, not the least of Rousseau's services to political thinking, and certainly one of the principal sources of his influence, is that he conceives of politics as a department of morality, bringing every institution to the touchstone of right and wrong, and entertaining no exculpatory pleas founded upon ancient use. So that, although the doctrine of the general will might, and indeed did, lead straight to the establishment of political tyranny, it was no part of Rousseau's real outlook upon life that such should be the result. 'That government should be permitted to sacrifice an innocent person to the safety of the multitude, I hold this maxim to be one of the most execrable ever invented by tyranny; none could be more false, more dangerous, more directly opposed to the fundamental laws of society.' There could be no clearer affirmation of the limits which ethical feeling imposes upon the exercise of material power.

Another feature of Rousseau's political thought, difficult to reconcile with the collectivist theory of the State, is his steady belief in the rights of property. 'It is certain that the right of property is the most sacred of all the rights of citizens, and, in some respects, more important than liberty itself'; and he goes on to speak of property as 'the true foundation of civil society and as the guarantee of the engagements of citizens'. In part this deference to the rights of property may have been due to the influence of Locke, who makes the preservation of property the prime end of the establishment of civil government, in part to Rousseau's enthusiasm for agriculture. That it was based on no deep speculative analysis did not prevent its being a very genuine and deep-seated feeling in Rousseau's mind, nor was its inconsistency with other parts of his political doctrine a bar to its subsequent influence. The French Revolution was not directed against property, but against privilege, and both Danton and Robespierre defended private ownership to an acclaiming audience: indeed, the preservation of property was one of the dearest objects of the newly enfranchised peasantry of France.

Again, it does not seem as if Rousseau ever consciously thought of the State as Power : he thought of it as Will, and this word to him carried with it no relentless associations. He defends his ideal State as a benignant democracy acting through a popular legislature and an executive of experts—for he was no believer in the democratic control of foreign policy—and he preferred that it should be of a modest area, choosing to assume that public spirit must necessarily be more vivid and intense in a small State, and that languor and indifference were congenital to the citizens of great countries. In such a preference he may have been specially influenced by his patriotic regard for the prowess of the small republic of Geneva, to whose achievements in peace and war he has dedicated a noble panegyric; but it is doubtful whether local pride would have been sufficient to determine his views, had not the general political condition of Europe afforded them a plausible measure of support. To the observer of the eighteenth century the case for the small State was by no means desperate: the whole of Central Europe was a mosaic of political fragments, and there seemed no reason then to expect that the little republics and principalities of Germany and Italy would ever be combined into national States. Indeed, the decay of Spain, the debility of France, the anarchy of Poland, the palace revolutions of Russia furnished some ground for thinking that the true solution for all the political troubles of Europe was to be found in some scheme of federation which would combine the advantages of the small with those of the great States. Among these advantages Rousseau was never tempted to reckon mere material wealth. He thought that poor nations had always fought and would always fight better than rich ones, that commercial prosperity was a curse in disguise, that the representative system was an imposture, and that true ideal democracy could only be practised in miniature. The idea of a nation organizing itself as a standing army was utterly foreign to him, though he may truly be described as the spiritual father of all the conscripts. 'For a new people whose public interest is still vigorous, all the citizens are soldiers in time of war, and there are no soldiers in time of peace.' So little did he anticipate the age of Krupp.

If the worth of a publicist is to be assessed by his power of divination, by his capacity of picking out from the confused mass of contemporary experience the shaping forces of the future and of seeing the world as it will surely become when these forces have acquired a further degree of momentum and influence, then Rousseau will not take a very high rank. It would be impossible to find in his writings any appreciation of the importance either of Colonial development, or of the relations between the New World and the Old, or of the influence likely to be exerted by physical science upon human affairs, or of the national as apart from the civic spirit as a factor in the formation of great nations. He thought that Europe was destined to be conquered by the Tartars; he believed that economic development was injurious to military power; he concluded that England was on the road to ruin for the same absurd reason which led him to argue that the disaster of the Lisbon earthquake was due rather to the sins of the Portuguese than to the cruel caprices of Nature. It was a sufficient indication of decay that London was a big city, that big cities were wrong, that agriculture constituted the strength of a nation, and that the size of London was inconsistent with a flourishing state of the farming industry. Such a verdict indicates a lack of elementary economic knowledge. We need not quarrel with Rousseau for sharing the ordinary physiocratic view as to the importance of agriculture as a source of wealth, but it is a serious disqualification in a publicist —even in one whose concern in public affairs is mainly guided by ethical considerations—to condemn commerce and industry *ab initio*, to hold that industrial development is unfavourable to the growth of population, and that the agricultural industry itself is not considerably helped by the markets for its produce which the development of great towns inevitably opens out to the farmer.

Nevertheless, as Burke may be regarded as the intellectual parent of the British Empire, so to the genius of this vagabond son of a Genevan watchmaker we may attribute the outlines of that French Republic which, for a second time, has astonished Europe by the intense and ardent quality of its patriotic devotion. We doubt whether there is another instance in the history of literature of a writer who has combined so many fantastic ideas and unrealized prophecies with a central core of political doctrine which has become so closely intertwined with the intellectual process and habit of a great nation. For this influence it is customary to assign literary reasons, as if any assemblage of literary qualities, however imposing in range and brilliance, would in itself suffice to explain a result so solid and permanent. The truth is that Rousseau's doctrine won upon its merits, the least of which was that, being subversive of an outworn and unpopular system, it chimed in with the rising spirit of revolt. But what gave to it an abiding influence was the fact that it traced with Euclidean precision the outline of a new form of State founded upon the popular will, controlled by the nation in the general interest, and raised clear of those sinister and sectional interests which had so long perplexed the course of public affairs in Europe.

One of the implications of this new polity was a scheme of national education:

'Un enfant, en ouvrant les yeux, doit voir la patrie, et jusqu'à la mort ne doit plus voir qu'elle. Tout vrai républicain suça avec le lait de sa mère l'amour de sa patrie; c'est-à-dire, des lois et de la liberté. Cet amour suit tout son existence: il ne voit que sa patrie, il ne vit que pour elle; sitôt qu'il est seul il est nul; sitôt qu'il n'a plus de patrie, il n'est plus; et s'il n'est pas mort, il est pis.' [1]

These sentences taken from a treatise written in old age, with a characteristic note of rhetorical exaggeration, represent one important side of Rousseau's teaching on education. It is the duty of the State to form the mind and character of its citizens, and an obligation rests upon parents to see that their children are duly indoctrinated with respect for the laws and institutions of their own country. The practical consequences which, both in Europe and America, have flowed

---

[1] *Considérations sur le Gouvernement de Pologne.*

from the application of these principles are too complex to be lightly assessed, and have not been unattended by drawbacks. If the civic festivals of the Revolution were comparatively innocent (though generally tedious and ultimately mechanical), the Napoleonic application of the doctrine was a disaster to intellectual liberty, only less fatal because the system was less efficient and thoroughgoing than that which has been inflicted upon the political mind of Germany by the educational control of a military empire.

There remains the curious paradox that this apostle of civic training composed an elaborate treatise on education from which it would be difficult to gather that the inculcation of civic duty was any part of the business of the instructor of youth. Émile is educated privately, and with no direct reference to any constituted theories of public policy. He learns no republican catechism, he is drawn to no public games or festivals, and he receives an amount of individual attention which is inconsistent with any general scheme of national pedagogy. Dr. Vaughan argues that in all this there is no real incompatibility of doctrine, seeing that, in the opening pages of the treatise, Rousseau avows his conviction that a public education is always to be preferred wherever a true public life exists. If then Émile is to be educated by a private tutor, it is because ' the civic spirit, the very idea of the fatherland and the citizen, has been swept away'. It is, however, worth noting that Émile receives little or no instruction which might not be given in a modern elementary school. His education, in other words, though administered on refined principles of psychology, is popular and general in its extent. He learns reading, writing, and arithmetic, singing and drawing, the principles of undenominational religion, national history taught orally by narrative. He receives physical and technical instruction, is taught by object lessons, is encouraged in the practice of observation, so that, without any direct patriotic training, he may yet become a useful member of society. The Committee of Public Safety thought so well of the programme that they attempted to carry it into practice in the schools of the French Republic.

The day has gone by when a philosopher, eminent for his abstract meditations, receives an invitation to legislate for a community in trouble about its soul. But in the eighteenth century there was a wide and innocent belief in the virtues of philosophy, and the illustrious author of *Émile* and the *Contrat Social* received two separate calls to prescribe for the maladies of a State. The first summons came in the summer of 1764 from Buttafuoco, a Corsican soldier of distinction, who appears to have been acting at the instigation, or with the authority, of Paoli. The letter of invitation could not have been couched in more gratifying terms.

'Our island,' wrote Buttafuoco, 'as you have very well said, sir, is capable of receiving a good system of laws. But it needs a legislator. It needs a man of your principles, a man whose happiness is independent of us ; a man who knows human nature from top to bottom; who, husbanding a distant glory, may be willing to work in one age and to enjoy in another. Condescend to trace the plan of a political system and to co-operate in the felicity of a whole nation.'

Rousseau replied with great good sense that he lacked experience of affairs, ' which alone throws more light upon the art of government than all the meditations in the world', and that six months in Corsica, did his health permit, would give him more instruction than a hundred volumes. But, since a voyage was impossible, he asked to be supplied with ample materials for a judgement, adding to a well-conceived list of requirements that it was very much better to have too much than too little, and that no information capable of throwing light upon the national genius of Corsica could be too detailed. This is not the procedure of a visionary, but though the *Projet de Constitution pour la Corse* (written in the autumn of 1765) is clearly based upon the evidence, apparently none too copious, which had been supplied by Buttafuoco, it is, in effect, a charming dream. The Corsicans are advised to abjure currency and commerce, to avoid town life and to spread themselves evenly over the surface of the island, irrespective of inequalities in the fertility of the soil. Forced labour and dues in kind supply the needs of this primitive and stationary community of peasant farmers. An agrarian law fixes a limit to property, sumptuary laws rigidly curtail expenditure, for the spirit of the polity is not so much freedom as equality. 'Il faut que tout le monde vive et que personne ne s'enrichisse, c'est là le principe fondamental de la prospérité de la nation.' No Corsican is to enrich himself. Had Rousseau ever, among his protracted meditations, considered the extent and quality of the interference which would be necessary to prevent a Corsican from enriching himself, or from pursuing any other elemental human ambition (conquest, for instance) to which he had a mind? But we may be sure that any objections, founded upon the imperfections of human nature, would have been brushed aside with serene and implacable logic. He would show the Corsicans what they should do, but whether they were likely to be wise or foolish was none of his affair.

The most careful and detailed of the political writings of Rousseau was an *œuvre de circonstance*, composed in old age and posthumously published. The *Considérations sur le Gouvernement de Pologne* was executed by request during that period of troubled uncertainty in Polish politics which immediately preceded the First Partition. To Rousseau no task could have been more congenial than to write prescriptions for a spirited people who had taken arms against the autocratic Empress of Russia and were famed through Europe for their inveterate habit of anarchy. The Poles seemed to have the root of patriotism, the promise of nationhood. He is, accordingly, remarkably tender to the traditions and institutions of a race so singularly distinguished from the general level of European cynicism and selfishness. He will allow the dear people to keep their serfs, their nobles, even their monarchy. He acknowledges that they suffer from anarchy, and that two of the causes of anarchy are the *liberum veto* and the right of confederation. Yet he will not condemn these curious vestiges of barbarous antiquity. The *liberum veto*, 'a brilliant right rendered pernicious by its abuse', is to continue under limitations and safeguards, one safeguard being that it is to be confined to fundamental laws, another that the single voter who blocks a law must answer by the loss of his head if, six months later, his action is not endorsed by a tribunal.

The right of confederation was legalized civil war. Rousseau applauds it as 'a masterpiece of policy, the buckler, the asylum, the sanctuary of the Constitution'. So decisive a means of expressing the general will must not, at any cost, be sacrificed. It was the opinion of the most reasonable party in Poland that the sovereign cure for the ills of the kingdom would be the establishment of a strong hereditary monarchy. 'It is a great evil', observes Rousseau, 'that the chief of the nation should be the born enemy of liberty,' an observation hardly calculated to encourage monarchical sentiment. Nevertheless, a monarch Poland must have. Republics are only suitable to small States and, though it is desirable that Poland should be divided into thirty-three provinces united by a federal tie, the federation will be of the size which demands the supervision of a monarch. At all costs, however, the monarchy must be elective. 'An elective monarch with the most absolute power would be better for Poland than an hereditary King who was a cipher.' Rousseau is aware of what, indeed, was notorious throughout Europe, that one of the chronic sources of intrigue and disorder in Poland consisted in the elective character of the monarchy. He proposes as a remedy that the monarch should always be a Pole and that he should be chosen by lot from the Senators. Sensible as some of his suggestions are, it would, on the whole, be difficult to conceive a series of recommendations less calculated to establish the tottering State upon firm and stable foundations.

And yet, in these 'reveries', as Rousseau himself calls them, there is a ground-note of truth and wisdom, of which his own generation in particular stood in special need. He realized the manifold and unexplored potencies of the national spirit. He tells the Poles in effect that, if they have the heart of a nation, they are unassailable, so that Russia may conquer but never digest them. To enhance the reputation of the military calling, he advocates a citizen army on the Swiss model, and in a remarkable passage praises the martial spirit which pervades the citizen soldiers of his native land. 'I remember the time at Geneva', he says, 'when the burgesses manœuvred much better than the regular troops,' adding a regret, strange in a professor of pacifist opinions, that the magistrates had discouraged them.

Indeed it will generally be found that the unsound or questionable provisions in this eloquent and curious treatise spring from just this pervading consciousness that the body politic is a dead thing without national feeling. The weak elective King who is carefully deprived of patronage so that he may not corrupt his subjects, the frequent but short-lived Diets strictly bound by instructions from their electors, what are these but instruments intended to promote the reign of public virtue? Unfortunately, the prescriptions made up to cure the patient can only be safely taken if the patient is already cured. Rousseau assumes that the lazy, turbulent nobles of Poland are already spotless patriots, eager and able to discharge public duties to the advantage of the State. For such a people three brief codes, intelligible to every schoolboy, will be amply sufficent. 'Are not all the rules of natural law better graven in the hearts of men than all this nonsense of Justinian? Only make them honest and virtuous and I answer for you that they will have law enough.'

'Only make them honest and virtuous.' Is it then so simple to induce honesty and virtue among Poles and the neighbours of Poles? Is it true that a large community of modern men, rendered honest and virtuous by the alchemy of a wise political tractate, will be content to live under a few simple laws such as may not overtax the memory of average schoolboys? Abolish commerce, currency, scientific inventions, destroy the towns and scatter the inhabitants broadcast through the country in self-sufficing agrarian communities, so that there is little intercommunion and clash of interests—then perhaps the ideal might be realized. The *Lex Salica* was brief enough, and there is no need for a complicated criminal jurisprudence when cattle-stealing, murder, and rape are the only crimes. But in Poland, where, in Rousseau's own true and penetrating phrase, 'the nobles are everything, the burgesses nothing, and the peasants less than nothing ', where the very alphabet of a State sense had still to be learned, was it reasonable to expect that the casuistry of human needs and misdoings could be so easily exhausted? 'Le bon sens suffit pour gouverner un État bien constitué ; et le bon sens s'élabore autant dans le cœur que dans la tête.' An admirable phrase, provided that it be understood that it is never good sense to give to complicated things a false appearance of simplicity.

Among the many golden sentences strewn about Rousseau's political writings there are none which in his own country exercised a more decisive influence than those in which he declares the true character of law :

'Le premier et le plus grand intérêt public est toujours la justice. Tous veulent que les conditions soient égales pour tous, et la justice n'est que cette égalité. Le citoyen ne veut que les lois et que l'observation des lois. Chaque particulier dans le peuple sait bien que, s'il y a des exceptions, elles ne seront pas en sa faveur. Ainsi tous craignent les exceptions ; et qui craint les exceptions aime la loi.'[1]

In this shining little chain of unbreakable argument lies the gospel of Jean Jacques, and the sufficient explanation of his everlasting power over men.

[1] *Lettres de la Montagne*, IX.

Ollivier's Memoirs[1]

M. ÉMILE OLLIVIER has written an apology for his political career in sixteen volumes, nine thousand pages, and a million and three-quarter words, and if the weight of an apology is to be measured in a grocer's scale his must be one of the weightiest apologies in literary history. It might perhaps be inferred from this that M. Ollivier was a party to transactions which it is impossible or at least embarrassing to defend, that his political course has been far from straight, and that his fame is so thickly obscured by clouds that only by gargantuan puffings and blowings can it be restored to its proper translucency. Such a conclusion would be hasty and erroneous. The writer of this prolix apology can afford to open his public career to the inspection of any jury of moralists without a twinge of misgiving. Whatever may have been his failures and his faults, nobody can say that they were the fruit of a mean, jealous, or double-dealing nature. M. Ollivier is the most diaphanous of men and the least malicious of memoir-writers. He has the full orator's allowance of vanity, but it is as the vanity of the sunflower, large, easy, and expansive. He can admire Thiers, who eclipsed him, and find qualities to praise in Jules Simon, whom he regarded as an old ally sundered by treachery. He has been a hard but never a rancorous

---

[1] 1. *L'Empire Libéral.* By Émile Ollivier. Sixteen vols. Paris: Garnier, 1895–1912.

2. *L'Évolution constitutionnelle du Second Empire.* By H. Berton. Paris: Félix Alcan, 1900.

3. *The Rise of Louis Napoleon.* By F. A. Simpson. London: Murray, 1909.

4. *Les Trois Coups d'État de Louis-Napoléon Bonaparte.* Vol. I. *Strasbourg et Boulogne.* By A. Lebey. Paris: Perrin, 1906.

5. *Louis-Napoléon Bonaparte et la Révolution de 1848.* By A. Lebey. Two vols. Paris: Félix Juven, 1907-8.

6. *Napoléon III avant l'Empire.* By H. Thirria. Two vols. Paris: Plon, 1899.

7. *Rome et Napoléon III.* By E. Bourgeois and E. Clermont. Paris: Armand Colin, 1907.

fighter, and has preserved a sweet core of geniality through misfortunes which would have dropped acid into a less wholesome nature. Nobody can read these volumes without feeling attracted to their author. They have none of those subtle and delicate harmonies which are so enchanting in the best prose of all; they are neither witty nor humorous, and they are sadly lacking in restraint, plan, concision; but they move along at a high level of clear and masculine eloquence; they are never languid or feeble; and who can refrain from admiring the unconquerable youth and buoyancy of heart which has prompted a man, after his political career had been broken beyond retrieve, to plan at the age of sixty-nine, and to execute between the ages of sixty-nine and eighty-seven, so gallant and extensive a vindication of the faith that was in him?[1]

M. Ollivier's apology takes the form of a general history of the Second Empire and of its intellectual and political antecedents. He wishes to show that Liberalism was an essential part of the Imperial idea, and that he was fully justified in his belief that France could enjoy a wide measure of political liberty under an Emperor of the lineage of Napoleon. And this object is combined with a purpose which is still more directly relevant to M. Ollivier's political reputation. The Cabinet of which he was the nominal chief plunged France into the war of 1870; and not the least among the motives which have led to the composition of this elaborate book is the desire to recount the true causes of that plain and palpable catastrophe. The name Ollivier is associated with a great defeat. There was a time when no Frenchman could speak a good word for the Minister who, on July 15, 1870, announced from the tribune that he entered the Prussian war 'with a light heart'. Many were the imprecations heaped on that 'light heart' of M. Ollivier. No party would defend him. To the Royalists he was a demagogue, to the Republicans a renegade, to the Imperialists the quack doctor who had injured a sound

[1] This favourable impression has been recently strengthened in the mind of the writer by the perusal of the charming letters published in the *Revue des Deux Mondes* (June and July, 1919).

constitution. When the first great defeats were announced, M. Ollivier was hurled from office and shot through descending levels of opprobrium and contempt into the oblivion from which an unresting spirit of self-assertion armed with an industrious and enduring pen has enabled him triumphantly to emerge.

The writer of these memoirs was born at Marseilles, July 2, 1825, and first came into public notice in 1848, when Ledru-Rollin sent him and his father into the departments of the Bouches-du-Rhône and Var as joint commissioners of the newly-founded Republic. Educated in the Radical tradition of France, Émile Ollivier had been familiar from early youth with some of the leaders of Republican opinion. His father, Demosthenes Ollivier, was the friend of Armand Carrel the Republican-Bonapartist, of Pierre Leroux the Republican-Socialist, of Ledru-Rollin the Republican pure and simple. 'Above our childish heads', says the autobiographer quaintly, 'resounded the grand words, God, Humanity, Plato, Jesus.' We are left to infer that the atmosphere of the Ollivier household was compounded of that sentimental and comprehensive idealism which is the special feature of the Revolution of 1848 in its early and exuberant phases. In such a home the young Ollivier naturally grew up to be a Republican, but not, though perhaps this may be the result of temperament rather than of surroundings, a Republican of the most austere and exclusive sect. One key to the inner shrine of Jacobinism he never possessed. He was neither an atheist nor an anti-clerical. On the contrary, much as he deplored the development of ultramontane tendencies in the Church, he was as a youth, and has ever since remained, a loyal Catholic. He tells us how as a boy he found his favourite intellectual pasture in Bossuet and Pascal, and how during his progress as Republican commissioner he created something of a sensation by calling on a bishop. Such Liberalism was rare among Ledru-Rollin's commissioners, but the brief life of the Second Republic afforded little scope for its exercise. The triumph of Louis Bonaparte dealt a shattering blow to the Ollivier family. The father was sentenced to Cayenne, then exiled ; and the avenues of public life seemed to be effectively closed against the son.

In the sudden and complete eclipse of public liberties Émile Ollivier found a refuge and eventually a reputation in the practice of the law. The bar has been a great school of political oratory in France. The leaders of the Gironde were barristers, Gambetta and Jules Favre won their first laurels at the bar, and M. Ollivier, who stands as far removed from the d'Aguesseaus and Pothiers of his profession as Lamennais from Aquinas or Erskine from Coke, learnt to love the sound of his eloquent voice first at Lyons and subsequently in the historic halls of the Île de la Cité. Then in 1857 he resolved to rid himself of the scruple which prevented the strait sect of Republicans from entering political life. The friend of Michelet took an oath to the Imperial Constitution, was elected to the Chamber by the third circumscription of the Seine, and found himself leader of a small company of five who alone represented the Republican principle in an Assembly manufactured by prefects and governed by emotions of servility and fear. The programme of the 'Five' was Liberalism. In domestic affairs they advocated the repeal of the Coercion Acts, the freedom of the press, the publication of parliamentary debates, parliamentary control of legislation and finance, elected municipal councils for Paris and Lyons, the abolition of official candidatures and governmental pressure at elections. In foreign policy they stood for the principle of Nationality; in the ecclesiastical domain for the free Church in the free State. To all Five it was common ground that the Empire could never consist with liberty, and that the true object of a Liberal Opposition was to sap its foundation and to prepare its fall. From this position Jules Favre, who was perhaps the most eloquent and resourceful of the Five, never departed; but Ollivier was cast in a less obdurate mould, and by swift and continuous gradations the Republican son of a Republican proscript became the apostle of the Liberal Empire. Of the agencies by which this transformation was accomplished there is naturally a full, though not a complete, account in these memoirs. It is clear, for instance, that the Duc de Morny, the Emperor's half-brother, took special pains to conciliate the vigorous young iconoclast, though it is impossible to determine with accuracy the weight which is to be attributed to the seductions of this adroit politician. But the course of public affairs probably counted for more with M. Ollivier than the personal influences to which the stalwarts of the Republican cause attributed his lapse. In 1860 the Emperor declared an amnesty for political offences. M. Ollivier's 'heart was appeased', and henceforward he began to think more favourably of the possibilities of the Empire. When on November 24 of the same year the Emperor so far relaxed the rigour of his system as to permit the publication of parliamentary debates and the power of discussing the Address, M. Ollivier discovered, as he tells us, 'a sovereign capable of understanding liberty'. He still declared himself a Republican, but in vague and eloquent language promised his support to the Emperor if he would realize the liberal programme of the Hundred Days. When Morny asked him whether he was content with the concessions he replied, 'If it is the end, you are lost; if it is a beginning, you are established'. It proved only to be a beginning. The elections of 1863, despite all that the prefects could do to prevent it, brought new strength to the Opposition and restored Thiers to public life. Blow after blow rained down upon the Government defences. The Mexican expedition was shown to be unnecessary, expensive, a violation of the principles of nationalities; the Opposition demanded the withdrawal of the French troops from Rome, and claimed that the interests of France were being sacrificed to the clericals. In these attacks M. Ollivier joined, but he was now no longer the most conspicuous star in the Assembly. The wider experience and the more brilliant eloquence of Thiers gave the Orleanist leader a position among the opponents of the Government to which none of the young generation could aspire; and perhaps this fact may have exercised a certain unanalysed influence over the attitude of the Liberal leader. Be this as it may, in 1864 M. Ollivier quarrelled with the Left over a bill to legalize strikes, and in the following year cast his vote—*un vote d'espérance*—for the Address. He was now drawn into the Imperial circle. On May 6, 1865, he dined with the Empress at the Tuileries, learnt that at sixteen she had been a Fourierist, and explained to her that his task was to convert a revolutionary into a constitutional democracy. On June 27 he had his first interview with the Emperor. 'I was charmed,' he wrote that evening in his diary; 'he was gay and open, ready with his smile, and so simple that he puts you at your ease at once; not talkative certainly, but an agreeable talker. His eye is quick, fine, caressing, his appearance cold but without stiffness. His nature strikes me as delicate and feminine.' In 1866 the breach with the Republicans was complete. Ollivier founded a Third Party pledged to support the Empire and to urge it down the path of liberal reform. Three years later a following of forty-two had swollen to a hundred and fifteen.

It is claimed for this design that it was not only sound in principle, but that it was within measurable reach of winning a great and durable success. M. Ollivier contends that a Republic was not really desired by France, that the monarchical parties were impossible, and that the requisite union of force and liberty could only be secured by the harmonious co-operation of those two incommensurables—a parliamentary government and an Empire founded by a *coup d'état* and consolidated by a plebiscite. He further argues with much circumstance that such a policy was the natural and logical outcome of Bonapartism. The great Emperor was himself quite outside the ordinary category of European dynasts. He was the child of fortune; his throne depended not upon legitimacy, but upon the will of the people; and the most durable achievement of his government had been to secure to France the social conquests of a popular revolution. During the Hundred Days, perceiving that a change had come over the political climate, he issued a Constitution, better, in the opinion of Thiers, than any other which France had obtained in all her revolutions; but the first experiment in a Liberal Empire was shortlived. The battle of Waterloo, which, as Napoleon observed at St. Helena, was as fatal to the liberties of Europe as the battle of Philippi was fatal to the liberties of Rome, ushered in a period of autocratic reaction. All over

Europe the liberal spirit was proscribed, and in the stupid excesses of the restored governments the banished Emperor discerned the future hope of his dynasty. In the St. Helena conversations he portrayed his liberal intentions and the democratic elements in his rule. He stood for liberty, equality, nationality, peace. If he had not been a Constitutional monarch from the first, this was not due to any inherent incompatibility between the Empire and Constitutionalism, but to the necessity of quieting the ferment of revolution, and then to the stress of a war which he would gladly have avoided. The day would come when Europe would need a government founded upon the principles of Bonapartism and capable of securing for them the respect which they deserved. A generation elapsed and part of the prophecy was realized: the French had returned to an Empire based upon the *plébiscite*. However despotic may have been its primal aspect, such a government contained the precious and necessary seeds of liberty. There was the authority of the *plébiscite*, there was a Chamber elected on a scheme of universal suffrage, there was an Emperor who had shown in his early writings that he possessed a grasp of Liberal principle and an eye for social reform. M. Ollivier contends that a free Constitution was the necessary complement of the Imperial idea. It was not indeed part of his conception that the Emperor should be an irresponsible figurehead. Rouher, who stood for autocracy, said that it was plainly impossible that the Emperor should reign but not govern, and M. Ollivier appears to think that a Chief of a State—active, initiating great lines of policy, and responsible to the people at large—could co-exist with a Ministry chosen from the dominant party in the elected Chamber and liable to be removed from office by its vote. Whatever may be the difficulties inherent in such a dualism, they had not time to develop themselves under the Liberal Empire. M. Ollivier's dream had hardly assumed a palpable form before it was rudely and finally shattered; but while it lasted the dream was bright. In December 1869 he was invited to form a responsible Ministry. The Constitution was remodelled, so that it became, as M. Ollivier remarked to the Emperor, 'the most truly Liberal Constitution which had existed in France since 1789'. The press was freed from its shackles; the parliament recovered complete control over every department of public policy; and the great scheme of Liberal reform was on May 8, 1870, endorsed by seven million votes of the French people. 'If I had then been carried off by fever like Cavour,' remarks M. Ollivier, 'I should have been unanimously applauded as one of the rare statesmen of the nineteenth century whose design had been accomplished in its entirety.' Unfortunately the first achievement of the Liberal Empire was to accept that disastrous encounter which for more than a generation lowered the military prestige of France. 'A cyclone which I could not foretell, and against which I was not allowed the time to struggle, beats down upon my work, crushes it, and casts me among the vanquished who are condemned to ostracism.' But for that unseen calamity M. Ollivier announces that 'without phrases or charlatanism of any kind' he would have slain anarchical or despotic Socialism by a vast scheme of social reform. A sketch of this imposing but uncompleted design is vouchsafed to us. It includes a reform of the civil, penal, and procedural codes; the abolition of collateral inheritance, and the legal emancipation of women. M. Ollivier was a true Liberal. He hated tyranny in all its forms, whether it were the tyranny of the trades union over the workman or of the State over the Church or of the Church over the State. He wished to respect the freedom of contract and to sanction the formation of religious as well as of commercial and civil associations. The Latin genius is averse to compromise, and political movements in France have been too often armed with terror in place of argument. M. Ollivier's policy was framed on a basis of confidence. He trusted the capacity of women to manage their own investments, and of priests to shape their own dogma. Above all, he trusted the Emperor, who is exhibited to us as 'the faithful interpreter of democratic France, ambitious of adding one last stone to the radiant pyramid of glory and generosity' erected by the genius of his illustrious uncle. So confiding is M. Ollivier that he believes that a Bonaparte could adapt himself to a philosophy of affairs which might have emanated from the brain of John Stuart Mill.

It is obvious that Napoleon III understood M. Ollivier: it is not so clear that M. Ollivier understood Napoleon III. Having persuaded himself that the Emperor was a Liberal, he finds his own honest and Liberal countenance reflected everywhere in the stream of Imperial policy. His handling of diplomatic affairs is an illustration of this amiable but misleading tendency. The Crimean War, by sowing dissension between Austria and Prussia, undoubtedly paved the way for the liberation of Italy, but what are we to say of this version of the motives which led the Emperor to embark on it?

'The Emperor had no hatred for the Cossacks and did not even cherish any ill will against the Tsar for his impertinence. He had no superstition for the balance of power; indeed, he intended to destroy it; and the Turk interested him as little as the Ottoman Empire. His object in making war was to restore the prestige of France in that quarter of the world which had witnessed our bitter humiliation of 1840. He wished to put an end to the Holy Alliance of the North, to make a rupture between Russia and Austria which would pave the way to the policy of nationalities—to the freedom of Italy and perhaps to the freedom of Poland.'[1]

Did Napoleon III really take up arms against the Muscovites for the principal reason that he might the more effectually rescue the suffering Lombards and Venetians from the Austrian yoke? Would he have expected such a story to find credence with the Empress or with Rouher? And when M. Ollivier swallowed it, was he not thereby encouraged to pay an even more elaborate compliment to his Minister's credulity? The Mexican expedition was not upon the face of it an enterprise calculated upon national or Liberal ideals. The French Government attempted to impose an alien Emperor upon the Mexicans by force of arms, hoping that a clerical autocracy so founded and supported would arrest the advancing tide of the Protestant Yankees. No episode in the whole history of Empire was more difficult to accommodate to the conscience of a man like M. Ollivier, who believed in

[1] *L'Empire Libéral*, iii. 188.

Rome for the Romans, Germany for the Germans, Mexico for the Mexicans, and France for the French. Yet a good conjurer can show us a bird where we expected to see a six-penny piece. We learn that the underlying thought of the Mexican expedition was not the Jecker contract, nor the claims of the Vatican, nor the outcry of the Mexican clericals, nor the desire to profit by the Civil War in America to extend French influence in the western hemisphere, nor the fabulous gold mines of the Sonora, nor any of the many sinister motives which were so freely attributed by the opposition press; it was, purely and simply, Venice. The idea of the Mexican expedition was so to smooth the ruffled plumes of Austria that she would consent to cede Venice to Victor Emmanuel. 'The ghost of Venice', as Nigra wrote to Ricasoli, ' roams along the corridors of the Tuileries.' In his subtle and circuitous way the Emperor was still pursuing the fair phantom of Italy, and Frenchmen were dying on the parched uplands of Mexico, as they had died in their snow-bound cantonments round Sebastopol, that the land of Dante might be free.

M. Ollivier is, however, constrained to concede that some passages in the diplomacy of his hero do not admit of this exalted interpretation. There were 'aberrations' from the straight path of altruism. The acquisition of Savoy and Nice was apparently sound nationalism, a restoration of lost members rather than a conquest, but no such apology can be discovered even by M. Ollivier for the designs upon Belgium, Luxemburg, and the Palatinate. These projects were regrettable 'aberrations' from the nationalist ideal, but no part, we are told, of the permanent fabric of Imperial diplomacy. ' Save in a moment of illness and folly in 1867 . . . the Emperor had not even a vague inclination to take Belgium . . . under pressure of public opinion he may perhaps sometimes have desired a rectification of frontier towards the Palatinate.' We are convinced that upon this point M. Ollivier is mistaken and that a rectification of the eastern frontier of France was a fixed part of the foreign policy of the Second Empire.

That M. Ollivier should have fallen into an error on a

matter so important is partly due to his eagerness to minimize the incompatibility between his own political ideals and the practice of the Empire, and partly also to the peculiar confusion and uncertainty of his master's policy. The Emperor's mind was full of vague, grand, and imperfectly harmonized ideas. He had a genuine sympathy for the Italians and Poles, and cherished a belief that it was the predestined task of the Empire to assist in the emancipation of suffering nationalities. At the same time he was ambitious for France. He understood enough of French human nature to know that it wanted glory, and he knew enough of French history to find the quarter where conquest would be most glorious and glory would be most grateful. From the very beginning of his reign he had made up his mind to revise the treaties of 1815. He spoke upon the subject with Prince Albert in 1858, casting and recasting the map of Europe and Africa in his conversation with the freedom of a Bonaparte; and amid all the vacillations of an uncertain and divided policy he never wholly lost sight of the waters of the Rhine. The complexion of affairs did not, however, permit a frank and thorough pursuit either of the one aim or of the other. Napoleon could not sacrifice the temporal independence of the Papacy to the Italian Kingdom and at the same time retain the loyalty of the French clericals; and the designs on Belgium and the Rhine were of so revolutionary a character that they could only be tentatively and secretly pressed as part of a general scheme of reconstruction. The problem of alliances was as complex as the objects of policy were various and confused. The English alliance, consistent with emnity to Russia and help to Piedmont, was at variance with any scheme for extending the frontier to the north-east. On the other hand, an understanding with Austria, while it would gratify the clericals and check the Prussians, would carry dismay into all the Liberal and nationalist circles in Europe. The Emperor was torn between conflicting sympathies and opposing counsels. Persigny was the friend of the English, Drouyn of the Austrians, Morny of the Russians. Ollivier gives it as his opinion that the capital fault of the Empire was that it did not make a firm friend of the Tsar after the Crimean War. Napoleon listened to everybody and trusted nobody. Like Louis XV he sent abroad secret agents and wove his own web of secret diplomacy. Walewski was kept in ignorance of his master's secret meeting with Cavour at Plombières and of the offensive and defensive alliance which was there entered into. No ambassador and no Minister. knew of the Triple Alliance between Austria, Italy, and France which was so nearly concluded in 1869. 'A declaration from one of my Ministers', observed Napoleon to Von Goltz, 'would not be important. I alone know what the foreign policy of France will be'—a perfectly intelligible position, but one not easily to be conciliated with parliamentary control.

The truth of the matter is that Napoleon III was ill-fitted for the rôle of a constitutional monarch, not because he was devoid of public virtue or popular instincts, but because he could not divest himself of certain ingrained habits of mind, partly due to his antecedents as a plotter, partly to his early practice of autocracy, which are incompatible with true parliamentary government. His reputation both as a man and a statesman has suffered abrupt and unusual vicissitudes. After a period of almost unqualified censure and contempt, a marked tendency has set in to portray the Emperor not indeed as a model of domestic virtue—that would be plainly impossible —but as more generous and less Machiavellian than he had been depicted, to discover in him a certain width of view and elevation of aim, a kindliness of disposition, even a warmth of heart, wholly incompatible with the cruel and calculating egotism ascribed to him by such writers as Kinglake and Victor Hugo. This tendency, which is part of the general revival of Napoleonic studies and has been powerfully assisted by the writings of M. Ollivier, has recently found an English exponent in Mr. Simpson, who has derived from a careful study of Louis Bonaparte's early life a great, perhaps an excessive, admiration for the character of his hero. That Louis Bonaparte possessed in early life an inflexible faith in his destiny, that his tenacity was proof against failures which would have dashed the courage and ruined the prospects of nine out of ten pretenders, that in the midst of a good deal of trumpery display and vulgar self-indulgence he showed industry and resource, that he played a •remarkably bad hand with surprising skill, always keeping himself in view when it was most opportune that he should be noticed, always projecting his mind into the future and cleverly guiding it into the grooves of the social progress, will not be denied by any one who studies the pages of Mr. Simpson or those of his French precursors, MM. Thirria and Lebey. But was he of the stuff out of which constitutional monarchs are made? Was he loyal? Was he capable of trusting his Ministers? Had he those habits of judicious compromise and quiet influence which are essential to the successful conduct of a constitutional monarchy? Above all, was he prepared to make a permanent surrender of autocratic power, or were his concessions accompanied by half-formed and cloudy resolutions of withdrawal which the energetic pressure of a reactionary camarilla might at any moment cause to solidify in action? It is to questions such as these that M. Ollivier supplies an unsatisfactory answer.

The early life of Louis Napoleon would, of itself, constitute a weighty reason for distrusting the solidity of the Liberal Empire. For the profession of constitutional monarchy there can be no worse training than a youth expended in conspiracy. Now whether or no Louis Bonaparte was in 1831 an enrolled member of the Carbonaro Society or only in avowed sympathy with its aims, it is certain that he graduated in Italian conspiracy and that for eighteen years conspiracy of the most secret kind was the main strand of his existence. And this conspiracy belonged in no small measure to the type which is most repugnant to a delicate conscience. For about five years Louis Bonaparte's main object was to debauch the loyalty of the French army. He began by composing a treatise on artillery and by circulating it as widely as might be among the French officers of that arm. Then in 1836, when his name had acquired some notoriety, he made an attempt to corrupt the garrison of Strasburg, was arrested, pardoned by the King, and dispatched to America. Having failed with the great eastern garrison, he and his friends next turned their attention to the army of the north. In 1840 they crossed the Channel, a live eagle tied to the mast of their vessel, and descended on Boulogne. The affair was a ludicrous and ignominious failure. The Pretender was this time put upon his trial and sentenced to lifelong imprisonment in the insalubrious castle of Ham. Here, exhibiting the finer side of a character singularly compounded of good and evil, he addressed himself to the cultivation of those branches of knowledge which seemed likely to commend him to the rising generation. He composed a pamphlet on the extinction of pauperism which drew a warm eulogy from George Sand, advocated protective duties on sugar to conciliate the beetroot industry, and recommended a study of the Prussian military system to keep his name before the soldiers. Louis Blanc visited him in prison and found him interested in Socialism; Lord Malmesbury, another visitor, reported that five years of confinement had not emptied his mind or relaxed his faith. It is, however, probable that both in mind and body he was permanently affected by his imprisonment at Ham, that he here grew into those vague, dreamy, and indecisive habits which became the perplexity of his advisers and the calamity of his country, and that it was here that were sown the seeds of that serious malady without which Prussia might now be a less powerful State, and France a more weighty factor in the balance of Europe.

We are not here specially concerned with the moral aspect of Louis Bonaparte's early escapades. His defenders invite us to believe that he was justified in attempting to overturn a government which was supported by brute force alone. That the July monarchy was 'wholly without the spirit of improvement', and that it 'wrought almost exclusively through the meaner and more selfish instincts of mankind', is the verdict of John Stuart Mill; but admitting all the allegations which have been brought against it, such as that it was sprung upon the country by a small knot of politicians and journalists, that it was neither brave, nor glorious, nor progressive, that it entirely failed to strike the common imagination or to enlist the affections of France, it may still be asked by what right a young gentleman, with not as much as fifty friends in the country, embarked upon an adventure which could only have one of two issues—instant failure or a costly civil war. The government which Louis Bonaparte sallied out to overthrow was not ideal; but at least it enlarged the liberties of the country and rallied to its support an array of parliamentary talent such as France had not seen before and has never since enjoyed. Moreover, in 1836, when the first assault was made upon the fidelity of the army, the government of Louis Philippe had not yet developed into a rigid system that stationary and unintelligent resistance to reform which brought about its downfall twelve years later. There was at that time every reason to believe that the frame of the constitution might be gradually adapted to the needs of a democracy. The hereditary peerage had gone; the franchise, though still far too narrow, had been expanded; and since property was safe and the principles of social equality had been secured in the institutions of the country, there was no grave reason for discontent. The plan of the building was tolerable, and its insufficiencies could be remedied by alterations and additions. A patriot would at least have waited until there was reason to suppose that the occupants themselves were determined to pull the old structure down and to rebuild upon a new and improved plan from basement to rafter.

That moment came in 1848; and out of the whirlpool of revolution Disraeli's 'Prince Florestan' swam ashore with a crown. He had arrived in London two years earlier, the hero of an escape which in its brilliant perfection of contrivance would have done honour to the invention of Dumas; and at the first tidings of the February revolution he crossed the Channel to take advantage of events. Finding the political skies vexed and unpropitious, he discreetly returned to his safe London harbourage to wait for a softer wind and a calmer sea. No very long draft was made upon his patience. Reputations are quickly used up in the furnace of revolution, and in the course of one short summer all the brightest flowers of the early spring were parched and drooping. Ledru-Rollin, ominously prominent in March, was a beaten man in May. Lamartine, who was expected to be able to sweep the country in April, was a spent force in October. Cavaignac, who had saved Paris in June, was reported in November to be assured of defeat for the significant reason that he was supposed to be specially identified with the Republic. All the odds were on the new man, who bore a famous name, who had kept himself free from paltry entanglements, who had steered clear of the dangerous shoals upon which so many light and flaunting barks had run to their destruction.

When it was decided that the President of the Republic should be elected not by the legislature but by the people, Louis Bonaparte was assured of victory. The eloquent and irresponsible tribute of two sublime sentimentalists was blazoned on his electoral manifestoes. Chateaubriand had written that no name went better with the glory of France, and George Sand, in allusion to the tract on pauperism, announced that the Napoleon of to-day personified the sufferings of the people, as his uncle had been the incarnation of their pride. The candidate himself behaved with rare discretion. He was watchful and silent, holding himself aloof from public debate or party war-cries, while shadowing forth that vague policy of comprehension which was the secret of his power. His maiden speech in the Chamber was a fortunate, perhaps a calculated, failure, for by giving the impression of stupidity he disarmed the vigilance of his foes. Like his uncle before Brumaire, he made himself accessible to men of every political colour, even to those from whom social order had most to fear. He told Proudhon that he was no dupe of the calumnies scattered against the Socialists, and left upon that acute and fantastic person the impression of a chivalrous head and heart, of a mediocre genius unlikely to prosper, and finally of a man whose professions it would be well to distrust.

The habits engendered in this period of watchful strain were not easily thrown off. We may freely agree with M. Ollivier when he tells us that the programme of the Liberal Empire was implicit in the *Idées Napoléoniennes* published in 1839, and that the whole course of Napoleon's internal policy was conducted on a long-meditated plan. The Liberal Empire was unquestionably a deduction of the intellect. Was it ever in any full sense a conviction of the heart? M. Ollivier quotes, in order to refute it, a passage[1] from the memoirs of Baron Haussmann describing a confidential talk with the Emperor in the park of St. Cloud on June 13, 1870, in the course of which Napoleon complained of the incapacity of his Liberal Ministry, and announced his intention of restoring autocracy at the end of the parliamentary session. There was no love lost between Haussmann and Ollivier, and the Empress has authorized a denial of this serious imputation upon her husband's loyalty. But the Empress was not present at the interview, and the story is so circumstantial and also so typical of the Emperor's wavering purpose that we cannot lightly brush it aside. The Court had never approved of his liberal concessions, and no fine ear was required to overhear its whispered discontent. Nor can we wonder if, in view of the pressure of the autocratic party and the manifold signs of public disquietude —the demonstrations in the streets, the lampoons in the press, and the tirades in the Chamber—the Emperor should experience moods of doubt and regret, moods in which his liberal experiment would appear to be a failure, and the prompt withdrawal of parliamentary government an imperious necessity of politics.

The difficulties which M. Ollivier surmounted in working his system of liberal ideas into the fabric of the Empire may have led him to think that the reconstructed edifice was more compact than it really was. In any case the Liberal Constitution was killed in an accident before it had time to prove its worth. Of the causes which led to this sudden ruin of his political hopes M. Ollivier has much that is valuable to relate. He was close to the central wheel of affairs; he kept a diary, and to the resources of a full memory he adds an acquaintance with the voluminous literature which has sprung up round the origins of the Franco-Prussian War. Many points which had been

[1] *L'Empire Libéral*, xiii. 522-5.

obscure to him at the time he has since been able to clear up in conversation or correspondence with important people. Of course M. Ollivier is human, and that he should absolve himself of any part of the blame is as natural as that he should find his principal scape-goat in the Prussian Chancellor. But his work is stamped with an air of candour and conviction, and his narrative is the fullest, the most scrupulous, and the most authoritative statement which has yet been published on the French side.

The causes of the Franco-Prussian War reach back to 1866. France could never forgive or forget the battle of Sadowa or the Treaty of Prague. She had expected to reap a golden harvest out of the collision between the Prussian and the Austrian monarchies, arguing that the struggle would be long and exhausting, and that the moment would surely come when the Emperor would impose his mediation and claim his reward. But these plausible calculations were shattered by the swiftness of the Prussian triumph. The King of Prussia had made himself master of all Germany north of the Main, while the Emperor of France had gained nothing, not a Belgian fortress nor a German hamlet. A surprising and unpleasant series of contrasts became suddenly evident even to the most listless eye ; the Head of the French State tranquilly composing a life of Julius Caesar while the Head of the Prussian State was forging the most powerful army in Europe ; the prize of Venice shaken out into the weak arms of Italy from the superabundant cornucopia of Prussian victory ; the prize of Mexico abandoned with every circumstance of humiliation at the imperious command of an Anglo-Saxon republic ; on the French side a chain of diplomatic rebuffs in Denmark, in Poland, in Bohemia, on the Prussian side nothing attempted which the power of the State was not able to carry to a conclusion ; on the one hand evidence of intellectual design, on the other of vague, ill-calculated and inconsistent policies. The Opposition led by Thiers rubbed in the sore. They proclaimed that France had been lowered in the scale of nations, that Sadowa was a national defeat, and that if ever the Prussians should attempt to cross the Main it would be the duty of the French Government to go to war. This opinion was by no means confined to the Opposition. Rouher and the Conservatives were equally clear that under any circumstances an attempt to draw the South German States into the Hohenzollern net would be a *casus belli*.

M. Ollivier drew a distinction. As a champion of the doctrine of nationalities he could not consistently oppose the unification of Germany if it were accomplished by the free act of the German people. In his view the principle of nationalities was sacred, and the balance of power was not. He would fight to protect the South Germans from Prussian coercion, but he thought it both wrong and futile to oppose a spontaneous union of North and South, even if such a union should change the European balance unfavourably to France. But these views were sparsely held. Neither Daru nor Gramont, who successively reigned at the Foreign Office during the Ollivier Ministry, agreed on this point with their *chef de cabinet*. M. Ollivier, however, was not the man to dissemble his opinions, and having arranged for their publication in the *Kölnische Zeitung* (March 13 and 24, 1870), was satisfied that his pacific intentions were known to the German public.

The Liberal Cabinet came into power on December 27, 1869, and almost at once began to make cautious and secret advances to Prussia through English channels with a view to mutual disarmament. Daru told Lord Clarendon that France was willing to take the initiative with a reduction of ten thousand men on her annual contingent; but Bismarck would not listen for a moment to this kind of palaver. He said that the Tsar's health was uncertain, that he could not count on the Tsarevitch, and that the North German confederation might find itself confronted with an alliance between Russia, Austria, and the South German States. The project dropped, and early in May 1870 M. Ollivier heard from Benedetti, the French ambassador in Berlin, that Prussia would be impelled by the pressure of the smaller Northern States to annex the South as soon as she could do it with impunity. Nevertheless, M. Ollivier persisted in believing that the peace could be kept and that a struggle with Prussia did not enter into the schemes of

his master. Those who have attributed Machiavellian projects
to the Emperor have been wont to lay stress on the *plébiscite*
of May 8, and upon Gramont's summons to the Foreign Office
on May 14. M. Ollivier assures them that they are completely
mistaken: No thought of war crossed the Emperor's mind
when he determined to submit the amended and liberalized
constitution to the verdict of the electors. He was not asking
for a fresh lease of authority in view of foreign eventualities;
he was, on the contrary, giving a reluctant assent to the demands
of his Liberal advisers. So little did he wish for the *plébiscite*,
that in discussing constitutional reform with M. Ollivier he had
made it an express condition that no *plébiscite* should be taken.
Nor did the Emperor's success at the polls and on the morrow
of the *plébiscite* deflect the policy of Court and Cabinet from
its pacific grooves. Gramont indeed had been since 1861
ambassador at Vienna, from which post of vantage he had
narrowly watched the onward march of Prussian greatness, and
Gramont, though neither senator nor deputy, was on May 14
brought to the Foreign Office. It has been usual to assume
that the Duke was a firebrand pitched into a pacific Ministry
by the joint action of the Emperor and Rouher in order that
matters might be carried with a high hand. To all such surmises M. Ollivier opposes a categorical denial. Gramont was
no firebrand, and it was M. Ollivier who recommended Gramont
to the Emperor, not Napoleon who imposed him on Ollivier.
From the first the bourgeois Minister fell under the charm of
the finished aristocrat. 'I met him at Prince Napoleon's. He
appeared to me to be seductive, enlightened, instructed.
He showed me his dispatch of 1866.' M. Ollivier does not
conceal the fact that upon the most important point of foreign
policy he thought differently from the man to whom he entrusted
the portfolio of foreign affairs. Gramont intended to resist the
union of Germany at all costs, Ollivier would draw the sword
only on proof of Northern coercion. For the present, however,
the cracks were plastered over, and the Cabinet hung on, mark-
ing time and keeping an open mind as to the future.

The Emperor had been more provident than his Ministers.
When Gramont went to Vienna to take leave of his embassy

he was shown to his amazement the text of a treaty which his master had been negotiating for the past year behind his back. The draft was of the greatest moment, nothing less than a scheme for an offensive and defensive alliance between France, Austria, and Italy; but it was unsigned and unratified because Victor Emmanuel exacted as the price of his adhesion the evacuation of Rome by the French troops. The negotiations, however, were suspended, not broken, and the three sovereigns exchanged autograph letters to that effect. Indeed, on May 28 Lebrun was dispatched to Vienna to hold a secret military conference with the Archduke Albert. But of all this the *chef de cabinet* was kept in the darkest ignorance.

It was early in June, while Lebrun was at Schönbrunn concerting military operations with the Austrian Archduke, that Bismarck requested Marshal Prim to renew his offer of the Spanish Crown to Prince Leopold of Hohenzollern. As far back as the spring of 1869 the Prussian Chancellor became aware that Napoleon was preparing a triple alliance against him, and in the Hohenzollern candidature he descried a chance of precipitating a conflict before the scheme of his enemy was matured. The pride of France would never tolerate a member of the Prussian Royal Family on the throne of Spain, even though that Prussian was a Roman Catholic and more nearly connected by blood with the French Emperor than with the King of Prussia. Bismarck was well aware of this. The Hohenzollern candidature had been discussed confidentially in Berlin in 1869, and the Prussian Foreign Office was put in possession of the French objections. So when on July 3 the news came to Paris that Prince Leopold had accepted the offer of the Spanish throne, subject to the confirmation of the Cortes, the French Cabinet instantly flew to the conclusion that here was a plot carved and polished by a cunning hand for the humiliation of France. They agreed that the Prince would not have accepted the throne without the consent of King William, and they received with imperfectly veiled incredulity the assurances of Von Thile that the Prussian Government had not stirred in the matter. An instant conclusion was arrived at that the candidature must be broken off before the Cortes met on July 20, otherwise the enemy would be Spain not Prussia, and while France was occupied in punishing the innocent, the guilty party would go off with the loot. A Council was held at St. Cloud on July 6 to consider the whole situation and to frame a plan of action. M. Ollivier, exhibiting a curious misunderstanding of the state of Europe, argued for a Russian alliance ; Gramont, speaking from closer knowledge, urged a treaty with the Austrians ; finally the Emperor for the first time divulged his secret negotiations with the courts of Vienna and Florence. As he read out the autograph letters which had passed between the three crowned heads, it must have been plain to every one that the withdrawal of the French garrison from Rome was the true crux of the problem of alliances. But no question was more delicate than the maintenance of the temporal power of the Pope ; and not a voice was raised to propose its discussion. The Council proceeded to debate the terms of a declaration to be made to the Chambers. The plan of such a manifesto had sprung up in M. Ollivier's brain and receives no little commendation from his pen. Gramont had drafted a paper which was both hot and strong, and M. Ollivier made it hotter and stronger. Then it was read out to the enthusiastic plaudits of the Legislature. The war fever caught hold of the city. In the Chambers and the press it was loudly proclaimed that Prussia had thrown down the glove and that France must take it up. Five days passed of anxious negotiation and heated polemic. Then late in the evening of July 11 an unofficial telegram reached Paris that Prince Anthony of Hohenzollern had been induced to renounce the Spanish throne in the name of his son. When the news was spread abroad in the following afternoon, a feeling passed over Europe that the crisis was surmounted. The King of Italy returned to his mountains to hunt; his ambassador in Paris congratulated Napoleon on a 'great moral victory', and Macmahon was ordered to suspend the embarkation of the African troops. 'Oui, c'est la paix,' said the Emperor, and in many quarters it was held that it was peace with honour. Guizot said that he could never remember a greater diplomatic victory for France, and Bismarck has recorded in his 'Thoughts and Recollections' that since Olmütz Prussia had experienced no greater humiliation.

No disease is more contagious than the war fever, nor is there one less susceptible of sudden cure. Up till 3 p.m. on July 12 the French Ministers had been strung up to regard war as inevitable, and now that intelligence had been received of Prince Anthony's vicarious renouncement they could not suddenly divest themselves of the suspicions and animosities which the conflict had excited in their minds. When Olozaga, the ambassador of Spain, came to Gramont with the news, the French Foreign Minister, so far from regarding the affair as settled, held that it had been rendered still more difficult of solution. In the telegram which had been addressed by Prince Anthony to Prim there was no word either of France or of Prussia. The Prince had been induced to renounce the Spanish throne in the name of his son (who was thirty-five years of age) upon the representations of Strat, the Roumanian envoy who had been dispatched to Sigmaringen from Paris on the initiative of Olozaga and with the secret concurrence of Napoleon. The telegram was *en clair*, and all the representations of Benedetti, the French ambassador, had been unavailing to induce King William either to command or to counsel a retreat. Gramont, in whom the punctilio of a professional diplomatist was blended with a deep conviction of Prussian duplicity, considered that the honour of France required something more than the bare renunciation of 'Le Père Antoine'; but M. Ollivier, more easily satisfied, said that if the candidature were seriously withdrawn the affair was at an end, and that he would be no party to pressing fresh demands upon the Prussian Court.

Fortunate would it have been for France if M. Ollivier had been able to persist in this decision and secure its acceptance. The Triple Alliance was still in the region of dreams, and France had everything to gain by postponing the conflict, if conflict there must have been, until she had secured an ally; but a spirit of mad unreason had seized upon the Chambers,

and when it was known among the deputies of the Right
that M. Ollivier thought well of the prospects of peace, there
was a loud explosion of anger and a formal inquiry from the
tribune as to the guarantees which the Government intended
to demand to prevent a repetition of similar complications.
The ominous phrase ' guarantees ' launched by Clément
Duvernois passed like wildfire through the town on to the
Palace of St. Cloud. In that atmosphere of high tension and
irresponsible vainglory the one fear was that war might be
averted. Four years before the country had stood aside,
and Prussia had comfortably eaten up North Germany.
Was that humiliation to be repeated? Was the pretended
resignation to be taken as serious and France to be again
fooled into torpor while Prussia massed fresh battalions and
swallowed fresh territory? If so, the Empire would perish,
and Bourbaki, melodramatically throwing his sword upon
the billiard table, allowed it to be known that the tragedy
of peace would be deepened by a general's resignation. The
Emperor was not proof against so much clamorous disappoint-
ment, and with the first shades of evening was pushed into the
crowning indiscretion of his life. Though it had been settled
that nothing should be done till the Cabinet meeting on the
following day, July 13, he concocted with Gramont a message
to Benedetti at Ems to the effect that it seemed necessary
that the King of Prussia should associate himself with Prince
Anthony's withdrawal, and that he—the King—should give
an assurance that he would not authorize any renewal of the
Hohenzollern candidature. The momentous telegram was
dispatched at 7 p.m. Later in the evening, after some
deputies of the Right, among them Jérôme David and
Cassagnac, had been to the Palace and put fresh powder on
the fire, an Imperial letter was sent to the Foreign Office
instructing Gramont to accentuate the dispatch. But the
first telegram had reached Benedetti, and before he heard
again from Paris he had seen King William and pressed the
demand for guarantees.

It was hard upon midnight before M. Ollivier, calling
at the Foreign Office, heard that a telegram had been sent

and that another was projected. He was placed in a position of great difficulty. A new and dangerous turn had been given to the Government's diplomacy behind his back and without the knowledge of the Cabinet. An English Minister, placed in M. Ollivier's position, would certainly have resigned his seals rather than render himself responsible for a policy diametrically opposed to the course which only a few hours before he had openly professed to be alone suited to the needs of the situation. M. Ollivier did not resign. He contented himself with advising his Foreign Minister to soften the tone of the dispatch to Benedetti, and himself wrote a short paragraph which he seems to have expected that Gramont would substitute for the original text. Then he left the room 'troubled and anxious'. There was every reason in the world why he should. In that brief interview he had allowed himself to be driven from a sound position. He had advised that the Prussian King should be asked to give a guarantee that he would not permit Prince Leopold to throw over Prince Anthony's renunciation. It is true that such a demand was slightly less exacting than the demand contained in the dispatch which had been sent off at 7 p.m.; for M. Ollivier's proposed guarantee was limited in point of time to the situation of the moment, whereas the dispatch of 7 p.m. required King William to give an indefinite guarantee against any renewal of the candidature. But this does not greatly attenuate M. Ollivier's lapse. He had assumed responsibility for the provocative demand for guarantees, and he had not even made it clear to Gramont that the limitation of the guarantee to the present case was the uttermost point to which he would consent to go.

M. Ollivier did not come to his decision to cling to office without anxious consideration and a sleepless night. The simile of the lightning conductor and the thunderbolt, which had once before done duty in a political crisis, came to his mind and brought relief. He would remain in the storm centre as the lightning conductor. He reckoned himself certain of a majority in the Council, less certain of the Chamber, where he might be overthrown by a coalition of the extreme wings; but with the Emperor's support he might conjure the storm. At first it almost seemed as if his calculations would work out. At the Council meeting on the morning of the 13th a pacific close followed upon the forked lightnings of a passionate opening. When everything appeared to be at its worst, Lebœuf calling imperiously for the reserves, the Emperor supporting the demand for mobilization, a servant entered with a letter from Lord Lyons, who spoke of the immense responsibility which the Government of the Empire would incur, should. it enlarge the field of discussion. The Emperor read the letter aloud and the debate was resumed, every member speaking in his turn, and M. Ollivier rising again and again to protest against mobilization. At last the Emperor swung round, dragging Gramont in his train, and the peace party won a victory by eight votes to four. It was too late to withdraw the request for guarantees, but if guarantees were refused the Council would be content with a token of the royal concurrence in Prince Anthony's act. When the evening telegrams came in and it was known that King William had given his entire and unreserved approval to the withdrawal of the Prince, M. Ollivier believed that the crisis was over, and that France would not and should not insist on guarantees. 'Maintenant c'est véritablement fini,' he observed. But Gramont's mood was different: 'c'est peu,' was his ominous and laconic verdict upon the latest intelligence from Ems.

Disillusion followed hard upon the heels of confidence. On the morning of July 14 Gramont burst into M. Ollivier's room with a little leaf of yellow paper in his hands—a telegram from Berlin telling of a certain special supplement of the *North German Gazette* which described how the French ambassador had molested King William on the promenade at Ems, how the King had refused to see him and had announced through his aide-de-camp that he had no further communication to make to him. It was the famous Ems telegram which Bismarck had condensed and caused to be published that he might scatter abroad the impression that his Prussian master had received and resented an affront from the ambassador of

France. This time M. Ollivier saw clearly. 'They wish', he said, 'to force us into war.' At 12.30 the Emperor came to the Tuileries, driving through a sea of angry, impatient faces. The Council opened with a demonstration. 'After what has passed,' cried Gramont, throwing his portfolio on the table as he took his seat, 'no Foreign Minister worthy of his place would hesitate to declare war.' Lebœuf said that the Prussians were buying horses in Belgium and that there was not a moment to spare. And then the ball was thrown to and fro. The dispatches of Benedetti had given the impression that King William had been courteous, and a sovereign was certainly within his rights in declining to give audience to an ambassador. On the other hand, how could the Special Supplement, containing, as it did, an official telegram, only to be supplied from official sources, be otherwise construed than as a deliberate provocation? The same men who had hoped for peace the day before now held that peace was improbable, and at 4 p.m. it was unanimously determined to call out the reserves. Forty minutes later Lebœuf left the Tuileries to take the necessary steps.

Then ensued one of the most dramatic revulsions in the history of that tormented day. A fresh dispatch arrived from Benedetti giving to the language of the King of Prussia a less peremptory form, and sending a sudden spasm of indecision through the veins of that haggard and harassed assemblage. Perhaps they had been precipitate, had neglected expedients, might yet honourably withdraw? In the general agony Gramont threw out an idea which was caught up as an instrument of salvation—an appeal to a general congress. With tears coursing down his cheeks the Emperor bade Ollivier, his ready writer and rhetorician, pen a Declaration of appeal to the Powers, and when at last this had been approved the Council dispersed. It was 6.30 p.m. The tired men stumbled out into the evening air.

Not many minutes elapsed before M. Ollivier's beautiful Declaration began to burn a hole in his pocket. As he reflected in the cool air on the decision which had been taken in the heat of an exhausting Council, he thought it cowardly. Returning to the Chancery, he summoned his wife, his brothers, and his secretaries, and read out to them the 'pathetic and eloquent' document which was intended for the consumption of the Legislature on the following day. Cries of astonishment and indignation went up from the domestic circle which had been thus hastily initiated into a secret of the State. And if such was M. Ollivier's return to his dovecote, we may imagine the discomfort of the Emperor among the war-hawks of the Palace. 'What!' cried the Empress to Lebœuf, 'do you also approve this cowardice? Dishonour yourself if you must, do not dishonour the Emperor.' In a paroxysm of penitence a fresh Council was summoned to meet after dinner at St. Cloud.

It was one of those delicious summer evenings before August has parched the leaves, when the air is hot but not heavy, and the stars shine softly overhead, throwing their pale reflections into the slow, languid waters of the Seine. Here and there groups of men and women strolled and chatted along the quays and shaded alleys of the Bois de Boulogne. A serene peace brooded over Paris. M. Ollivier drove to St. Cloud and found that the Emperor's thoughts had taken the same course as his own. The Congress was unsatisfactory; neither the Chambers nor the streets would stand it. 'Mud would be thrown at our carriages,' said the Minister, 'and they would hoot us.' After some moments of silence the Emperor answered, 'See in what a plight a government may sometimes find itself. Even if we had no motive for war which we could avow, we should nevertheless be obliged to resolve on it to obey the will of the people.' The conversation was interrupted by the arrival of the other Ministers, and for the first time the Empress took her seat at the Council board. Lebœuf began by explaining that he had called out the reserves, but that this should not affect the issue; he could recall the order and resign. Then Gramont read the latest telegrams. They showed that the refusal of the King of Prussia to receive Benedetti was being officially communicated to foreign governments. The Council determined that the reserves should be called out. There was no occasion for voting, nor did the Empress open her lips. The final step was left for the morning. At 9 a.m. on July 15 the Cabinet met again at St. Cloud, and again the Empress was present. The mood of Paris was angry and unmistakable, and as the Ministers drove to the Palace they were assailed by cries of 'À Berlin' and 'Vive la guerre'. When Gramont had finished reading the Declaration the Emperor clapped his hands. The war was voted with unanimity, the Empress alone neither speaking nor casting a vote; but it is charac- teristic of Napoleon that as his Ministers were on their way to the Legislative Assembly he received Witzthum, the Austrian Minister at Brussels, who was going to Vienna, and asked him to request Francis Joseph to summon a congress that peace might be preserved. But the die was cast. The Chamber vociferously applauded the intrepid spirit of the Cabinet, and by an imposing majority voted a credit of fifty millions to the war.

Such, in bare outline, is the painful story. Thiers puts the responsibility for the war upon the blunders of the Liberal Cabinet; the Emperor more wisely divided the blame between himself, his Ministers, and the Chambers; M. Ollivier brings into special prominence the bellicose attitude of the Conservative party, which at the critical moment sacrificed a great diplomatic advantage by pressing the Emperor to ask for guarantees. It is clear that the French might have honourably avoided war after the withdrawal of the Hohenzollern prince, and that in this sense Bismarck spoke the truth when he told Lord Goschen that the war was not of his making. It is also clear that nothing gave Bismarck greater pleasure than the news that the French were producing fresh demands. But what a satire is this exhibition of inconsequence, hesitation, and division upon the vaunted solidity of the Liberal Empire! The most critical decision in the whole course of the negotiations is taken by the Emperor and the Foreign Minister without the knowledge of the Cabinet, and the Chief of the Cabinet accepts a policy which he does not approve, because when it comes to his ears it is already irreversible. In spite of all that M. Ollivier has written, Gramont's handling of the problem was either wholly incompetent or quite inconsistent with peaceful desires. M. Ollivier is generous to an honourable colleague, from whom he was divided more widely than he seems to imagine; but, at least, at this great crisis of national destiny the two Ministers were united in a common failing. Neither of them kept his head.

A Leaf from a Corsican Note-Book

IT was very cold at Vizzavona. Though the second week of April was nearing its close, the snow lay deep upon the road and the wind whistled through the pine forest which clothes the lower slope of the Monte d'Oro. Trudging up the long causeway from the station the party from Corte felt that it had been suddenly transported from Corsica into Switzerland. We were cold and we were hungry, for the hour was close upon two, and we had touched no food since our light breakfast at eight o'clock in the mountain stronghold of Boswell's Paoli.

At last we gained the hotel, a low shabby building posted on the top of the pass opposite the gleaming summit of the mountain, with a glass veranda, pleasant enough doubtless in summer-time, but in this Arctic temperature very properly deserted by the visitors. The one permanent occupant of the hotel, a young Dane, born and bred in Iceland, who had chosen this desolate spot as suited to the composition of a doctor's thesis upon the origin and nature of genius, was crouching over a wood fire in the little salon. A few French motorists shivered by, eager to exchange this disconsolate spell of winter for the palms, the oranges, and the sunlight of the coast. With the keeper of the hotel such speed was a note of human frailty, for he was himself a Dane, with the grave and stoical habit of the North.

The importance of Vizzavona lies in the fact that it is the highest point in the long diagonal line of communication which connects Bastia on the north-east with Ajaccio on the south-west of the island. Every traveller who wishes to combine

Bastia, Corte, and Ajaccio in his tour must pass over the pine-clad shoulders of the Monte d'Oro, and, save in the summer months, must be prepared to find the forest of Vizzavona deep in snow. The stout Genoese fort which stands upon the little spur just opposite the hotel, and is visible for many a mile to travellers ascending the valley from the south, shows how much the old masters of the island thought of this position, and incidentally also how little they cared for aesthetic effect. Indeed, no one must expect architectural beauties in so poor a land as Corsica. From the earliest extant monuments o the sixteenth to the latest achievements of the twentieth century, there is not a single biluding which reaches respectability. The country learnt nothing from its conquerors, and contributed nothing of its own. In Corfu and elsewhere the Venetians have left some fine military and civil memorials in stone of their ancient Empire. Not so the Genoese ; and a baser and more squalid use of splendid stone and marble can hardly be imagined than that which in Corsica defaces some of the loveliest scenery in the world.

The proper course for an Englishman halting at Vizzavona is to ascend the Monte d'Òro, a peak over nine thousand feet above the sea, whence a view can be obtained not only of the whole island, but also, under favourable conditions, of the shores of Italy and Tunis : and as a guide can be hired for ten francs, and the time for the ascent is certainly not above four hours, the expedition is easy and inexpensive. But with a howling wind, a black sky, and a prospect of a fresh snowfall in the evening, the conditions were none too favourable, and we decided to pass on southwards in the morning, and to visit those places in the valley of the Gravona which are connected with the early history of Napoleon Bonaparte.

The villages in the upper part of the valley lie some hundred feet above the roots of the mountains upon the western or left-hand side as you descend, and occur wherever the great wall of granite flings itself back into a horseshoe curve, supplying water for man and beast, and a gentler slope for wood, pasture, and tillage. Of these villages the first, as you descend, is Bocognano, which lies some eight kilometres from the head of the pass. About a quarter of a mile above the main street of the village there is a round knoll, green and terraced, sprinkled with white fruit blossom and the shimmering grey-green of the olive, and crowned by a tiny hamlet of white stuccoed red-tiled cottages. A clear mountain-stream brawls beneath it on the south ; on the north there is a fine grove of Spanish chestnut shading the green slope of the great western bastion of the valley. This little hamlet is Poggiolo, the mountain residence of the Tusoli, in whose house Napoleon spent a night on a famous occasion. I climbed the hill under a warm midday sun, and found myself in a small piazza, face to face with a square, two-storied house of granite, quite ugly, and in every way undistinguished save for the extreme solidity of the material out of which it was built. The front door was of solid chestnut, whitened with age, and above it there was an empty niche, which may have held a Madonna or a saint. A stone balustrade ran along in front of the house from end to end. The walls, which were thick, were plastered with stucco, and the whole house was clearly built with a view to coolness and as a shelter for the eyes against the dazzling summer rays, for there were but two windows giving on the front. The floors were of stone, the shutters and great beams of the roof hewn from the chestnut grove on the estate. Such was the house of Napoleon's relatives, the first to be built in Bocognano, so my peasant guide informed me. 'Maintenant c'est presque rien,' and indeed it is now serving to receive the cast-off rubbish of the hamlet.

Whether the chance peasant will know anything about the Bonaparte traditions of his village is a matter upon which you cannot lay a bet with any approach to safety. Formerly, I should imagine that things were otherwise, but one of the many results of Napoleon's career is that more than anything else it has contributed to make Corsica, not only in constitutional law, but also in sentiment, a province of France. The young people emigrate to Algeria or Tunis, and embrace in great numbers (so vivacious is the military spirit of the island) the career of arms. The hill villages are becoming dispeopled, and here and there a smart white château tells the tale of a successful emigrant who has returned from the colonies with a fortune and with a very reduced interest in the concerns of his humbler neighbours. For the historical inquirer, the only course is to enter into conversation with the very old inhabitants. They at least may remember what their juniors have forgotten, or have never even learnt. In Bocognano, which was one of the Bonaparte villages, this method of approach brought instant success. The first two people whom I happened to accost, a fine old grey-bearded peasant in a brown velveteen coat, and the courteous lady who sells picture post-cards in the main street of the village, were both loyal members of the Bonaparte *clientèle*. 'The father of my grandfather', said the old man, 'sheltered Lieutenant Bonaparte at Tavera when he was escaping from Bocognano. My name is Jacques Mancini.' And the lady turned out to be descended on one side from the Poggiolis, a family of whom some words must be said hereafter.

The escape of Lieutenant Bonaparte from Bocognano, in May 1793, is the principal romance of this valley. The island was divided into two bitter factions—the friends and the enemies of Paoli. The great liberator, once the idol of republicans all over Europe, had been denounced to the French Convention as a royalist, a traitor, and a pensioner of England, and a decree was issued for his arrest. Such an insult levelled at such a man threw the Corsican patriots into a frenzy, and bands of armed peasants flocked into the mountain citadel of Corte, where the old general might securely defy the French Commissioners at Bastia to do their worst. Lieutenant Bonaparte, then in his twenty-fourth year, and noted throughout Corsica for the zeal of his Jacobin convictions, was at Ajaccio, where Paolist feeling ran dangerously high. He determined to cross the island and join his political friends at Bastia. So, setting out from the coast on May 3 with his faithful henchman, Santo Ricci of Bocognano, he pushed his way up the hot pass, threaded the forest of Vizzavona, and dropped down upon Corte, where it was his intention to beard Paoli in the grim old palazzo which Boswell has described. The plan was audacious to the point of impudence, more especially as it had become known to the Directory at Corte that Lucien Bonaparte was openly boasting of having procured Paoli's disgrace. Friends warned Napoleon that his life was unsafe, and that he must retreat to Ajaccio without delay. He jumped upon his horse and rode for his life. At nightfall he reached Bocognano, and was received by the Tusoli; but his enemy, Marius Peraldi, was riding post-haste upon his heels, and on the next morning, as the young lieutenant was about to resume his journey, he was taken by a band of Paolists and shut up in the inn to await the pleasure and vengeance of his foes.

The traveller who passes through Bocognano must infallibly lunch at the Hôtel de l'Univers, for, despite its ambitious title, it is a clean and modest country hostelry. Here he may fare on excellent potatoes, steamed in their jackets, and on a delicious *bruccia*, as the national dish of curds, made with goat's milk, is termed. Then they will give you an omelette and fresh butter and excellent bread, and jam made from the native apple. And fortified by such a collation you may be prepared to survey, for it is but a few steps up the hill, a large slatternly green-washed building pretentiously labelled 'Gendarmerie Nationale'. In the wall which looks down the valley towards Ajaccio you will be shown near the ground a window, out of which, on that May morning, somewhere about the hour of déjeuner, Lieutenant Bonaparte is said to have made his escape, with the help of Santo Ricci and other faithful friends, from the village of Bocognano.

The story of this adventure has been told by so many lips, and with so many variants and embellishing touches, that the historian may well despair of fixing every detail with certitude. The most illustrious of the narrators is Napoleon himself, who told Antommarchi at St. Helena that he managed to cajole his captors to allow him to stroll about in the open air, and that, seizing a pretext to withdraw, he made a sudden dash into the country. But the most elaborate and circumstantial account is the result of a judicial inquiry held at Bastia in 1855 for the purpose of ascertaining the identity of 'the man of

Bocognano', to whom, in virtue of the seventh codicil of the Emperor's will, dated April 25, 1821, a sum of twenty thousand francs had been bequeathed. At this extraordinary scrutiny no less than eighty witnesses were examined. What lies must have been told! The story which the Court decided to believe may, perhaps, be a tissue of inaccuracies, but since it is the best we have, there is no option but to follow it.[1]

Once away, he must have crossed a little garden slope, jumped the brook at the bottom, and then run for his life uphill for three or four hundred yards. Whether he had to climb the two stone walls which at present cross the line of his retreat I cannot say; but that the slope was then, as now, sprinkled with chestnut trees is more than probable, and that shots were exchanged before the fugitives crossed the ridge I learn from the lips of an old peasant who showed me the ground. Once over the crest the fugitives must have dashed down the old road which twists and twists till it meets the point where the grand new carriage road, after taking a lower and more leisurely circuit, now crosses the deep gorge of the Gravona by a solid and respectable bridge. If you pass over the river by the bridge, and climb the hedge on the other side, you will light upon a little path which leads down to the stepping-stones. Pursue that path, for there is none more delicious. The gorge is cool, steep, and narrow, clothed with solemn ilex and dark arbutus and silvery erica, and, at the bottom, there is a stream of clear and swift waters, with deep pools and tiny waterfalls and great slabs and blocks of granite strewn about its course. It is over these stones that Lieutenant Bonaparte must have passed; but if the stream were as full on that May evening as it was when I saw it, he did not pass dry-shod.

A few miles down the valley, and in another recess of the mountain barrier, stands the little village of Tavera. The black goats were browsing on the sunny green pastures, the stream was rustling merrily down to the fuller waters of the Gravona, and the white plaster and russet tiles of the

---

[1] See Marcaggi, *La Genèse de Napoléon*, whose account of this incident seems to me preferable to that given by Chuquet.

village looked gay and pleasant in the brightness. The village, which stands about a hundred feet above the railway line and the main road, is reached by a winding path of stone, walled-in on either side, and so narrow that a donkey laden with faggots is quite sufficient to obstruct all progress. Go right through the village, past the white-washed church, and strike transversely across the oaks and chestnuts towards the little white mortuary chapel of the Mancini family on the brow. Then, by a broad and broken path, over rough slabs of granite and under the grateful shadow of an ilex avenue, you will eventually reach the hamlet of Cazarac. Here a certain traveller met a very old lady, full of intelligence and curiosity, and graced with all the gentle and courteous manner of a mountain race. She took him into her cottage, fetched him a bottle of light red wine, and then, after half an hour of hospitable intercourse, conducted him to the fountain at which Lieutenant Bonaparte is recorded to have drunk upon the occasion of his famous flight from Bocognano. At Tavera he had been received by the ruling Mancini, probably on the site of the grand new house which is now the principal glory of the neighbourhood. Then he struck up the hill and plunged into the *macchia*, following a little path some half-way up the mountain-side, which my elderly friend showed me. At what hour of day the fugitives reached Cazarac I could not ascertain, but that the Mancini gave the Lieutenant a cup of milk and that the fugitives pressed on rapidly down the valley is vouchsafed on the testimony of Laurent Campana, the most credible of all the eighty witnesses in the great judicial inquiry of 1855. In any case Lieutenant Bonaparte took to the *macchia*, and to those who so proceed it is vouchsafed to enjoy a fragrance of aromatic herbs so sweet and powerful in the keen mountain air that, having once experienced this pleasure, they must needs hope ever afterwards to be able to recall it.

We did not follow the fugitives in this part of their retreat, but, since time pressed, took the shortest possible route, which is that of the railway, from Tavera to Ucciani. Here, too, the village is perched on a little spur of the great hills about a kilometre above the railway line. We ordered coffee at the inn, and, sitting in the evening sunlight on a bench outside, soon attracted a gathering of boys and men. Inquiries as to the Bonapartist legends of the place were at first singularly fruitless. The innkeeper, who looked like a Levantine, knew nothing whatever, and several likely old gentlemen proved equally sterile. At last an antique inhabitant was produced with all the prestige of eighty summers, and an assurance that he contained the necessary information. He came forward to our table and gravely took a seat. A soft felt hat was on his head, a black cloak was thrown over his shoulders, and though his clothes were old and threadbare, he had the bearing and manners of a finished gentleman. He began in excellent French : ' There was a very old man in this village whom I just remember. His name was Silvani, and he belonged to my family, for I, too, am a Silvani. We called him *il prete*. Now he knew Napoleon very well in youth, and Napoleon inquired after him at St. Helena. The Silvanis were very faithful to the Bonapartes. One of them was almoner to King Louis of Holland. Yes ; Napoleon used to stay very often at Ucciani, sometimes with the Silvanis, sometimes with the Poggiolis, and sometimes in the house of Leonati, which is now destroyed. On the occasion to which you refer, when he was fleeing from Bocognano, he stayed in the *maison Leonati*. All through his life he had many *fidèles* in Ucciani.' All this the old man said very simply and quietly, catching at times for breath. As for himself he had been a soldier ; most of his life had been passed in Algeria, a finer country than Corsica ; but he had fought in the war of 1870 and was at the battle of Sédan. A battered old gentleman, with cataract in both eyes, yet finding some consolation for the afflictions of life in his afternoon glass of lemonade and game of cards in the village inn.

He led us up to the house of the Poggioli, a stout ugly granite building, and showed us the window of the room in which Napoleon slept. An English farmer would never consent to inhabit such a building, and it would be condemned by every district council or sanitary authority in the land. Yet Napoleon slept there, so tradition affirms, and according to M. Chuquet (who in this matter contradicts my old friend) slept there on the occasion of his flight, being received by the Poggioli of the day who was then mayor of the village. There can be very little doubt that M. Chuquet is right, for in his last will and testament Napoleon left a sum of thirty thousand francs to the Poggioli who had helped to save his life upon his memorable escape down the wild and beautiful valley of the Gravona.

The next day horses were brought and the fugitives rode straight down to Ajaccio. The other alternative would have been to cross the mountains at Ucciani and to drop down upon Bastelica, a stiff walk of about two hours and a half, at the end of which Lieutenant Bonaparte would have found himself in a region noted for its loyalty to his clan. The village of Bastelica, set in a horseshoe of snow-veined granite mountains, the middle slopes of which are clothed with beech and chestnut, and the lower regions bright with apple-blossom and the sparkling green of an Alpine pasture, is one of the loveliest in Corsica; and it is not surprising that its fresh air and easy access to the highest peaks should attract visitors from Ajaccio during the blaze of summer. But unlike Evisa and Vizzavona, Bastelica is not the product of tourist agencies. On the contrary, it is the historic storm-centre of Corsican history, the birthplace of Sanpiero, the valiant champion of Corsican independence in the sixteenth century, and the scene of one of the classic battles of that age. Seven times has Bastelica been burned, once by the Saracens, once by the Pisans, and five times by the Genoese. An old resident told me that he remembered in his youth the charred houses which bore witness to the last burning of the eighteenth century. Yet, save for the accident of Sanpiero's birth, the reason for the importance of Bastelica is not immediately apparent. It lies in a cup at the head of a valley, but the valley is to some extent a *cul-de-sac*. There are, of course, paths across the mountains, but no one pass so important as that which connects the valley of the Gravona with the region of Corte. The true reason for the importance of Bastelica would seem to lie in the fact that it is the summer pasturing ground for the goatherds and shepherds who, during the winter months, are scattered abroad through the levels of the long valley which broadens down into the sunny and fertile Campo del Oro on the shores of the Gulf of Ajaccio. Even now the population of Bastelica is doubled every June by the incoming of the herdsmen with their flocks and goats from the lower levels of the vine and the olive. Bastelici all of them, for the canton stretches from the mountains to the sea, they collect in their Highland capital during the fighting season of the year, and in the days when fighting was half the business of life were so posted as to be able to dispute the entry into one of the richest valleys in Corsica. Now the herdsmen of this region were friendly to the Bonapartes who possessed land in the Campo del Oro, and were no doubt good customers for the curds and chestnut cakes, the sausages and homespun, which are the principal products of the uplands. It would therefore have been a natural course for Napoleon, had he been hard pressed at Ucciani, to escape by way of Bastelica; but that he did not do so is clear. There is no tradition. The mayor, the apothecary, 'le grand Joseph', the spacious innkeeper, who looks as if he had stepped out of a picture of Vandyke, roundly deny that Lieutenant Bonaparte stopped at Bastelica in his flight. The old men of the place know nothing of him here, and we may be safe in concluding that if they know nothing there is nothing to be known.

It is curious how little attention is paid by the French Government to the old houses which are connected with the early history of Napoleon. One would have thought at least that some *plaque* would mark the dwellings in which the Emperor had slept in his boyhood, or which are known to have been in the possession of his family. But neither is this pre-caution against oblivion adopted nor is any attention paid to the upkeep of the structure. A few miles outside Ajaccio, on the slope of a flowery hill, stands the country house of the family, the house of Milelli, from which the fiery young radical lieutenant indited his fierce letter to Buttafuoco. When Gregorovius was in the island in 1852 he was shown the oak (or rather ilex) in the garden of Milelli under which Napoleon would sit dreaming or working, with the azure waters of the bay far below him and the steel-grey mountains beyond.

The ilex has now disappeared, and the visitors must be content with a dubious stump in the midst of weeds and asphodel. The tall, gaunt house is a slatternly olive farm; and the garden in front of it, if a tangled mass of weeds can be so described, is ornamented with the family washing. Great blocks of granite strewn here and there among the olives and ilexes give an air of disordered grandeur to the scene. When we visited the spot groups of girls were gathering the olive harvest, and the *padrone*—his hands, face, and shirt black with olive-oil, and in possession of no language but the Corsican dialect—was far too much occupied with his important business to attend to the wants of unintelligible tourists. Nevertheless, being courteous, as are all Corsicans, he led us down to the sorry remnant of Napoleon's tree and plucked us a branch of oranges from the garden. And so laden, we returned up the pretty country path, with its hedges of white cistus and wild peas, and lupins and golden broom, to the carriage which awaited us in the Casteluccio road.

It is now nearly a hundred and fifty years since Corsica came under the dominion of France, and the conquerors have not been idle in the interval. They have built roads and bridges and hotels, and have so effectually spread the knowledge and practice of their language that it is now rare to find a Corsican, unless he be well past the middle age, who cannot understand a few words of French. That a race so distinct in its individuality and so proud of its peculiar traditions should have allowed itself to be absorbed in an alien civilization is due to three governing causes: the living memory of Genoese oppression, the career of Napoleon, and the facilities offered by the French connexion for the profession of arms and for colonization in Algeria and Tunis. Of these influences by far the most important is the fact that Napoleon was born at Ajaccio. In giving Napoleon to France, Corsica more than wiped out the memory of the field of Ponte Nuovo; and there is not a Corsican who does not feel that all the glories of the ancient monarchy pale beside the brilliance of his national hero. We cannot wonder that the Corsican is a Bonapartist. In the little mountain village of Tolla it was my good fortune to make friends with Jean Baptiste Marti, a gendarme in the *Gendarmerie-à-pied* under the Second Empire. He was a tall old man, with a complexion of the freshest pink, an aquiline nose, and light blue gleaming eyes, and, like all Corsicans, he was full of movement and gesture. His life had been spent under arms, and he showed a gunshot wound on his right leg, which still gave him trouble in rainy weather. For many years he had served in Algeria, and then, like many another Corsican, was enrolled in the Emperor's bodyguard. Often and often had he seen Napoleon III chatting with his officers in the barrack, or had stood on duty in the Tuileries admiring the brilliant uniforms of the men and the gay dresses of the women during an Imperial function. He could tell of all the Marshals of the Empire, of the defence of Paris against the Prussians (during which he received his wound), of the outbreak of the Commune, and the victories of the Versaillais. He had seen M. Thiers direct a gun from Mont Valerien, had taken part with his fellow Corsicans in a desperate charge up the hills of Meudon, and had done his share of street fighting against the Communards. Of all these incidents and experiences he would speak with simple and flowing eloquence, and with a touching devotion to the cause of the Corsican dynasty. And many a grey stone village in these wild hills may show such a man as he.

Among the early friends of the great Napoleon was a certain Nunzio Costa di Bastelica, a lieutenant in that second battalion of Corsican volunteers, of which Bonaparte was elected Lieutenant-Colonel in 1791. 'The brave Costa' helped the mother and sisters of Napoleon to escape to the sea on the starless night of May 30, 1793, and earned the eternal gratitude of the young artilleryman. Gratitude on the one side was matched by devotion on the other, and Costa left descendants as loyal as himself. The author of the 'Ajaccienne', which is the National Anthem of Corsica, is a Costa di Bastelica, and when the band strikes up

Réveille-toi, ville sacrée,
Dans ton orgueil et ton amour;
La Sainte Famille est rentrée,
Les exilés sont de retour.
Les voici—Victoire!   Victoire!
Qu'il soit fêté dans sa maison,
L'Enfant prodigue de la gloire,
Napoléon!   Napoléon!

every head is bared, and men and women sink upon their knees. There has been nothing like this in Europe since the Roman Emperors were worshipped with public rites. And meanwhile, on a high ridge, far above the chattering city of Ajaccio, stands a villa built out of the material of the Tuileries by Count Pozzo, descendant of that life-long enemy of Napoleon, who carried his Corsican feud into the wide field of European politics, and helped to prompt the great revenges of Alexander of Russia. Standing as it does insolently on its hill-top and assaulting the eye of every traveller who sails into the harbour by light of day as something notable and compelling, it seems to typify the victory of the dynasts, to answer the strains of the band, and to confound the devotion of the kneeling crowd.

Lord Acton's Historical Work[1]

IT was a natural idea to collect the writings of Lord Acton, for, though many men of his time were more famous, few left behind them a larger legacy of unsatisfied curiosity.

[1] 1. *Lectures on Modern History. The History of Freedom, and other Essays. Historical Essays and Studies. Lectures on the French Revolution.* By Lord Acton. Edited by J. N. Figgis and R. V. Laurence. Four vols. London: Macmillan, 1906–10.

2. *Letters of Lord Acton to Mary Gladstone.* Edited by Herbert Paul. London: George Allen, 1904.

3. *Lord Acton and his Circle.* By Abbot Gasquet. London: George Allen, 1906.

4. *The French Revolution: a Political History*, 1789–1804. By A. Aulard. Translated from the French by Bernard Miall. Four vols. London: Unwin, 1910.

Though he was a man of the world and polished and pleasant in society, there was always something remote and mysterious about him. He did not fall into any of the received types who are to be found in London clubs or in country-houses and college halls; and it was not easy to give him a label. His religion—for he was a member of the Roman Communion—cut him off from the pleasant but somewhat·narrow convention of English public-school and university life. His education had been lonely, peculiar, and exotic. Descent and marriage made him half a foreigner; much of his life was spent abroad at Tegernsee or at Cannes; and he did a thing which must always be véry rare among Englishmen of ample means and high station—he devoted the. devouring industry of his days and nights to the single-minded pursuit of knowledge. A good deal of pleasant antiquarian erudition has come out of English country-houses, as Sir William Dugdale's monumental folios may testify; but Lord Acton's learning was not the product of these old-fashioned pieties of the soil. He was a *savant* not of the English but of the newest and most scientific German type, and yet with none of the narrowness which marks much learned work in Germany, for he was a specialist, not only in one, but in many periods of history.

Possessing the tastes and equipment of a great continental professor, he moved in the world of fashion and affairs, and stood near, though not very near, to the wheels of government. He was the stepson of Lord Granville, whom he accompanied on a mission to Moscow, the friend and confidant of Gladstone, and a Lord-in-Waiting to Queen Victoria. Like Gibbon, he had sat in Parliament. He had known many makers of continental history; and, being a complete master of colloquial French, German, and Italian, he was able to converse with them freely and on even terms. It was often said that Lord Acton's memoirs, if memoirs he wrote, would furnish a banquet of rich and curious miscellanies which could not easily be matched. Nobody, it was reputed, was more fond or retentive of gossip, not only by reason of the natural curiosity of his mind, but from a rooted conviction that the historian must be prepared ' to take his meals in the scullery ', uniting the appetite for small things with the appetite for big ones, and carrying his trained and rigorous habit of thoroughness into the observation of passing events and living people. And yet this ravenous devourer of historical and contemporary knowledge died on June 19, 1902, having published during a long and busy life a few articles and reviews, some of them anonymous, most of them hidden away in obscure and half-forgotten periodicals, a preface to Machiavelli's *Prince*, and an inaugural lecture delivered at Cambridge upon his appointment to the Regius Chair of Modern History. Such was the literary output of a man who, in the opinion of competent judges, was more original than Seeley and as learned as Döllinger or Stubbs.

We have now more work by which to appraise him. The essays and papers prove, as is so often the case, to weigh heavier than was at first surmised, and fill two handsome octavo volumes. A course of lectures upon Modern European History delivered from the Cambridge Chair was published in 1906 ; and now, eight years after Lord Acton's death, Dr. Figgis and Mr. Lawrence, two Cambridge scholars who have borne the pious labour of editing their master's literary remains, give to the world his Lectures on the French Revolution. We have two volumes of Essays, two volumes of Lectures, and two volumes of Correspondence. The lectures are without annotation, and lack the refining touches of an author's revision. The two volumes of correspondence are not the winnowing of the whole mass, but special fragments illustrative of two disjointed episodes and friendships. In time other letters, the letters to Gladstone, for instance, may be printed ; for the present, six volumes constitute the accessible sum of Lord Acton's published writing.

It is not a great mass of literature, and yet it is sufficient to exhibit not only a mind of extraordinary range and power, but also a very rare and exalted nature. There is a mournful French saying, *tout savant est à moitié cadavre*; and the pedestrian qualities which form the necessary groundwork of the learned life—the acquisition and arrangement of material —are too often developed at the expense of the human qualities of insight and appreciation which are the soul of history. Now Lord Acton had all the mechanism of the professional historian. He read exhaustively upon each successive topic which he took in hand, annotated his reading, and collected and tabulated his annotations. His immense magazine of exact knowledge was so disposed that every part of it was ready for use when occasion demanded. If you asked him a question about books, his mind seemed to be constituted in bibliographies. He told you what were the best books to read, what parts of them were most valuable, from what sources the author had drawn, to what extent he was credible. He could mention having seen such and such a pamphlet on such and such a shelf at a Paris bookseller's ten years before. The visitor to the noble library which is now the possession of the University of Cambridge will find everywhere, as he prowls round the shelves, the same marks of meticulous annotation, tokens of a mind in which myriads of facts garnered from every quarter of the spacious realm of knowledge were bound together into an organized and intelligible whole.

A man would be hardly human if, with this great business capacity for the arrangement of knowledge, he did not sometimes err in assuming a corresponding quality in his readers. In some of Lord Acton's historical articles the knowledge is so recondite, so closely packed, so overwhelming in weight and quality that the mind of the reader recoils. In others the author is submerged in his own quotations. But, however difficult and abstruse Lord Acton may be, he is never dry. His work is exciting even when it baffles, like the music of a new composer who has cut himself loose from the conventions and evolved a technique of his own.

Great learning has its own dangers. One of the most common is that it leads to a paralysis of the judgement. There are so many authorities, so much has been written on every side of every question, that men who have fully mastered the literature of a subject are generally the least ready with a confident award. That failing, if it be a failing, was not Lord Acton's. Those who knew him only by report as the man whose golden harvests were never reaped will be surprised when they come to close quarters with his literary remains. They will learn that, if he published little, it was not because he was deficient in deep feeling or strong opinion, not because he was overmastered by his accumulations, or lacking in powers of literary expression. They will discover no traces of the scholar's diffidence, no delicate blends of light and shade, nothing of the temper which led Renan to declare that truth was a matter of *nuances*. Lord Acton can wield the sledge-hammer as well as the rapier. He abounds in superlatives, the supreme reward of an exhaustive induction, and moves in a world of his own values. His verdicts are for the most part confident and magisterial ; and this not only from the force of settled conviction, but because he conceives it to be part of the historian's duty to distribute censure and praise to the dead—strong censure to the sinners and high praise to the saints. Thus Solon is 'the most profound political genius of antiquity', Sixtus V 'the ablest of modern Popes', Napoleon 'the most splendid genius that has appeared on earth', Alexander Hamilton 'the most scientific of conservative thinkers', Siéyès 'the most original of the revolutionary statesmen'. The Persians, the Greeks, and the Teutons are 'the only makers of history, the only authors of advancement'; and the religious standpoint of the author is revealed in the view that the history of the Middle Ages is 'the history of the gradual emancipation of man from every species of servitude in proportion as the influence of religion became more penetrating and more universal'.

The literary judgements are as clear-cut as the historical. The author of the *Imitation* is 'the greatest religious writer that ever lived'. Montégut. is 'the first of literary critics', Burke 'the author of the noblest political philosophy in the world', Bernhardi 'the ablest of the German writers on Napoleon'. George Eliot is 'justly esteemed the most illustrious figure that has arisen in literature since Goethe died'. These are not the awards of a timid or grudging judgement. We are reminded less of the cool and balancing Ranke than of Treitschke, 'vehement, certain, and overwhelming'.

Such a comparison would, of course, be unfair to Lord

Acton. Treitschke is one of the most brilliant writers of contemporary history that ever lived, but he had the mind of a partisan, and wrote to the Bismarckian brief with a hardihood untempered by scruples. With less instinct for politics—for there was a certain unworldly *naïveté* in many of his judgements of contemporary men and affairs—Lord Acton had a wider range, a nobler purpose, a more generous and disinterested intelligence. The Berlin professor is a great political pamphleteer; the Englishman essentially a theologian and philosopher.

'This is my quarrel with Seeley' (he writes after reading the *Expansion of England*), 'he discerns no Whiggism, but only Whigs. And he wonders at the mistakes of the Whigs when he ought to be following up the growth and modifications of their doctrine, and its influence on the Church, on Toleration, on European politics, on the English monarchy, the Colonies, finance, local government, justice, Scotland and Ireland. . . . He does not like to go straight at the impersonal forces which rule the world, such as predestination, equality, divine right, secularism, congregationalism, nationality, and whatever other ruling ideas have grouped and propelled associations of men.'[1]

Lord Acton was not a philosopher in the technical sense of the term ; that is to say, he had little interest in pure dialectic, and, we should imagine, none of that special aptitude or desire for the free sceptical exercise of the logical faculties which is the mark of the true metaphysician. On the contrary, the natural proclivity of his mind was to cite authority rather than to risk an adventure of the reason. The process by which he won his ultimate categories is obscure, for they were settled before he began to write, and were not subsequently disturbed. But, if he was not a metaphysician, his prime interest in history was metaphysical. It was the idea that mattered, the impersonal force working itself out through the drifting myriads of brief, blind, feeble, human lives. The circumstances of his creed, family, and training enabled him to view the course of human development with a singular detachment from patriotic or sectarian ties. He came to the

[1] *Letters to Mary Gladstone*, pp. 7, 8.

conclusion, when a lad of seventeen, that Döllinger and no other must teach him history, and, vanquishing the preliminary reluctance of the Munich professor to receive another idle English pupil, spent several years under Döllinger's roof. Here, under the most liberal Catholic in Germany and the most profound historian in Europe, he learned the widest interpretation of history consistent with the profession of orthodox belief.

It was an age of giants in historical research. The general tone was severe, disinterested, scientific; and it would have been a matter for wonder if a pupil trained in that laboratory of mighty workers, the disciple of Boeckh and Ranke and Riehl, had gone to the past for anything less important than truth. From the width and plentitude of his knowledge, Lord Acton could afford to concede points to an adversary. He has nothing to say for the antagonists of Luther, and censures Dr. Creighton for being too lenient to his Popes. He regarded it as a special weakness of Catholic apologists that they would defend bad men and bad measures. If a pope was a poisoner, there was nothing to be gained for the Catholic cause by concealment. The Church, which has survived the fact, would survive the publication. Catholic as he was, Lord Acton did not refrain from plain speaking. He wrote of the Council of Trent that 'it impressed on the Church the stamp of an intolerant age, and perpetuated by its decrees the spirit of an austere immorality'.

The two impediments generally most fatal to the pursuit of truth were thus removed. Lord Acton was a Catholic, but a critical Catholic; an Englishman, but a cosmopolitan Englishman. The tendency of many movements must, of course, be differently judged by a Protestant and a Catholic writer; and no special power of discernment is required to determine the camp to which Lord Acton belonged. No Protestant historian, however fully he realized the unreason of 'cuius regio eius religio', would describe the Reformation 'as a great movement against the freedom of conscience'. No Protestant student of English social and constitutional history would quite go so far as to write, 'The Catholic Church has bestowed on the English the great elements of their political prosperity—the charter of their liberties, the fusion of the races, and the abolition of villeinage'. He would reflect that human patience has its limits, that some Saxon ladies were probably fair, and some Norman lords probably impecunious. But, after making every deduction for the fact that Lord Acton writes history from a strongly-defined theological standpoint, that he regards the course of human affairs as the triumphant vindication of God's purpose through the instrument of the Catholic Church, that he has no tolerance for naturalistic explanations of spiritual developments, that he agrees with Döllinger in thinking that the dissidence of the Protestant Churches is their sufficient condemnation, no historian of a strong religious temperament has ever stood so near the centre of judicial indifference.

It was not for nothing that he sat at the feet of 'the keen, grave, unemotional professor' at Munich or joined in the struggle against the promulgation of Infallibility, when the Vatican Council, which in his eyes was 'the first sufficient occasion which Catholicism had enjoyed to reform, remodel and adapt the work of Trent', betrayed the hopes of the liberal Catholics. The history of the Roman Church in his own lifetime, marked as it was by a succession of grave and revolutionary events, by the loss of the temporal power, by the Syllabus of 1864, and by the Council of 1870, made it an urgent matter for serious minds to discriminate between the vital and unessential portion of the Catholic tradition and establishment. Lord Acton did not shrink from conclusions which drove straight across the prevailing currents of official policy; and, being thus forced into an opposition minority, he was the more ready to appreciate the spiritual case of the dwellers and wanderers beyond the Catholic pale.

The standpoint of an historian who is both a strong Liberal and a convinced Roman Catholic is certainly unusual, and needs a special line of defence. The idea of most ordinary persons is that human liberty has grown in proportion as ecclesiastical power has decreased, that the Roman Church in particular, with its Inquisition, its Index, its Council of Trent, its Order of Jesuits, has been by far the most formidable enemy which the cause of free speculation in Europe has had to encounter ; and that, on any survey of the world made since the beginning of the eighteenth century, it is evident that freedom, civil and intellectual, is more fully enjoyed under Protestant than under Catholic governments.   The ordinary man will say, 'Compare North America, England, Holland, Germany, with Spain, France, and Italy.   In the Protestant zone there is, upon the whole, just "that assurance that every member shall be protected in doing what he believes to be his duty", which Lord Acton defines as the essence of liberty.   In the Catholic zone the case is notoriously the reverse.'

To all such observations Lord Acton would oppose a picture of human progress in which the quarrels of the sixteenth and seventeenth centuries are contracted to their due proportions. If we do not grossly misapprehend him, he held the prime essential of liberty to be that the Church should be separated from the State.   This condition was not realized in the ancient world, nor yet in Lutheran Germany and Sweden, but it was realized throughout Europe during the Middle Ages.   When Christ said, 'Render unto Caesar the things that are Caesar's and unto God the things that are God's', He inaugurated the reign of freedom on earth.   The spiritual and temporal spheres, confounded in the economy of the ancient State, were henceforth severed.   A barrier was raised against absolutism by the birth of a society bound together by spiritual ties, and developing itself according to the rhythm of its own being. And so, while the barbarian invasions of the fifth century resulted in the formation of military monarchies all over Western Europe, no fatal blow was dealt to liberty.   On the contrary, liberty is the product of the mediaeval world, with its system of states in which authority was restricted by privileged groups and powerful classes and, above all, by 'the acknow-ledgement of duties superior to those which are imposed by man'.

It is to the existence of this mediaeval dualism between Church and State, and in particular to the collision between the Empire and Papacy in the eleventh century, that Lord

Acton would attribute the rise and development of a philosophy of political liberty. The *Libelli de Lite Imperatorum et Pontificum*, which fill two volumes of the *Monumenta Germaniae*, are not often disturbed even by professed students of the Middle Ages. Yet here is the first link in the long chain of liberal tradition which, passing through Guelph and Ghibelline alike, 'connects the Hildebrandine controversy with the Long Parliament and St. Thomas with Edmund Burke'. Nor was it merely in the matter of political theory that the Catholic system manifested its liberalizing influence. The Church was the mother of institutions as well as the exciting cause of political speculation. Was not the oldest parliamentary system in the world based upon the framework of the Councils of Toledo?

Such, in outline, is Lord Acton's view of the relation between Catholicity and liberty in the Middle Ages. He holds that the Church, while generally allied with the mediaeval monarchies and working through them, contributed to curb tyrannical caprice, to uphold the moral law, and to promote and support subordinate groups and associations within which individuals might freely develop their special aptitudes; and he further holds that without the separate agency of the Roman Church a liberal philosophy of the State would not have arisen. It is true that heresies were cruelly suppressed, and that gentle, cultivated, and pious souls approved the oppression and the cruelty. It is, however, Lord Acton's view that the persecution of the Catholic Church was never aggressive (were not the 'Dictatus Papae' aggressive? were not the Crusades aggressive?), nor founded upon the doctrine that a deviation from theological orthodoxy is punishable as such. If the Albigenses were exterminated it was not because their theology was unsound, but because they menaced the social order. It was left to the apostates of the sixteenth century to base the necessity of intolerance upon the simple ground of religious error.[1]

If this view is correct, then the Reformation, in its primal

[1] These views were expressed before the appearance of Mr. Lea's *History of the Inquisition* in 1887.

aspect, far from enlarging, greatly restricted the sphere of liberty. The Reformation brought in its train bitter disputes, cruel persecution, long dragging wars. Monarchs became more despotic; theologians became more intolerant; the State encroached upon the spiritual sphere. The leaders of the Protestant revolt were no preachers of liberty or toleration. On the contrary, many advocated passive obedience and preached the duty of persecuting religious error. Lord Acton is specially severe upon Luther, and holds that the reason which caused him to force the rupture with Rome at the Diet of Worms was the belief, due to Lorenzo Valla's tract on the Donation of Constantine, that the Pope was Antichrist. Of Lutheranism he wittily remarks that, 'born of the union of princes and professors, it retains the distinct likeness of both its parents, not altogether harmoniously blended'. The union of princes and professors, the Erastian theory of Church government, was (he says) the first product of the Reformation and the deadly blow to freedom. Of pure religious impulse there was probably less than is generally imagined, for Scotland is the only country where the Reformation triumphed in opposition to the State, as Ireland is the only country where, having the support of the State, it fell short of victory. But deficiency of religious zeal was amply balanced by the strength of the secular appetite; and Thomas Cromwell was not alone in suggesting to his royal master that by attacking the wealth of the Church a ruler might become great and powerful.

The early triumphs of the Protestant revolt were stemmed by a great rally of the Catholic Church. Of many of the agencies by which the Counter-Reformation was effected Lord Acton was frankly critical. He condemns the Index of Prohibited Books. He notes with relief that the persecutions of the Holy Office of Rome did not extend beyond the reign of Urban VIII. He deplores the fact that the doctrine of the Church should have been formulated afresh in an intolerant age. But he is nevertheless concerned to show how even among the Jesuits, the professed advocates of authority and submission, a liberal philosophy was entertained until 1620; how 'the greater part of the political ideas of Milton, Locke, and Rousseau' may be discovered in the ponderous Latin of the Spanish Fathers; how impossible it was found to compress original minds by the iron rules of St. Ignatius; how Sarasa anticipated Bishop Butler in proclaiming the infallibility of conscience; how Masenius shared the dream of Leibnitz for Christian reunion; and how Petavius 'first described the history of dogma, and cast every system into the melting-pot of history'.

The most crucial passage in the history of modern liberty is the French Revolution. Lord Acton had more than once published opinions with regard to it, and was understood to have mastered as much of the literature of the subject as any Englishman, alive or dead. When he was appointed to the Cambridge chair, he lectured upon the subject during four successive academic years. His discourses made a great impression. They were written with scrupulous care and were charged with an austere and pregnant eloquence foreign to graduate practice and undergraduate expectations. Even now, when they are given to the world unfinished, without annotation, somewhat lacking in proportion—for we have read more than two-thirds of the volume before the Tuileries are attacked, and the Convention, the Terror, the War, and the Vendée are still before us—we are able to appreciate the zeal of the Cambridge audience. Here and there the reader may think that a judgement is unduly sharp and peremptory, that the influence of books on men is overrated, or that Lord Acton has too easily succumbed to the temptation of accepting new or recondite testimony. Nothing written is infallible; least of all should we expect infallibility in a course of lectures written for the instruction of the young and untouched by the edged tools of an author's revision. But that in this volume we have the best account of the French Revolution yet written by an Englishman is a proposition which no competent student will dispute.

The ruling thought of these lectures is the essential incompatibility of liberty and equality. In Lord Acton's view the French Revolution, aiming at equality or 'government by the poor, payment by the rich', missed the priceless boon of freedom.

Democracy without the safeguard of 'a multiplicity of check-ing forces' inevitably turns to tyranny; and the Revolution, sweeping away as it did all the intermediate bodies which stood between the State and the individual—the wealthy Church, the powerful nobility, the proud and exclusive judicial corporations, the trade guilds and the rest—paved the way for a mechanical despotism, more pervasive, more scientific, more plausible, and therefore very much more dangerous, than the old clumsy monarchy of France. This, of course, is a very common view to take of the French Revolution; and it has been expounded with great pomp and power by M. Taine, who belonged not to the Roman Catholic communion but to the fellowship of Positivists and Freethinkers. But the thing which makes Lord Acton's view of the Revolution different from Taine's is that, whereas Taine, writing under the fresh and immediate impression of the French Commune, could scarcely find anything in the Revolution to commend, Lord Acton manages to combine his general disapproval of the result with a great deal of unreserved and generous enthusiasm for the aims and intentions of the Constituent Assembly.

'By right of the immense change they made in the world, by their energy and sincerity, their fidelity to reason and their resistance to custom, their superiority to the sordid craving for increase of national power, their idealism and their ambition to declare the eternal law, the States-General of 1789 are the most memorable of all political assemblies. They cleared away the history of France, and with 2,800 decrees they laid down the plan of a new world for men who were reared in the old. Their institutions perished, but their influence has endured; and the problem of their history is to explain why so genuine a striving for the highest of earthly goods so deplorably failed. The errors that ruined their enterprise may be reduced to one. Having put the nation in the place of the Crown, they invested it with the same unlicensed power, raising no security and no remedy against oppression from below, assuming or believing that a government truly representing the people could do no wrong.'[1]

A partial explanation of the miscarriage of these high en-deavours is to be found in the political philosophy of the period.

[1] *Lectures on the French Revolution*, pp. 188-9.

Lord Acton, who goes back to Fénelon, 'the Platonic founder of revolutionary thinking', and even accords to that mild philosopher more space than he is able to find for Rousseau, remarks that none of the intellectual precursors of the Revolution in France were in reality Liberals. Montesquieu was an intelligent Tory, Voltaire an assailant of the clergy, Turgot a reformer and the inventor of the idea of progress, Rousseau a democrat, Diderot a Freethinker. 'The one thing common to them all is the disregard for liberty.' Lord Acton would not, we presume, have denied that the weight of enlightened opinion in France was against arbitrary imprisonment, secret trial, and religious disabilities, and so far favourable to liberty. What he means is, that one wing of enlightened opinion wished to procure these objects through an intelligent but untrammelled despotism, and the other through an intelligent but untrammelled democracy. In particular, he notes it as a specially unfortunate circumstance that, owing to the anti-clericalism of the period, no attention had been given to the very complicated questions which are connected with the relations of Church and State. The leaders of advanced opinion, being estranged from Christianity, had got into the habit of treating Church questions with levity and indifference. They had never seriously examined under what conditions a Church may be established or disestablished, endowed or disendowed; so that, when the ecclesiastical problem became suddenly urgent, there was no formed body of intelligent opinion concerning it. The ideal of the omnipotence of the State, derived from Rousseau, swept everything before it.

America, with its famous constitution of checks and balances, might, one would have thought, have come to the rescue; but the America which influenced France was the aggressive America of Otis and the War of Independence, not the circumspect America of the Philadelphia Convention. The theory of resistance, the theory that political power comes from the people, the jealous dislike of the judicial and executive authority, the preference for a Single Chamber, were transmitted from America to France. But the philosophy which informed the debates in the Philadelphia Convention was sealed up in private note-books;

and the great Federal constitutions had only been in working for two months when the States-General met at Versailles. Nobody knew how the American experiment would stand the test; nobody knew the true explanation of its provisions. The cause of federalism, though it had been commended by Montesquieu and Rousseau, never really had a party behind it in France; and 'the one immortal tribute of America to political science' was entirely lost upon the statesmen and agitators who shaped the course of the French Revolution.

Lord Acton's enthusiasm for checks and balances leads him to single out for enthusiastic praise a statesman who is generally mentioned in terms of depreciation often descending to ridicule. The Abbé Siéyès was undoubtedly an exceedingly clever man. He came to the front, as everybody knows, during the elections of 1789 with a pamphlet, perhaps the most famous and influential in all history, *Qu'est-ce que le Tiers-État?* A man who has the capacity of expressing in the most effective form, and at the most opportune moment, the thought of a whole nation, is a considerable man. Siéyès understood from the first what the Revolution was about. The Commons, who had been nothing, were to be everything; and the Nobles, who had been everything, were to be nothing. At the same time he saw the danger of unbridled democracy. He insisted upon a restricted franchise based upon property, and shared Burke's view of the relations between the legislator and his constituency. Ten years later, schooled by bitter experience, he was prepared with more checks and chains for the animal whose riotous excess had driven him to hide his head during the Terror. He produced an elaborate piece of mechanism, which Bonaparte simplified and distorted to his own ends; but the operations of the earlier and more influential Siéyès were not so conducive to the kind of State which Lord Acton admired, for he destroyed the provinces of France, created the departments, and was in favour of the government of a Single Chamber. Lord Acton, viewing the body of his political thought without respect to periods, concludes as follows (p. 162):

'In his sustained power of consistent thinking, Siéyès resembles Bentham and Hegel. His flight is low and he lacks grace and distinction. He seems to have borrowed his departments from Harrington, the distilled unity of power from Turgot, the rule of the mass of taxpayers over the unproductive class above them, from the notion that labour is the only source of wealth, which was common to Franklin and Adam Smith. But he is profoundly original; and, though many modern writers on politics exceed him in genius and eloquence and knowledge, none equal him in invention and resource.'

This is a higher claim than has been made by Taine or Sorel or Vandal or Aulard; but it would have been endorsed by Mirabeau, who wrote to Roederer in the course of debate that Siéyès was a man of genius who inspired his veneration and tender love.[1]

Upon the subject of the breach between the Revolution and the Church we should naturally expect to learn much from Lord Acton. That it was injurious to the French character, that it has been the cause of a permanent rift between two sections of the French nation, that it has been provocative of a vindictive, illiberal spirit which has more than once disgraced the political annals of France, all this is part of the accepted stock of knowledge. But why did it happen? Was it inevitable? Who was to blame? Lord Acton's answer to these questions will, perhaps, surprise some of his readers. After showing the close connexion between the Gallican Church and the order of things which the Assembly was resolved to destroy, he goes on to consider the financial causes which led to the appropriation by the State of Church property, and the provisions of the Civil Constitution of the Clergy consequent upon that measure and devised to settle the government and finance of the disendowed Church. He does not deny that the change was sweeping, but he is concerned to show that the principle upon which the Civil Constitution was framed found support in some parts of the ecclesiastical tradition. Under the Constitution, the bishop was to be

---

[1] Roederer, Œuvres, iv. 172. Lord Acton had clearly consulted the Notice sur la Vie de Siéyès [Brit. Mus. R. 92]. Roederer, who reviewed the pamphlet in the Journal de Paris, February 12, 1795, had no doubt that it was written by Siéyès himself (Œuvres, iv. 204).

chosen by the departmental electors, the parish priest by the district electors. Lord Acton observes that the principle of election had been upheld by high authorities and had played a great part in earlier times. The right of institution again was taken away from the Pope—an act of aggression, but sanctioned, as we are reminded, by the august opinion of Bossuet. A more adroit exercise of diplomacy on the part of the King and his advisers might, we are told, have brought the Pope to accept a settlement in no way subversive of essential principles.

'The new dioceses, the new revenues, were afterwards accepted. The denial of papal institution was in the spirit of Gallicanism ; and the principle of election had a great tradition in its favour, and needed safeguards. Several bishops favoured conciliation, and wished the measure to be discussed in a National Council.' (*French Revolution*, p. 170.)

Even in Rome the feeling was not entirely hostile.

'It was the office of the King to negotiate with the Pope ; and he might have saved the Revolution, the limited monarchy and his own life, if he had negotiated wisely. . . . The judgement of the Italian divines was in many instances favourable to the decree of the National Assembly, and the College of Cardinals was not unanimous against it.' (Ib., pp. 170, 172.)

As it was, Pius VI rejected the Constitution, and drove the King to seek the help of Europe against his own people. The Church was divided into two camps. Some 23,000 clergy, about a third of the whole and not enough for the service of all the churches, swore to accept the new conditions. The nonjuring clergy were persecuted as a horde of traitorous rebels. The mischief was never wholly repaired, though the scars were plastered over when Pius VII conceded to Bonaparte what Pius VI might have granted to Louis XVI.

Lord Acton does not conceal his opinion that the real solution of the problem was to be found in measures of which hardly anybody at that time thought—that is, in disestablishment and separation. Another alternative, that of leaving Church patronage to the King acting through responsible Ministers, was rendered impossible by the unwise exclusion of the Ministers of the Crown from the Legislature. No expedient could have turned out more disastrously than that which was actually adopted ; but it is open to question whether the cancer of privilege could have been cut out of the body politic at a greatly diminished cost.

Following the example of most English commentators, Lord Acton casts the weight of his sympathies into the scale of those statesmen who, while anxious for radical reform in French social and political life, were alive to the necessity of a strong executive. He gives an excellent sketch of Mounier, the powerful provincial, who, like Washington, combined revolutionary doctrine with a conservative temper, but whose austere rigidity of character wrecked any slight chance which he might have possessed of carrying a Constitution upon the English model. It is less possible to write sympathetically of Mirabeau, whose private life was stained by profligacy and corruption, and whose public career was one vast intrigue. Lord Acton, who is by no means blind to these defects, and moreover thinks that Mirabeau never had a chance of success since he was distrusted throughout by King and Queen alike, finds eloquent praise for his talents and his outlook on the world of politics. He describes him as 'the most prodigious individual force in the world', and praises him as the friend of freedom and of federalism. 'When he spoke confidentially, he said there was no other way in which a great country like France could be free.' If this indeed was a genuine opinion, Mirabeau was discreet in suppressing it, since there was no more certain road to political extinction during the French Revolution than to advocate a course which could be represented as incompatible with the strength and unity of the State.

These personal estimates and constitutional discussions are blended together in Lord Acton's volume with a narrative of events always minute, condensed, and instructive, and sometimes reaching a high level of literary art. The story of the Tennis Court Oath, of the events leading up to the capture of the Bastille, of the march of the women to Versailles, of the flight to Varennes, of the attack on the Tuileries, of the revolution of Thermidor, are told in detail. There is a fine and sympathetic, but all too short, chapter on the Vendée.

Throughout we are left with the impression of complete familiarity, of great reserves of knowledge lying behind, and of judgements founded at first hand upon a careful sifting of evidence. An epithet seems to reveal the fact that Lord Acton had seen the memoirs of Chaumette, which were discovered by M. Aulard in 1893 and published in the *Revue de la Révolution Française*. A few sentences show that he knew the whole literature of the *Vengeur*.

The causes which led to the downfall of the monarchy are recounted in the best spirit of impartiality, the impartiality of a strong mind controlling and sometimes combating a deep flow of natural sympathy. In some discursive bibliographical remarks which have been collected in an Appendix, Lord Acton remarks that 'no man feels the grandeur of the Revolution till he reads Michelet, or the horror of it without reading Taine'. The sovereign merit of Lord Acton's lectures is that his repulsion from the horror has not prevented the grandeur from going unperceived. In his censure of crime he goes as far as Taine and much farther than Sainte-Beuve, who wrote a pathetic apology for the Girondins; but his judgement of the main lines of policy is unaffected by his condemnation of particular acts. He depicts the King full of vague affable benevolence, but from the beginning of his reign and at every crisis of his career dominated by the sinister counsels of a worthless camarilla. He exhibits Marie Antoinette as the evil genius of France, and lays to her account the principal onus of the war and a long train of treasonable acts after its declaration. His view clearly is that the doom of the monarchy was deserved, for that King and Queen, after squandering golden opportunities, conspired to bring havoc and disaster on their country. Yet he feels the pathos of their fortune, lit up as the darkness gathers by the far-shining courage and resolve of the Queen, once so light and reckless, but suddenly sobered by the tragic days of October, and revealing in her danger and humiliation something of that high and serious quality which had made her mother one of the greatest rulers in Europe.

From another point of view, the story of the downfall of the

monarchy has been told in greater circumstance by a writer
to whom Lord Acton is under obligations and to whose
unexampled knowledge of the literature he pays a fitting
tribute.   It is now twenty-five years since M. Aulard was
appointed to the Chair of the History of the French Revolution
at the Sorbonne; and most of the advance which has been
made in our knowledge of the period has been due either
directly to his personal labours or indirectly to the influence
which he has exerted over his pupils.   He is the principal
contributor to the *Revue de la Révolution*, has edited the
Acts of the Committee of Public Safety, besides other
important documentary collections, and has published several
volumes on his own account, the most important of which,
L'Histoire politique de la Révolution Française, has recently
become accessible in an English translation.   It would be safe
to say that what M. Aulard does not know about the French
Revolution, nobody knows.   He has digested the histories,
the memoirs, the debates, the pamphlets, the newspapers, the
official documents published or unpublished.   His whole life,
save for a brief excursion into the poetry of Leopardi, has
been occupied in reading and writing about this single subject,
this single period.   What morasses he has traversed, sustained
by his exuberant faith in the Jacobin cause!   We cannot recall
the name of an historical specialist in this country who has
thrown the work of an industrious life into so small a compass
of time.   Mr. Gardiner ruled the seventeenth century and was
called a specialist.   M. Aulard is a specialist in a period of
fifteen years.

A book written by such a man as this necessarily carries
enormous weight as a repository of exact and settled information.   Lord Acton, who knew everything about the Popes of
Avignon, and the Reformation, and Napoleon, and a vast deal
else besides, including astrology, cannot be expected to com-
pete with M. Aulard in his minute antiquarian knowledge of
the French Revolution.   M. Aulard is a much narrower, much
less interesting man, but on his own special field he can write
a more valuable monograph.   He could not have done what
Lord Acton has achieved in his Cambridge Lectures, for he

has not the span or penetration or solid strength of intellect to compress into a single volume the whole spirit and significance of a passionate and complex movement. But, keeping within the more restricted compass of his interests and abilities, M. Aulard can write excellent special studies. We doubt his capacity ever to compass a great history, for his work lacks the atmosphere, the grace, the finish and impartiality of the masters. But if he is not a Vandal or a Sorel, he is a fine example of the laborious, clear-headed French scholar, who has always something new to say, and can say it in apposite and vigorous language.

But his latest work, despite the title, is no complete history of the French Revolution, omitting as it does war, finance, diplomacy, personal adventure, and presenting a picture of these times from which the pathos, the tragedy, and the grandeur have been purposely omitted. M. Aulard, in other words, has not written a formal history, but rather a series of essays upon the development and transmutation of political ideas and public feeling in France during the fifteen years which divide the summoning of the States-General from the Empire of Napoleon. Such a theme exhibits all M. Aulard's special qualities. Now he is tracing the republican idea through pamphlets and newspapers; now the diffusion of the cult of the goddess of Reason; now the risings and fallings of the political barometer in Paris after Thermidor and Brumaire. We may dispute his judgement or sense of proportion and relevance, but never the abundance or accuracy of his facts. Whatever else may be written about the French Revolution, M. Aulard's book will hold its own as a repertory of exact and sifted knowledge.

The notion that the government of France could be other than monarchical was a plant of very slow and timid growth. M. Aulard tells the tale of the wise men, Montesquieu, Rousseau, Voltaire, and the rest, who wrote out political prescriptions during the *Ancien Régime*, not a man of them republican, or believing that a republican government was compatible with a large area of territory. With his extraordinary and exhaustive knowledge of pamphlet and newspaper literature, he is able to affirm that until October 1790 there is hardly a case in which open profession was made of republican principles. Then a little republican agitation grew up and died down in the Paris press. The Constitution was accepted, the Constituent Assembly was dissolved, the Legislature met, war was declared ; and there was still no mention of a republic. Robespierre professed his fidelity to the monarchical Constitution. Vergniaud and his Girondins were anxious for office under the Crown. It was never breathed in the Press that the throne must be overturned. The thing came with the shock of a thunderbolt. After the storming of the Tuileries on August 10, there was only one course open ; and it was taken on September 22, the day when the guns at Valmy apprised Goethe that a new era had dawned upon the world.

It is in his treatment of Danton and the Terror that Lord Acton parts company with M. Aulard. The French historian is a strong Jacobin and a zealous admirer of Danton, in whom he discerns the force, the courage, and the statesmanship which saved France at the crisis of her fate. Lord Acton cannot help remembering a certain story which used to be told by Louis-Philippe and may be found in one of Taine's foot-notes. The son of Philippe Égalité, who had been fighting on the frontier, was accosted by an ogre of a man in the room of Servan, the Minister of War, when the massacre of September was a fresh event. The ogre was Danton. He had heard that the lad had been denouncing the atrocities, and closed his lips with the peremptory avowal, 'C'est moi qui les ai faits'. Danton's patriotism is beyond dispute ; and the founder of the Republic must always occupy a conspicuous place in history. He had no sympathy with the levellers ; he saw the folly of a general crusade against the monarchs of Europe ; he was a strong man who wanted and made a strong government. If he countenanced terrorism, it was for patriotic ends, not for party advantage ; but an accomplice in murder, however able and patriotic, obtains no acquittal in Lord Acton's court.

It has often been pointed out that the Terror was closely connected with the war ; that it began with Brunswick's invasion in August 1792, rose to its height when the fortunes of France seemed most desperate, and slackened off when the public anxiety was relieved by the great victory at Fleurus. Like every other writer of recent date who has touched upon these times, Lord Acton notes this correspondence. He finds in the war not, indeed, with M. Aulard, an apology, but at least an explanation, for the eclipse of liberty, the concentration of public power, and the abandonment of all the early principles and maxims of the French Revolution. The fall of the Girondins marks the beginning of total darkness. For that vacillating and divided party, which has furnished so many heroes and heroines of romance, there is little but stern condemnation in the Cambridge lectures. They had no principle; they countenanced the massacres; 'they were not only weak but bad.' On the other hand, they alone stood between France and the Terror; and, this being so, 'no nation ever suffered a greater misfortune than that which befell France in their defeat and destruction'. It is admitted that the Girondins were incapable of governing the country or of conducting the war to a successful issue. How, then, was the misfortune so great? Condorcet wrote a little book on Human Progress 'that every man should master in order to understand his age'; Isnard was 'the first man who divined the prodigious resources and invincible energy of France'; and there was no lack of rhetoric or ingenuity in the party. The disease which destroyed them was timidity. They had no statesman tempered to the hot and perilous climate of revolution; and they rejected the proposed alliance of Danton, whose courage might have helped them to rule the Convention and to save France from the furies. Everything they touched was mismanaged—the war, the public administration, the King's trial, the conduct of parliamentary debate. An attack upon Robespierre was the immediate cause of their downfall, as it has been their enduring claim to posthumous regard; but Lord Acton reminds us that men who had condoned the massacres of September were not entitled to throw stones at villainy more calculating than their own.

Late in life, and having seen the frustration of many hopes,

Tocqueville wrote that there was only one thing which could not be created in France, and that was a free government; only one thing which could not be destroyed, and that was centralization. The Girondin ideal of decentralization and local liberties was finally extinguished in 1793; and federalism, which Necker from his exile declared to be the true solution, was 'dreaded as the superlative danger of the time'. The Jacobins fell back upon a system which was at least simple and intelligible—'that the mass of people should at all times assert and enforce their will, overriding all temporary powers and superseding all appointed agents'. Concentration of power was the note of their political ideal. Liberty was sacrificed to efficiency; and Napoleon, who knew efficiency when he saw it, gave office to 127 regicides.

The classic embodiment of the Jacobin spirit is Maximilien Robespierre; and a chapter in Lord Acton's History is reserved for the description of his eminence, his atrocities, and his fall. What was the precise degree of his eminence, or the precise measure of his atrocities, is a matter of unconcluded controversy. Hamel painted him as the saint of pure democracy; Mr. Belloc represents him as an honest fanatic, comparatively powerless, and consenting to the Terror because he thought it popular. Lord Acton, following the general tradition, depicts him as malignant and despotic. It is doubtless too much to say that, at the Feast of the Supreme Being, Robespierre 'had attained the loftiest summit of prosperity and greatness that was ever given to man'; for his power in the Convention and Committees, never absolute and uncontested, was already menaced by the forces which were successful in overthrowing it. But that his popularity in Paris gave him a singular advantage on the Committee of Public Safety we cannot doubt; and there is still the mysterious problem why or how such a man rose to the front of public affairs. His personal appearance, if the evidence of a picture may be trusted, was favourable rather than adverse. His forehead was broad, his deep-set eyes brown and sparkling, his face animated and convinced, with sensitive lips which could relax into a pleasant smile. But he was rancorous, cold, self-righteous, besieged with suspicions, without largeness or geniality of soul, the victim of dogmas amiable enough in themselves but perverted to the workings of an insatiable vanity.

'In the north of Europe' (writes Lord Acton), 'especially in Denmark, he had warm admirers. European society believed that .he had affinity with it. It took him to be a man of authority, integrity, and order, an enemy of corruption and of war, who fell because he attempted to bar the progress of unbelief, which was the strongest current of his age. His private life was inoffensive and decent. He had been the equal of emperors and kings; an army of 700,000 men obeyed his word; he controlled millions of secret service money, and could have obtained what he liked for pardons; and he lived on a Deputy's allowance of eighteen francs a day, leaving a fortune of less than twenty guineas in depreciated *assignats*. There is no doubt that he held fast to the doctrine of equality, which means government by the poor and payment by the rich. Also, he desired power, if it was only for self-preservation; and he held it by bloodshed, as Lewis XIV had done, and Peter the Great and Frederick. . . . His private note-book has been printed, but it does not show what he thought of the future. . . . Only this is certain, that he remains the most hateful character in the forefront of history since Machiavelli reduced to a code the wickedness of public men.' (*French Revolution*, pp. 299–300.)

With the Directorial Constitution and 'the whiff of grape-shot' Lord Acton's survey of the French Revolution comes to a close. The hopes of a royalist Restoration had been blasted by the failure at Quiberon and the death of the Dauphin in the Temple prison. Peace had been made with Tuscany, Prussia, and Holland; and the author of the *noyades* at Nantes had gone the way of Hébert and 'the glowing patriarch of irreligious belief'. A new Constitution, 'affording security for order and liberty such as France has never enjoyed', had been launched upon a trial destined to be brief and stormy. The peasants had doubled their wealth, and socialism had been averted by wholesale confiscations. The conquests of France surpassed the utmost successes of the monarchy under Louis XIV. 'By arbitrary control over promotion and the cheapness of French lives,' an energetic and honest engineer of no very

commanding ability had learnt the art of organizing victory.
The golden orb of Freedom had set in a sea of blood. The
death of the Dauphin left the hope of the royalist cause in the
hands of the *émigrés*; and the alternative to the Revolution
became again, what it was at the beginning, the rule of a
privileged caste and a legitimate sovereign.

The student who has mastered these impressive fragments
of an unaccomplished design must feel sad when he reflects
that behind the polished front of the printed page lay vast
stores of thought and knowledge which have perished with Lord
Acton beyond recall. What we have gained is much, what
we have lost is immeasurably more. In the history of the French
Revolution, where the issues are so perplexed, so controversial,
and so much obscured by wilful forgery, vague misrepresenta-
tion, and idle report, a narrative unsupported by critical discussions loses something of ts value. That Lord Acton
should have concluded thus and thus affords a strong presumption that it was so. Yet what would we not give to hear him defend
the authenticity of the famous memorandum which Favras is
said to have written, Talon to have possessed, Napoleon to have
coveted, and Louis XVIII to have burned! In a tourney
with M. Lenôtre and Mr. Oscar Browning over the flight to
Varennes, would he have victoriously established his contention
that the King was ruined by gluttony at Étoges? Would
Mr. Belloc have persuaded him that Carnot was a genius,
and M. Aulard that Danton was not the murderer of Mandat?
On these and many other delicate and doubtful points Lord
Acton would undoubtedly have commanded a respectful
hearing from his interlocutors, even if he failed to extort their
assent. But such colloquies and discussions can never be.
The massed battalions of the reserve stand shrouded in darkness, and the general is no longer here to marshal them into
action. Perhaps some day a young scholar will in a due spirit
of piety take down from their shelves at Cambridge the long
array of histories and memoirs on the French Revolution
which bear the traces of Lord Acton's reading, and when he
has mastered these, and the Croker collection of pamphlets in

the British Museum which Lord Acton read and greatly prized, will give us an annotated edition of the Lectures which will enhance their authority and furnish a fresh illustration of the genius and industry of their author.

Modern German Historians

THE admirable work [1] in which Mr. Gooch surveys the historiography of the nineteenth century reminds us not only of the extent to which the thought and knowledge of the world is indebted to the labours of historical students, but also of the catholicity and interconnexion of the historical movement. No country can claim a monopoly. Every country has made contributions corresponding to its wealth of scientific equipment and reflecting the characteristics of its peculiar genius. It cannot even be said that the primacy goes unchallenged, for if in the fifties and sixties, when Sybel, Mommsen, Häusser, Droysen, and Giesebrecht were at the height of their powers, the pride of place unquestionably belonged to the Germans, in the last decade of the century the most brilliant galaxy of historical talent was undoubtedly to be found on the banks, not of the Spree but of the Seine. Here the student might listen to Renan on the Hebrew Text of the Old Testament, to Sorel on European diplomacy, to Paul Meyer and Gaston Paris on the mediaeval literature of the Romance nations, to Viollet on the history of law, and to Aulard on the annals of the French Revolution. Taine was completing his brilliant historical work in the Origins of Contemporary France. Vandal, Houssaye, Masson were revealing the details of the Napoleonic age in a style which suffered little from the rich abundance of material. Luchaire had already made his name as the most finished exponent of French municipal antiquities. Rambaud and Anatole Leroy-

---

[1] *History and Historians in the Nineteenth Century*; Longmans, 1913. Cf. Fueter, *Geschichte der neuern Historiographie*; Munich: Oldenburg, 1911.

Beaulieu were established authorities in Russia. Hanotaux and Lavisse were widely known, the one for an unfinished fragment of high quality on the age of Louis XIV, the other for a series of valuable contributions to Prussian history as well as for his general powers as a teacher. Among the younger generation Langlois and Bémont were attracting notice for the solidity of their mediaeval studies, and when a 'Soutenance de thèse' was held at the École des Chartes, the great Léopold Delisle would preside over the jury, bringing from the Bibliothèque Nationale such a sum of minute and exact mediaeval scholarship as can seldom have been gathered in a single brain.

There is, however, a sense in which the nineteenth century may be claimed for the German historians, for not only was the critical treatment of authorities inaugurated in Germany, but in sheer mass of printed historical matter the Germans easily distance their competitors. It is, however, important to observe that the competence of the Germans in historical study is a fact of comparatively recent date. No English contemporary of Charles James Fox would ever have thought of Germany as a source of historical illumination. No German of that age would have looked to his own countrymen to furnish him with a history in the grand style. The great historical books which the world then read and has never ceased to read were not made in Germany, but in Italy, France, and England. There were Commines and Guicciardini, Clarendon and Burnet, Voltaire and Gibbon, and for the philosophy and economics of history, Vico, Montesquieu, Turgot, Adam Smith, and Burke. 'Read Burke,' wrote Stein to Gneisenau, 'it is the breviary of all wisdom'; and again, 'English literature especially deserves to be known because it furnishes us with the best historians', a verdict the more striking when we remember that it proceeds from the greatest Prussian statesman of his age, and from the founder of the *Monumenta Germaniae Historica*. Even if we take account of the preliminary work of editing and publishing chronicles and documents, in which the Germans have now acquired so great a mastery, there was nothing anywhere comparable for the imposing mass of its achievement to the patient labours

of the French Benedictines. 'Your bold progress', wrote
Ranke to Waitz in 1838, 'evokes my greatest sympathy and
joy. You are treading the paths of Baluze and Mabillon.'
That is a significant compliment. When Ranke wishes to
praise the greatest German editor of mediaeval historical texts,
he does not say, 'You are breaking fresh ground,' nor yet,
'The mantle of Leibnitz has descended on you.' He says,
'You are treading the paths of Baluze and Mabillon', of those
two French scholars of the seventeenth century who founded
the exact science of mediaeval charters and chronicles.

The true historical awakening of Germany sprang out of the
Napoleonic wars, and the movement has never lost all traces
of its origin. From Niebuhr and Savigny downwards every
German historian has made it part of his *professio fidei* to
denounce the French Revolution and all its works, and to
explain the evil which comes of pouring Jacobin wine into the
holy vessel of Teutonic civilization. There have been constitutional historians in Germany as well as antiquarian historians ;
and oceans of historical ink have been expended upon themes
as remote from the political passions of mankind as the fossil
in the rock or the star in the sky. But the political historians
of Germany have been what the political history of their
country has made them. They have been opposed to doctrinaire radicalism because it is the creation of the French Revolution. They have been liberal because they hated the French
despot and saw in the development of constitutional liberties
a guarantee for national power. Fervent advocates of Prussian
expansion, they favoured the exclusion of Austria from the
German confederation, facing such ridicule as might attach
to the label of 'Little Germans', and losing no opportunity of
exposing the waste of national power involved in the political
disunion of their country. Since a military monarchy was a
distinguishing mark of Prussia, they combined with their constitutional liberalism a strong faith in the Hohenzollern dynasty,
whose services to the German cause they depicted with
romantic enthusiasm. 'One cannot rebel', said Ranke, the
mildest and most candid of men, 'against historic right,' by
which he meant that a nation's future is determined by its past,

and that the way to political salvation lay in the conservation of Prussian institutions and in the spread of the Prussian spirit. Patriotic optimism threw its glow backward as well as forward. Learned gentlemen, forgetting the golden rules of evidence, attributed the results of the historic complex to the forethought of statesmen ; and the Great Elector was invested by the laborious Droysen with the attributes of a prophet of the Prussian mission to Germany, a mission as foreign to the mind of that age as the operation of X-rays or the Siberian railway.

The patriarch of all this historical movement was a Danish administrator, who, being called to Berlin a little before the battle of Jena, was entrusted with the direction of the Bank of Prussia. Niebuhr was a competent financier, a master of twenty languages, and the most profound and various scholar of his age. It is customary (though not entirely exact) to speak of him as a pioneer in critical method and as, in a sense, the founder of scientific history as that term is now understood. But the real importance of Niebuhr in the intellectual development of Germany does not consist in his learning or in his critical acumen or in his application of philological tests to decide historical problems; for in the generation of Wolf, Boeck, Savigny, and Grimm there was no lack of learned scepticism in Germany, and the Homeric poems had suffered violence before Niebuhr laid sacrilegious hands on Livy. It consists rather in his political spirit. He was the first of the Germans to approach history from the angle of a modern statesman and to discover in the past a discipline for character and a guide for public action. Thus the learning which gave to Niebuhr's Roman History an authoritative place in our English Universities until it was deposed by Mommsen is not really its chief title to be remembered. The learning commended but did not constitute the message. For Niebuhr the true interest of the history of Latium was that, presenting as it did ' a model of national development ', it served as an example to his adopted country of the methods by which a small people may achieve greatness. Even as Rome had gathered all Italy under her sway by a resolute exercise of prudence and courage, so might Prussia, shaking off the foreign tyrant and incarnating all that was valiant and manly in the German spirit, unite the scattered fragments of the German Confederation under her rule.

The impetus, once given, continued through the century, gaining volume as it went and bringing to the academic prophets of German unity and Prussian power an influence over public opinion which no prodigies of cold science could have secured. It was not so much the political doctrine which mattered, as the patriotic feeling and the stimulus to national self-respect. The work of a philologist and legal antiquary like Wilhelm Grimm was almost as important as the lectures of such a man as Häusser, whose eloquence continually touched the quivering nerve of living issues. From the historians Germany recovered a loving, perhaps an exalted, sense of her former greatness. She learned how in the distant past the Germans had broken down the Roman Empire, founded dynasties in France, Italy, England, Africa, and Spain, and refashioned the face of Europe. This people, laid helpless at the feet of Napoleon, had once been the great conquering and imperial nation of Europe. A German Emperor had ruled in Arles, and the Netherlands too had been part of his domain. One writer argues that Dante was a German; another places Paris in the list of mediaeval German cities. The old epics and songs, the old chronicles and legal customs, were made the framework for an infinite labour of affectionate embroidery. From Giesebrecht's eloquent and learned pages young people could read the romance of the Mediaeval Empire, of that great and tempestuous effusion of German chivalry which for many centuries filled Europe with its noise, and ultimately suffered the ruinous check which fate administers to those who chase shadows. And the later periods also contributed their quota to the sum of national self-esteem. Had not Luther given Europe the Protestant Reformation, and Kant the true theory of knowledge?. Even the enemy marched in plumes borrowed from Germany, for Bernhard of Saxe-Weimar and Maurice of Saxony, not to speak of certain paladins of Napoleon, such as Ney, Kellermann, Rapp, and Kleber, were all to be accounted among the sons of Odin.

All this exuberant stirring of national sentiment, though it often led to the expression of unripe opinion, was quite consistent with scrupulous workmanship. For the greater part of the century Von Ranke, 'that discreet and disinterested servant of the Prussian monarchy', provided an admirable exemplar of historical impartiality. His governing idea of the individuality of peoples grew out of a temperamental opposition to the French theory of a Universal Republic or Empire; and it was his main interest in history to define the distinctive character of each national group and then to describe their mutual action and interaction at the moments of universal history. The spirit of those alert and lively Venetian *relazioni*, the importance of which he was the first to discover, seems to have entered into this gentle and curious Saxon aristocrat. Wherever he moves, and he moves everywhere, he is always elegant, dexterous, well-mannered. Even the tempest of 1870 did not discompose him; and, while the guns were booming at Gravelotte and Sédan, Ranke was describing the origins of the Seven Years' War with the sobriety of a judge. The hotter tempers of Germany did not appreciate this Olympian detachment. They considered him lifeless and uninspiring; they thought, not without reason, that he gave an excessive air of calm and sunshine to the scene, and that, living by preference in the company of extinct diplomatists and courtiers, he missed the large sweep and passion of popular movements.

Ranke, however, lived to be a miraculous survival of an earlier age. The dynamic forces during the later half of the century were men of a very different type from that band of patriot scholars, of whom Dahlmann.may be taken as a conspicuous example, whose life hopes had. been crushed by the failure of the constitutional movement of '48. Mommsen, the greatest of all the new professors of 'Realpolitik', had begun life as a journalist, was even concerned in the disorders of the revolutionary period, and never ceased to manifest a fiery interest in the politics of the day. Always a liberal and even after 1870 a vigorous opponent of Bismarck in the sphere of domestic policy, Mommsen was at the same time a convinced and passionate imperialist. Whereas Niebuhr had regarded the foundation of the Roman Empire as 'one of the most afflicting spectacles in history', for Mommsen it was the salvation of the world, and its creator was the only man of genius produced by Rome. The *Römische Geschichte* was first published in 1854, and took the world by storm, not merely for its vigorous eloquence, its hard firm outline and massive knowledge, but also as a brilliant incarnation of the spirit of Prussian imperialism. An apology for Caesarism so thoroughgoing and confident had never been pronounced by a scholar entitled to a hearing. The old idols of Republicanism were swept down with a contemptuous gesture, Cato as a vain and obstinate dullard, Cicero as a despicable charlatan of the journalist tribe. The ideals of the aristocratic Republic were treated as beneath observation, for, as M. Guilland aptly remarks,[1] 'le vaincu pour Mommsen a toujours tort'. The great scholar was on safer ground when in later life he evolved the history of the Empire from the inscriptions, for here his survey was unblotted by the clouds of passion. But the earlier and more famous work is another illustration of Lessing's witty saying that nobody ever writes the history of any age but his own age.

A younger contemporary of Mommsen brought historical studies into more intimate relations with German politics. Heinrich von Sybel, a Westphalian by birth but a Prussian by adoption, was primarily a publicist, holding in common with Seeley that history should be practical and the historical workshop a laboratory of political hygiene. His own opinions, which were of the National Liberal type, vehemently Prussian and Protestant, were held and enunciated with great vigour during a long and busy life. As a political pamphleteer he was certainly unequalled in his generation, for he took large views and was the master of a manly and robust style, sometimes touched with irony and always marked by conviction. His best short pieces denounced the Mediaeval Empire as an extravagant and disastrous folly, and (at some expense of historic justice) depicted Austria as the destroyer and Prussia as the constant champion of German interests. But his fame rested upon two long historical books, each of which in a sense

---

[1] *L'Allemagne nouvelle et ses historiens.*

marked an epoch. We do not now read Sybel's 'French Revolution', which was in truth a political pamphlet designed to unmask the baseness and cruelty of the French, the cowardice and treachery of Austria, and the loyal courses of the Prussian monarchy in a distracted age. We do not read it, partly because its political estimates are biased, and partly because the book is dull and heavy, wanting alike in psychological insight and graphic power. But nevertheless we have all profited by Von Sybel's admirable researches. He was the first historian to attempt a complete study of the documentary evidence for the Revolution, the first to bring out the importance of the Polish question as a factor determining the course of European affairs, and the first who paid serious attention to the economic side of revolutionary history. Of the actors of the Revolution he wrote with a mind utterly empty of the intelligence which springs from sympathy, but often with the clairvoyance of hate; and after a course of Michelet's inspired rhapsodies, a draught of the Prussian mixture is still a useful antidote.

His second long work on the 'Foundation of the German Empire', being an unstinted eulogy of Bismarck, earned for him the dislike of his Imperial master and exclusion from the Archives of Berlin. The brief to which he wrote would have perplexed a moralist, but Von Sybel was too hardened a Prussian to permit himself the luxury of a fastidious conscience. He defends the Second Partition of Poland and is at elaborate pains to argue the Prussian case for the annexation of the Danish Duchies. Von Roon, who was a blunt soldier, did not see the need of professorial apologies. 'The question of the Duchies', he said truly, 'is not a question of right but a question of force, and we have the force.' To rob first and excuse afterwards was the classical process whereby Prussia had grown, and the successful thief was always more honoured than his apologist. 'Je prends d'abord,' said Frederic II; 'je trouverai toujours des pédants pour prouver mes droits'; and Bismarck had no more difficulty in finding his pedant than the robber of genius who established the greatness of Prussia on the stolen provinces of Silesia and Posen.

The graphic quality, which is so singularly lacking to Von

Sybel, was amply supplied in the work of a deaf and passionate Saxon who has been described by some as the Macaulay and by others as the Carlyle of Germany. Heinrich von Treitschke was a man entirely devoid of some properties generally held to be essential to the adequate writing of history. He was generally lashed up to a white heat of indignation, and consistently insulting to large and respectable bodies of the genus Man—to the English and French nations, to the Jewish race, and to all who professed socialist or radical opinions. Violent in his capacity for theological execration—for he preached his political doctrines with fanaticism—he created misgivings among many German scholars, including Ranke, who drew a line between the publicist and the historian. But the man was a genius. His history of the German Confederation from 1815 to 1848 is one of the most delightful and brilliant achievements of modern prose literature. The little courts and the big courts, the wandering idealizing students with their patriotic songs, their duels, their gymnastic clubs and sentimental absurdities, the newspaper men and the junkers, the special characteristics of manner, physique, and tradition by which the inhabitants of one part of Germany may be distinguished from those of another—all this and much more he paints for us with such wealth of illustration, such vitality, and with so easy a mastery of men and things, that there is no other historical book upon any period from which Germany and all that Germany means can be so well understood.

So far we have spoken of Treitschke merely as a great descriptive artist, but Treitschke was a great deal more; he was not even principally an artist, and of course still less a man of science. If we wish to classify this astonishing master of eloquence, we must think of him as a prophet, delivering, as all true prophets must, one message and one message only to his age, and repeating himself now in one form, now in another, but always on a sustained note of fiery and even reckless intellectual courage. And the message was in essence identical with the creed of Mommsen, Droysen, Sybel—the necessity for a strong Germany, united under the Prussian sceptre and informed by the Prussian spirit.

Of this doctrine Treitschke was certainly the most influential, even if he was not the most learned, exponent. His lectures at Berlin, spiced with malicious sallies at the English, the Jews, and the socialists, were one of the established entertainments of the capital and widely celebrated in the student world of at least six nations. Nobody could complain that the Professor's teaching was lacking in the quality of directness. He knew exactly where he stood and whither he intended to lead his flock. A single idea informed his whole teaching. If he praised Hegel as the 'first political head among the German philosophers', it was because the Hegelian philosophy glorified the State. If Byron was held up as a shining example to cosmopolitan decadents like Heine, it was because 'to the banished aristocrat England still remained the first country in the globe'. The State was the ultimate good, patriotism the supreme virtue; and the main problem for the teacher was to develop the State-sense in a people remarkably deficient in political coherence. What matter if there were some exaggeration? To a nation like the German the call of the State must be bawled through a megaphone.

In the light of this governing principle, common to Aristotle, Machiavelli, and Hegel, Treitschke expounded the ethics of German imperialism to a generation steadily becoming more and more conscious of its inner unity, its military strength, and its great future in the world. He did not hesitate to glorify war as a necessary and elevating influence on national progress, and at all times and seasons preached with reverential emotion the gospel of material power. For Prussia his enthusiasm knew no bounds, for he held that she had performed every great achievement in German politics since the Peace of Westphalia. The true test of a man, as of a nation, was capacity for sacrifice. But if we ask the oracle to what ultimate end, we obtain no very clear or satisfactory response.

That Treitschke has been the principal literary organ of a very brutal type of imperialism should not blind us to the many elements of real moral grandeur contained in the body of his writing. Perverted, overstrained, violently prejudiced, as he undoubtedly was, nobody has paid more unstinted reverence to the proud and heroic forms of human temperament. And the example of Carlyle is sufficient to show that a philosophy of politics fundamentally opposed to the specific Christian virtues may be so held and propagated as to exercise, upon the whole, a fortifying influence on the brain and will by bringing into relief the sterner beauties of human character, by insisting on the seriousness of life, and by exciting a more active sense of its duties and responsibilities. So it was with Treitschke, who, with less of mystic depth, had more of practical sense and elasticity than Carlyle. The generation for which he wrote welcomed and needed the stimulus of his genius; and, though in many ways his influence is greatly to be deplored, in others it was good, not only as giving to the study of politics a large and imaginative outlook, but also because it helped to arouse an intelligent interest in the conduct of public affairs.

The present constitution of the German Empire,[1] with its unequal federalism, its Prussian predominance, its aristocratic social structure, its vast system of militarism combined with universal suffrage, is so anomalous a mixture of mediaeval and modern principles that, were it not for the fact that Professors in Germany are State servants, we might be surprised at its having received a general measure of academic assent. Treitschke, like Alexander Hamilton, would have preferred a unitary state to a federation and was ill-pleased with the Reichstag. Yet, upon the whole, being at once aristocrat, militarist, and monarchist, he was well satisfied with the polity as it finally left the shaping hands of Bismarck. As we learn from Mr. Davis's excellent volume,[2] his early enthusiasm suffered some diminution with the passage of years. Free education, local self-government, a free acceptance of reasonable laws by the citizens of a national state—such was the ultimate residuum of his liberalism. For party strife and parliamentary government he cherished an infinite contempt, and regarded such institutions as entirely unfit for Germany.

Indeed part of his intellectual activity was devoted to

[1] Written in 1915.
[2] H. W. C. Davis, *The Political Thought of Treitschke*. Constable, 1914.

combating the notion, which was not uncommon in the middle years of this century, that the political salvation of Germany was to be found in English Constitutionalism. This or something like it had been the belief of the great Dahlmann, Treitschke's master in history and the creator of the still-born Constitution of 1848. And it was because English liberalism was at once so seductive and yet so incompatible with the Prussian spirit, that all who stood near to the mind of Bismarck determined to discredit it with every weapon at their command. How basely the campaign was conducted by their hero is concealed in many volumes by Von Sybel but amply revealed by the voluble Busch. Nor can we be surprised if the professor of patriotic history in Berlin did not fall short of his political chieftain in his efforts to weaken that sentimental attraction of the Germans to England which was 'really a deadly sin, nothing less than the sin against the Holy Ghost'. In this congenial operation Treitschke was assisted first by the patent sympathy of the English people for the Danes in the affair of the Duchies, and then by the English neutrality during the Franco-Prussian War. That Great Britain should refuse to strike in with Prussia appeared to him a crowning demonstration of baseness. ' The lust for mammon ', he writes, ' has stifled every feeling of honour, every feeling of right and wrong ; cowardice and sensuality take shelter behind that wondrous theological rhetoric which to us free German heretics is the most repulsive of all the defects in the English character. We seem to hear that reverend snuffle when we see the English press turn up pious eyes full of indignation against the unchristian and warlike nations of the Continent.' That every nation contains its cowards, its sensualists, and its hypocrites is a sad truth; but how Treitschke can have brought himself to think that it was a British interest to enter the Franco-Prussian War on the Prussian side passes belief. In his own words and on his own principles the British statesman who could have so far allowed sentiment to overbalance the overwhelming self-interest of the nation would have trebly ' sinned against the Holy Ghost'.

In so viewing history from the strictly patriotic and nationalist standpoint, without the barest attempt to understand either the general complex of international relations or the great and inspiring features of alien civilizations, Treitschke was unfaithful to that high tradition of scientific detachment which earned for the leading historians of Germany their wide audience and honourable name in Europe. But, if his object was to stamp a particular set of political views upon the main body of his countrymen, he may be pronounced to have been brilliantly successful. His picture of England was not more malevolent than Michelet's ; but, being less fanciful and executed in a series of strong confident strokes, it was far more telling with the public. The selfish island power, impervious to heroic ideals, which had stolen an empire while the world was asleep, the tyrant of the seas, the modern Carthage, the upholder of a barbarous system of international law, the land of hypocrites and shopmen, preaching and canting, yet buying cheap and selling dear and lusting for a ' Cotton millennium', the secular perturber of European peace, against whose insidious diplomacy the unvarnished simplicity of German nature would be for ever, save for some heroic remedy, exposed in unequal conflict, a nation brutalized by sport, demoralized by the obscuration of its ancient aristocracy, patently loose in patriotic principle and organic cohesion—such was the estimate of our people which he drew for Germany, and which in the lower regions of German opinion found an only too easy acceptance.

It would be unjust not to admit that there are many passages in Treitschke's writings which present a true appreciation of the more sublime qualities of the British genius, as also of some political virtues of the more ordinary stamp. But in general it may be said that his capacity for appreciating Englishmen steadily declined with his own advance in years, and that the England of his admiration was finally interred in 1832. In language both plain and emphatic he indicated his opinion that some time or other Carthage would cross the path of Rome, and that, though the struggle might be long and difficult, self-interest would be vanquished by valour and the purse defeated by the sword.

It would have been surprising and even discreditable if so great an event as the foundation of the German Empire, with its amazing procession of military triumphs and its great exaltation of patriotic feeling, had left no impression on the historical literature of Germany. And in fact the impression has been profound, the political process directing the pen of the writers, and the writers in turn shaping the public mind to appreciate and extend the process. Indeed it is not too much to say that the historians of the Prussian school have been the principal architects of the political creed of modern Germany. They have exalted material power and belittled the empire of moral sentiments. They have applauded war as an instrument of progress and national hygiene. Holding that aggression is a symptom of vigour, and vigour the sign manual of political virtue, they have championed every violation of right which has subserved the aggrandizement of Prussia. They have scorned small states because they were small and have applauded big states because they were big. And in their violent but not unnatural reaction against the quietism and happy contemplation of that old pleasant Germany for which Mozart wrote music and Goethe verse, and which still holds Europe in its manifold enchantment, they have exaggerated with Teutonic thoroughness the brutal side of politics as a thing much to be respected and a talisman calculated to conduct their too kindly fellow countrymen into an Elysium of indefinite ease and self-respect.

We too have had our prophets of the strong man and the strong state, of imperialist expansion and of ' our country right or wrong ', which is the British equivalent of ' Deutschland über Alles '. But no reputable British author has ever written of war as in itself desirable, or has conceived it as part of his serious business in life to breed and maintain the warlike spirit in his people. Nor has the doctrine of force ever become a master element in British political opinion to the extent which is now the case in Germany, and this for reasons rooted in history and national temperament. The Germans are in the main a military, the English a civilian nation. To Englishmen a standing army was once regarded as so great an obstacle to that political and personal freedom in which a true national instinct divined the secret of the greatness to come, that ever afterwards militarism has come to be considered as a retrograde force, allied to political tyranny, therefore to be jealously watched and circumscribed. Germany, on the other hand, has been made by the army, and too recently to permit of ingratitude. Yet a nation with a longer experience of political disputation would have been more critical of the Prussian apostles; and, if the habit of bringing policies, however gorgeous, to the touchstone of the moral sense had been as widely prevalent in Germany as, thanks to the resplendent genius of Burke, it has happily been in England, the baser notes of Treitschke's resounding organ would have been drowned in protest.

If we have thus concentrated our attention on the political historians of the Prussian school and on the important share which they have taken in shaping the public mind of their countrymen, it is from no failure to recognize that there is more than one department of historical study in Germany and more than one type of German historian. Even in the narrower sphere of political history the case for South Germany has not gone entirely by default, as Baumgarten's criticisms of Treitschke remind us; and books are still written by professors of modern history under the good old rubric of scientific serenity. Meanwhile outside the regions of modern polemic the indefatigable industry of the German race continues to make valuable contributions to the sum of knowledge. If the exploration of the papyri is for the most part carried on in London and Oxford, the greatest living historian of antiquity is a German. Liebermann, a Jewish scholar it is true, has given us the best edition of the Anglo-Saxon laws, Krumbacher the only Byzantine bibliography; in the sphere of Biblical criticism, German scholarship, though no longer without serious rivalry, is still sufficiently active to provoke a reproof from the Imperial partner in the Divine concern. But, while it is important not to minimize our continuing indebtedness to German historical science, it is equally necessary to avoid overstatement. The Germans have been pioneers in the organization of learned enterprise, but have nothing better of their kind than the dictionaries associated with the names of

Murray, Stephen, and Lee. They created the academic study of history, but are now equalled, if not surpassed, by the severe and polished standards of Paris. The countrymen of Savigny can still boast of great legal antiquaries, but of none so brilliant as Maitland and Esmein. Jhering was a genius, one of the rare Germans who have sown original and fruitful ideas ; yet it will be generally admitted that in range and illumination and fertility Maine was his superior. Indeed, if we weigh the historical product of the nations not by the brute mass of knowledge which it contains but by the quality of its insight, the true balance of its judgement, the wealth of its original perceptions, the charm and brilliance of its manner, we shall find ourselves asking questions which, in the interests of the international comity of scholars, had better not be asked, and will not confidently be answered. Was Stubbs as learned and yet more actual than Waitz ? Has anybody equalled De Tocqueville in social analysis ? What historian is fairer than Lecky, wiser than Gardiner, more imaginative than Carlyle, more full of threads to guide than Guizot, more brilliant in narrative than Macaulay and Vandal ? Among the many excellent German historians of Greece is there a political judgement as massive as Grote's ? We cannot dogmatize, but this at least we know, that whoever would pass from the ancient to the modern world must tread that great Roman causeway the stones of which were so soundly laid by the genius of an Englishman some hundred and fifty years ago, that neither the traffic of scholars, nor any sudden tempest in the climate of intellect, is likely to leave it cracked and unserviceable.

Imperial Administration[1]

I HAVE undertaken to address you this afternoon upon the administrative system of the British Empire, but in truth the British Empire does not possess an administrative system. Rather it may be compared to a league of states, each separately equipped with its own body of administrative agents, and, save for the office of Colonial Governor, and a common but undefined obedience to the Parliament and Cabinet of Great Britain, bound, one to another, by no bureaucratic tie. It would, no doubt, be possible, even with no radical change in the constitution of the Empire, to create the rudiments of an Imperial administration. Thus, if (to take a long stretch of fancy), after consultation with the Governments of India and the Dominions, a Zollverein were established for the whole Empire, it would be necessary to create an Imperial customs service, and it is probable that the members of that service would be recruited on a common plan, paid at a common rate, and made amenable to a common discipline. Diplomatic agreements might similarly be made with respect to other spheres of Imperial policy, such as naval defence, which might similarly involve the appointment of administrative agents common to the whole Empire and responsible to the control of the Parliament of Great Britain. Such agreements, however, would last only so long as they were agreeable to the temper of the Dominion Governments who had entered into them, and the administrations founded on them would share the same uncertainty. An Imperial administrative system in the true sense of the term could only be created as the result of the prior creation of a true Imperial legislature, of a legislature, that is to say, composed of representatives from all parts of the Empire, and charged with the duty of legislating upon all matters of Imperial concern.

How far it is desirable to create such an organ is a question

[1] A lecture delivered in the Great Hall of King's College in the autumn term of 1915.

which falls outside my present scope. I will merely remark upon the fact that the Parliament of Great Britain is singular in being without representatives from the Colonies and outlying parts of the Empire. I do not know whether a Turkish Parliament continues to deliberate in Constantinople, but, if it does, representatives from Basra in the Persian Gulf, who have voyaged to the capital via Bombay, Aden, and Port Said, are participating in the work of the assembly.

My object to-day is to direct your attention to the machinery which actually exists, to comment upon its leading characteristics, and to explain in bare outline some of the gravest among the many problems of administrative mechanism which are occupying the minds of our statesmen beyond the seas.

Administrations fall, in the main, into two types, those which are and those which are not responsible to immediate parliamentary control. For the purposes of clearness, though the phraseology is far from being accurate, we will designate them as responsible and irresponsible administrations. The Civil Services of Canada and Australia are responsible because they are under the immediate eye of a democratic Parliament. The Civil Service of India is irresponsible because, although ultimately subject to the Parliament of Great Britain, it is exempt from interference from any popularly constituted body in India, and possesses therefore a liberty of action considerably in excess of that enjoyed by the administrative agents in our self-governing Dominions. Then, again, an important distinction may be drawn between two types of responsible administration. There is the permanent Civil Service, and there is the party Civil Service. The Civil Service of Great Britain is permanent. Once appointed, the Civil Servant, although his tenure is technically ' during pleasure ', practically retains his office until his appointed time of retirement, unless disqualified by misconduct. But before the reforms of 1883 the Civil Service of America was not permanent. The whole personnel of the administration changed with each swing of the electoral pendulum, and all the experience gained in public work was immediately lost to the country. In other words, in America the Civil Service was the creation of a party, born when the party came into power, dying when the party was beaten at the polls. It was the creature of an electoral victory, the sport of electoral chances, the spoils of a successful electoral campaign. Whereas a permanent Civil Service tends to correct the native inexperience of democratic government, a party Civil Service tends to confirm it.

The Dominions of the British Empire, enjoying the benefits of responsible government, have not been exempt from the most insidious danger liable to beset the public service of a democratic and parliamentary state. The Canadian Civil Service, in particular, bore a particularly bad reputation for political jobbery until the great cleansing of 1908, a result to be attributed partly to the infection of American example, but even more to the economic situation of the country, to the ease with which large fortunes were made in business, and to the comparative unattractiveness of the public service as a career for able and highly educated men. To those who travelled in Canada before the establishment of the Civil Service Commission in 1908, and even in the years immediately succeeding that great and necessary measure, nothing was more surprising than the universal belief that every Government servant had been jobbed into a post the duties of which he was incompetent to perform. I well remember how at a dinner-party in Quebec a lady expended in my hearing much compassionate vocabulary upon the lot of the passengers on board a certain vessel which, having developed a case of small-pox during its passage across the Atlantic, had been put in quarantine in the St. Lawrence. My hostess was not thinking of the delay. Her pity was solely aroused by the fact that the passengers would be inspected not by a proper doctor, but by a médical officer in Government service who, though she was careful to add that she knew nothing of him personally, would certainly be rough, ignorant, and wholly unequal to his task.

Experience has shown that in other communities besides Canada it has been necessary to take special precautions to prevent party leaders from using the Civil Service as a means of scattering small rewards among their humbler political adherents. In the Commonwealth of Australia elaborate precautions are taken under the Act No. 5 of 1902 to secure that the control of the Civil Service shall be withdrawn from the politicians and placed in the hands of a Commissioner who can only be removed on an address from both Houses of Parliament. But though Australia and Canada have thus shown themselves alive to the necessity of protecting the public services from political jobbery, it cannot be said that the Canadian and Australian bureaucracies have as yet been able to command a very high measure of general respect. This is due partly to the absence of any provision for recruiting men of superior education into the public services, partly to the lack of a pension scheme, but partly also, as I have already explained, to the greater attractions of a business career in a young country. Youth, however, is a fault which Time itself will remedy.

We shall be the less inclined to wonder at the somewhat rudimentary administration of our Dominions across the sea if we reflect upon the fact that until the middle of the nineteenth century the bureaucratic element in our own Government was small and unobtrusive. In the Napoleonic Wars, Great Britain was supreme at sea, but the proceedings in the impeachment of Lord Melville show that there was at that time no permanent civil staff of the Admiralty, and that such clerical work as was required was provided at the expense of the First Lord. Even as late as the Crimean War, the Duke of Newcastle, who was Secretary at War, worked in a small room in the Prime Minister's house, and it was not until the reforms ensuing on the close of the campaign that we can properly date the beginnings of the modern civil staff of the War Office. The story of the rise of the British Civil Service has yet to be written; and is indeed one of the most important unwritten chapters of our history. The bureaucracy has grown with the sudden swiftness and luxuriance of tropical vegetation after tropical rains, and the country has been covered by a forest of officials almost before it has observed that there has been any change at all in the constitutional landscape.

This late emergence and swift development of a paid bureaucracy is due partly to the long survival of a great and wholesome political tradition, and partly to the complex results of industrial revolution and Imperial policy. All through the eighteenth century, and, indeed, even up to the establishment of County Councils in 1889, the bulk of the administrative and judicial work of the counties devolved upon the shoulders of the unpaid magistracy, upon the Justices of the Peace, who represented the rough common sense, the prejudice, and the high standard of personal honour which characterize the rural aristocracy of these islands. Their services were rendered cheaply, honestly, and on the whole industriously, but though they had adequately supplied the needs of a comparatively simple rural society, they were unequal to the severer and more elaborate conditions of a densely populated industrial empire. Indeed modern industry, coupled with Imperial policy, created new tasks for government, requiring specialized ability and accumulated experience. Government by experts gradually succeeded government by amateurs as the sphere of State action extended itself. And in the grant-in-aid an instrument was discovered which rendered the closest inspection of the central bureaucracy an endurable and even a welcome necessity to its beneficiaries. The powerful and permanent bureaucracy which has now become so important a feature in our system functions under a quadruple safeguard. It is recruited in the main by open competition, a safeguard against jobbery and the grosser forms of incompetence. It is divided into a superior service drawn from the best men at our Universities and an inferior service drawn from men of good but average education. It is brought into continual contact with parliamentary life and parliamentary criticism by the questions addressed to ministers in Parliament. And, lastly, it works under the direction of parliamentary chiefs. The Civil Service of Great Britain is never permitted to forget that it is in a true and literal sense a body of servants whose work is liable at any moment to be brought under the master's eye. That it has escaped or can entirely escape the characteristic vice of all bureaucracies cannot perhaps be confidently affirmed, but if it is comparatively free from that senseless surplusage of reglementation which is common in autocratic countries, the cause is to be found in the last two of the four safeguards which have been mentioned, the parliamentary critic in the House, and the parliamentary chief in the office. In other words, administrative questions cannot be considered in a purely dry light; they must be viewed in a political light. And it is an essential part the skill of an experienced civil servant to feel how a measure will represent itself to the vision of Parliament, and with what modifications it may be made acceptable. The machine is continually up against the living forces of opinion, which, despite all party discipline, make themselves felt in the House of Commons, and since the members of the Civil Service are obliged to furnish answers to parliamentary questions and apologies for departmental action to their parliamentary chiefs, they acquire a wide kind of political education, tending perhaps towards a certain spirit of caution or even timidity, but based upon a close apprehension of the views, prejudices, and aspirations of the country.

In the Crown Colonies, and more particularly in India, the spirit of the administration is widely different. Here the administration is the Government, and nothing else particularly matters. Questions, indeed, may be asked in London about Indian affairs, but nobody is particularly interested in them, and the Indian Budget night is notoriously regarded as one of the least interesting occasions of the session. The affairs of India are in the hands of the Government of India ; they are managed by the Viceroy and his Council, and by the Governors and Lieutenant-Governors of the several provinces acting through the various branches of the Indian Public Services. Proposals may come from the Indian Government to London, and be vetoed by the Imperial Government. The large lines of Indian policy may be shaped by a Secretary of State in the India Office ; and a powerful Secretary of State may make his influence felt very strongly on the direction of Indian affairs, if he encounters no serious opposition from the Government of India. But, in reality, the last word lies with Indian official opinion, in the sense that a measure would not be forced upon India against the united opposition of the Indian bureaucracy, the Indian Viceroy, or the Indian Governors and Lieutenant-Governors. The Secretary of State exercises a useful and impôrtant function. He supervises, he suggests, he sometimes initiates. He is the most important conduit through which English parliamentary opinion reaches and affects the Government of India ; and for every change which needs an Act of the Imperial Parliament, he must be consulted and his consent secured. But the work of administering India is not done in London. It is done in India itself. It is for this reason that the organization of the Public Services of India is a matter of such great importance. There are, it is true, since Lord Morley's rule at the India Office, legislative councils, composed both of an official and of a non-official element, and even in the smaller executive councils it is now usual to include a non-official Indian member, but, great as is the political value of these institutions as establishing a connexion between the British Government on the one hand, and the Indian intellectual class on the other, they are debarred from one of the principal functions of a Western Parliament. The Indian councils cannot turn out a Government, and cannot make a Government. The Indian Civil Service is the Government. It may accept amendments, it may withdraw a measure in face of criticism which it judges to be well founded, it may profit by the suggestions of non-official members, but it is master in its own house. Cabinet Councils, Government majorities, diplomatic agencies in the Native States, administrative agencies in British India—all are provided by the Indian Civil Service, that wonderful bureaucracy recruited by a competitive examination in London, which is expected to turn out judges, revenue officers, heads of administrative departments, pro-consuls, legislators, political officers or diplomatists, and under the new régime, parliamentarians as well.

The supremacy of the Indian Civil Service among the public services of India is one of the leading facts which every student of Indian administration has to take into account. The Civil Service is the political, the governing service of the country. The members draw larger salaries and higher pensions than the members of any other branch of the public service. In the Table of Precedence, an Indian civilian will always rank above a member of any other Indian service of similar age and standing. The other services are excrescences, later developments due to the increase of specialization, grafts upon the parent tree, which is the Civil Service of John Company, now for many years taken over by the Imperial Government. The Indian Medical Service, the Indian Forest Service, the Public Works Department, the Education Department, the Police Service, have in every generation possessed officers of ability and distinction, but however distinguished an officer of these services may be, he is always subordinate to the head of the district, who is a civilian.

This pre-eminence enjoyed by the Indian Civil Service in India is perhaps most clearly illustrated by the position of the Secretariat. In view of the fact that parliamentary government does not exist in India, it might have been expected that the Governor or Lieutenant-Governor of an Indian province would rule with the assistance of a Cabinet composed of the administrative heads of the different departments, that the Education Service would supply him with a Minister of Education, the Public Works Department with a Minister of Public Works, the Forest or Agriculture Department with a Minister of Agriculture. This, however, is not the case. These departments indeed do possess official heads, but they are not part of the Provincial Government. Their work comes up, in the first place, before a Secretary to the Government, who is always a member of the Indian Civil Service, and no large proposal can be carried into effect without the imprimatur of the premier service. Some day, with the growth of specialization and complexity, this hegemony may be broken down. At present it is practically unimpaired. So far as there is an attack upon the position of the Indian Civil Service, it comes not from the specialist services of later origin, but from the Indian Bar. There is a very wide demand that the Indian Civil Servant shall no longer rise to the judicial posts of District, Sessions, and High Court Judge, or exercise magisterial functions, and that the Indian judiciary should be filled by a separate form of recruitment. When the Public Services

Commission toured round India, the cry for a separation of the executive and judicial functions was heard, most loudly indeed in the province of Bengal, where there is a powerful Indian Bar, but whenever and wherever Indian evidence was taken. It was argued that under the present system of union of functions, the judge came to his work with an administrative bias, that it was anomalous that the head of the police who brings the criminal to trial should also be the judge who sends him to prison, and that the justice of a civilian judge is amateur justice, good enough in barbarous times, but increasingly unsuitable to present conditions. On the other side it was contended that unless the district officer was also magistrate, his prestige would be gravely diminished in the eyes of the native population, that a substantial British element in the judiciary was essential, otherwise the administration might in times of racial tension be gravely hampered, and that though a civilian judge might know less law than a barrister imported from England, he would, through his administrative experience, know a good deal more about the Indians.

On all sides it would be admitted that the union of the executive and judicial functions is unsuited to highly developed communities, and in India the functions are already separated in the Presidency towns. On the other hand, the system of patriarchal justice possesses the advantages of cogency, economy, and simplicity in rude and primitive districts where public opinion gives very little support to the suppression of crime, and the amount of intricate civil jurisdiction is comparatively small. For this reason, the union of functions is likely to continue for a considerable time to come in the undeveloped parts of India, as also in Nigeria. On the other hand, it is likely, owing to the growing pressure of the barrister class, to disappear by degrees, and in places even before the time is ripe.

The relation of the political to the specialist services is another problem which is already discussed and is likely to come into greater prominence, as the technical side of administration develops. In India the Civil Servant is, as has been said, the most highly paid agent of the Government. In

Nigeria the civil engineer commands a higher rate than the head of the district. If an administrative system had to be created for India for the first time to-day, it is very unlikely that it would assume the shape which a long train of historical circumstances has given to the present system. There would be a single Civil Service of India, divided into a number of branches, executive, judicial, medical, agricultural, and the like, each recruited at the rate at which work of the type required can be supplied. There would be no one service so prominent among the other services as is the Indian Civil Service, or so exclusively entrusted with the central functions of advice at the head-quarters of Government. The executive head of the Government would have a wider choice of secretaries and advisers. There would be more equality in pay and prospects between the different branches of the public service, more interchangeability, a less rigid system of administrative caste.

One of the necessary features of British administration in the tropics is that it is difficult to get any public work per-formed except upon the service system. Ordinarily speaking, you cannot get an Englishman to come out to India to do a particular piece of work lasting one, two, or three years, however highly you tempt him, for if he comes he loses his connexion at home and may not be able to recover it. A University Lecturer may be brought out to teach in an Indian University for the cold weather, but hardly for any longer period short of a working lifetime. Consequently the best chance of obtaining good European service in a tropical country is to devise a system which will catch men young, train them for tropical service, and keep them in work until the age of retirement is reached. It is on this system that the Government of India obtains its doctors, its college teachers, its bacteriologists, its forest officers. And no other system is possible. If a new branch of public work is opened, the first ambition of the officers employed is to be formed into a regular service, with fixed expectations of emolument and a recognized place in the official Table of Precedence.

The critics have not been slow to descry the dangers, temptations, and anomalies incidental to the working of this highly disciplined professional hierarchy. If a Professor of History goes on leave from a Government college, the State may name a Professor of Mathematics belonging to the Imperial Branch of the Education Service to officiate in his place, and the same Professor of Mathematics may shortly be transferred elsewhere to teach Geography or English Literature almost irrespective of his qualifications. Again, the system has developed a very close and jealously guarded doctrine of vested interests—the higher posts in each service being regarded as the perquisite of the Service, as a prize against which recruitment has been made, and, consequently, not to be abolished until the vested interests of every person recruited against them have been satisfied. *Esprit de corps* is no doubt a valuable feature of public life, and there is no *esprit de corps* so strong as that of the Indian Public Services. The Indians themselves not unnaturally regard these services as manifestations of the European spirit of caste.'

One of the outstanding features of the employment of a European agency in a tropical country is its costliness. A European will not serve in India or in other tropical countries at the rate for which he will render the same service at home. He must be remunerated for exile, for the journey to and from, for the expense of keeping up two establishments, in which, if married, he is almost necessarily involved. He is a very costly article to import, and since he requires a pension on retirement, he is a charge on the revenues of the country long after he has ceased to render it any active service. Consequently the British administration in India is the costliest in the world, and a not unnatural mark for Indian critics, who complain of the heavy financial drain which it involves, and, in particular, of the large sums devoted to the payment of pensions.

The answer to these financial complaints is that if the administration of India requires a European leaven, the Indian taxpayers must be prepared to pay the price, without which the leaven cannot be procured. At the same time, the costliness of the European agency is a very powerful argument in favour of reducing it to the lowest possible figure consistent with continued efficiency, and this has for long been an acknowledged maxim of British policy.

A whole series of very difficult problems has arisen out of the costliness of the European. A European and an Indian are employed to do the same work. Should they receive the same pay? If they do, then the Indian is greatly overpaid, and the Indian taxpayers proportionately overburdened. If, on the other hand, the Indian is paid on a lower scale than the European, he feels aggrieved by the inequality of reward, since he is adjudged capable of doing the same work. The difficulty has become more acute owing to the fact that no uniform principle has hitherto been observed. Indian High Court Judges are paid the same salaries as their English brothers on the Bench, Indians who gain a place in the Civil Service competition in London are paid the same salaries as their English colleagues, but in most services the Indian receives two-thirds of the European rate of pay, and the vernacular press protests against the injustice of rewarding the same work by different rates of pay. It is not a very big question, save when measured by the friction which it generates.

Another problem which occupies a large part in all Indian discussions is the Indian proportion in the higher branches of the Public Service. In general, the Indians contend that the time has arrived when they may be safely admitted in very much larger numbers to the higher branches of all the Public Services, and one of the matters submitted to the recent Commission was the extent to which this desire could be gratified without injury to the efficiency of the Government. It would not be proper to me to divulge the conclusions to which the Commission has arrived, since they have not been given to the public,[1] but I may at least indicate the principal factors which enter into the consideration of the problem, since they are extremely familiar to the Anglo-Indian and Indian world. They are three in number: first, the extent to which a particular service may be regarded as 'a security service', i. e. as contributing to the security of the country; secondly, the extent to

---

[1] i. e. in 1915. The Report has now (1919) been before the public for some time, but effect has not yet been given to its recommendations.

which for educational reasons it may be desirable that a service should possess a substantial European element; and, thirdly, the measure of the facilities provided for the training of Indians to enter those services in which it is desirable that they should be employed in greater numbers. One thing is certain. A man in the higher branches of the Indian Public Services is a marked man. He is seen, he is criticized, he is generally doing notable and noteworthy things. It is necessary that he should be efficient, and it is to the interest of India that authority should be given only to hands which can rightly wield it.

The questions to which I have been alluding are so continually discussed in Indian newspapers that any treatment of them, however brief and perfunctory, will sound odious to the ear of the weary Anglo-Indian. Another question, undiscussed as yet, but likely to become prominent, is whether the scheme of Indian bureaucracy is likely to provide a sufficient stock of political talent in the generations to come. It is not without interest to notice that there is a good deal of weighty opinion to the effect that a peer imported from England governs a province better than a Lieutenant-Governor who has risen through the bureaucracy of the Civil Service. There have indeed been idle and ineffective Governors, and very brilliant and effective Lieutenant-Governors—but the weight of opinion seems to incline to the Governor. He is not so experienced in the particulars of Indian government. He is, in general, not so able or industrious a man. Of oriental languages and literature he knows nothing, whereas the Lieutenant-Governor generally knows a great deal. But he brings a fresh eye; his mind is full of Western improvements and analogies; he is not encumbered by too much knowledge of detail. His outlook is apt to be broader. He is often more conciliatory in his bearing to Indians, having less experience of the difficulty of governing them, and, in general, a good Governor will possess more of the distinctive political talent of handling masses of opinion and party groups than the man whose whole life has been divided between district administration and the secretariat. It may indeed be questioned whether a life spent in the Indian Civil Service is calculated, except in rare cases, to stimulate that part of political talent which consists in the study and guidance of political opinion, or in the framing of the large legislative proposals which are from time to time needed in actively thinking political communities. Until quite recently there was little need for such forms of talent in India, for if there was active thought among the Indians, it certainly did not revolve round the theme of politics. But the immemorial tranquillity of the East has now been disturbed, perhaps only for a time, perhaps never to be resumed, and we must make our account to meet an age of political discussion and criticism among men educated on the Western model, and using the Western philosophy to obtain their Eastern ends. Will that famous Indian Civil Service, which sends its sons upon their first arrival in India to five years of administrative work among the peasantry in some lonely district, the mother of so many strong and kindly fathers of the poor, rise to the occasion, and throw up men capable of guiding and inspiring the new India? It is a mistake to suppose that the oriental world is best governed by a policy of perpetual silence. Human nature is the same everywhere, and Indians, like Englishmen, are easily won by oratory, and seduced by the sweets of persuasion.

The problem of discovering and improving the political talent of the Government of India is made all the more urgent by reason of the rift which has sprung up between the British administration and the intellectual class of India. It is difficult to see how some such antagonism could have been averted once the decision had been arrived at to educate Indians in Western knowledge. From that moment it became clear that the governing bureaucracy would find itself in a dilemma. On the one hand, the Government Colleges would be providing an education in the philosophy, literature, and history of the democratic societies of the West; on the other hand, the political liberties which were the outcome of those intellectual conditions would be withheld. The paradox of the situation was illustrated very clearly a few years ago when Lord Sydenham's Government removed English history from the list of subjects necessary to be offered for the matriculation examination of the Bombay University amid a storm of protest from the Indian leaders of public opinion in the province, who found in English history a long lesson of successful resistance to authority. Nor is it to be wondered at if the rising tide of Indian nationalism, with its unpleasant accompaniment of bombs, dacoities, and other spasmodic deeds of violence, should have helped to involve the whole Indian educated class in a certain atmosphere of suspicion with those on whose shoulders the responsibility for the maintenance of order primarily rests. The bigger men on both sides can shake themselves free from the pervading feeling of racial distrust, and are anxious to promote the harmonious co-operation of the two races. But the Indian Civil Servant, partly because he is a representative of the official class *par excellence*, and partly by reason of his absorption in the exacting routine of his official work, is, in general (though there are many noteworthy exceptions), less fortunately placed than the lawyer or the missionary for making real friends in the circle of educated India. Many civilians regret this, and would welcome fuller opportunities of free and friendly intercourse with intellectual Indians. Others find an insuperable difficulty in establishing relations with men whose political outlook is so radically different from their own.

The new Indian Councils, by bringing the leaders of Indian public opinion into connexion with the official class, do, no doubt, afford valuable opportunities of ascertaining the drift and quality of the educated Indian mind. Government measures have to be defended against criticism; and in the course of debate the characters of the critics divulge themselves. One man shows himself to be steadfast and trustworthy, another to be slippery and fitful. A strong and skilful critic, like the late Mr. Gokhale, inspired general respect, for it was manifest that his conduct was guided by disinterested motives. And nowhere was there a more cordial recognition of Mr. Gokhale's fine qualities than among the members of the Anglo-Indian community. Again, the great difficulty of social intercourse between Englishmen and Indians in India consists in the absence of common topics, and the debates in Council provide common topics. They are not, it is true, so useful in bringing the races together as joint work at the Bar or on the Bench, for in the Councils the Indian element is mainly in opposition, and the opposition is often a source of irritation to the Government. But the Councils are a good deal better than nothing, and, though you may often hear them condemned as involving a serious waste of public time, no time is really wasted which contributes to amend the principal defect in the present political education of the Indian Civil Service, its failure to secure for the Civil Servant easy opportunities for an understanding of educated India. A little sympathy goes a very long way in India, and the finest district officer may fail when he comes to deal with a Legislative Council, by reason of the fact that he has expended all his available stock of sympathy on the peasants, and has none to spare for the journalists and lawyers.

In speaking of Indian administration, however, we should always bear in mind that in India, as throughout the Empire, we practise no uniform system. Our administration in India belongs, in fact, to two main types. There is the direct British administration of British India, and there is the indirect British administration of the Indian States, just as in Nigeria, besides the portion of the colony directly administered by Sir Frederick Lugard, there are the Moslem Emirates, in which the British influence percolates through native channels. Now the Native State in India is one of our most successful achievements ; and my impression (but please remember that it is merely the impression of a superficial and hasty observer) is that the inhabitants of a well-governed Native State are on the whole happier and more contented than the inhabitants of British India. They are more lightly taxed ; the pace of the administration is less urgent and exacting ; their sentiment is gratified by the splendour of a native Indian Court, and by the dominion of an Indian Government. They feel that they do things for themselves instead of having everything done for them by a cold and alien benevolence. And yet they obtain the advantages of the *Pax Britannica*, are protected against the caprices of a cruel despot, and derive benefit not only from the help of the British Resident, but also from the presence of Indian administrators who have received their early training in British India. A Native Indian State is, in fact, the most perfect experiment so far devised for bringing West and East together in a natural, pleasant, and wholesome way. The old oriental forms are preserved, the princely house, the princely court, the Durbar of splendidly robed oriental councillors, the princely bodyguard. The ordinary Indian seems to be more comfortable in a Native State, wears brighter colours, and goes more at his ease. And among modern Indian princes there is no little emulation in the matter of good works, such as the provision of schools and hospitals, so that these Western improvements come to be regarded there as popular possessions rather than as intrusive novelties, and are often, indeed, demanded by the public voice.

The success of these Native States depends upon the fact that they are encompassed by the atmosphere and institutions of British India. Remove the British Raj and it is only too certain that the princes would quarrel, that their subjects would be ground down with taxation, and that the revenues now devoted to objects of public utility would be squandered in guns and rifles. At the same time it is a question worth considering whether it might not be possible to extend the area of India now governed by this indirect method. In the public discussions as to the future of India, reference to the Native States, which occupy a third of the continent, is generally omitted, and it seems to be assumed that political development will take the form of an extension of self-government upon a Western rather than upon an Eastern plan. But the other alternative is at least worth considering, for it is possible that by the creation of new principalities in great tracts of country, such as Bengal, the devolution of authority might proceed in a manner at once more intimately congenial to oriental ways of thought and more advantageous to the maintenance of the British connexion.

Such a proposal, however, would meet with no support from the Indian leaders of political thought, who are apt to view the Native States as backward, if not as reactionary. They wish for a fuller share of power in British India, and have no interest in promoting a plan by which the area of British India would be curtailed. Nor in their ideals for the distant future do they entertain the project of a federation in which British India would be the predominant, and the Native States the less important partners. Yet the facts of the situation would seem to indicate that if ever India is removed from the category of dependencies into the category of dominions, the constitutional pattern of the new State must be a federation in which hereditary monarchies and principalities are included as constituent parts.

Upon the most important matter of all, upon the spirit which informs the British administration of that ancient oriental society where clashing creeds, long-inherited customs, and delicate sensibilities put our powers of governance to their most arduous test, a brief concluding word may be spoken. 'There is but one way', said General Gordon, 'to govern men, and it is eternal truth. Get into their skins. Try to realize their feelings. That is the true secret of government.' In India the secret has been known of old. In the instructions issued to the supervisors by the Council of Calcutta in 1769 we read as follows:

'Your commission entrusts you with the superintendence and charge of a province whose rise and fall must considerably affect the public welfare of the whole. The exposing and eradicating numberless oppressions which are as grievous to the poor as they are injurious to the Government; the displaying of those national principles of honour, faith, rectitude, and humility which should ever characterize the name of an Englishman; the impressing the lowest individual with these ideas and raising the heart of the Ryot from oppression and despondency to security and joy are the valuable results which must result to our nation from a prudent and wise behaviour on your part. Versed as you are in the language, depend on none when you yourself can possibly hear and determine. Let access to you be easy, and be careful of the conduct of your dependants. Aim at no undue influence yourself, and check it in all others. Great share of integrity, disinterestedness, assiduity, and watchfulness is necessary not only for your own guidance, but as an example to all others.'

Nearly a hundred and fifty years have passed since these directions, containing the heart of all true political magnanimity and wisdom, were issued by the Council of Calcutta to the Agents charged with the task of supervising the administration of Bengal. A very different theory of government in tropical and semi-tropical countries had been practised by other colonizing nations, but it is to the credit of the British administration of India that within the first decade of its exercise of political authority, it viewed the problem before it, not as the merciless exploitation of a lucrative estate, but as a responsibility for the lot of an oppressed and impoverished peasantry. In that spirit of paternal guidance and sympathy, the Government of India and of our dependencies has ever since proceeded. A slow Government, cautious to the point of timidity, suspicious of all new ideas outside the sphere of administrative improvement, but within that sphere swift, resolute, and enterprising, a Government unused to external criticism, and somewhat distrustful of external critics, but spotlessly pure, ceaselessly vigilant, studiously respectful of the religious and social traditions of the people, and single-minded in its devotion to the material and moral welfare of three hundred and fifteen million souls.

French Nationalism

THE spirit of Catholicism may be distinguished from the special quality of Catholic doctrine. The doctrine of Catholicism is universal. The spirit of Catholicism is a spirit of submission to the local pieties, inherited instincts, and particularizing forces of history. The doctrine of Catholicism posits a Universal Church; but the spirit of Catholicism, so far from being cosmopolitan, is intertwined with an unconscious tangle of exclusions and preferences accumulated in the passage of centuries and transmitted from a distant past. It would seem that the absolute submission which the Church requires of the faithful in the sphere of doctrine promotes a general temper of acquiescence in the sentimental legacies of time. The Catholic is naturally a Conservative. He feels the call of the blood and the imperious attractions of the soil. Without any process of analysis or questioning he is prepared to shoulder the burdens of history and to live upon the large force of impulse. He trusts democracy, but only when it follows its instincts, never when it uses its reason, and believes in the Army and the Church as divine agencies for the formation of character and the inculcation of habits of reverence and submission. A diffused and equable philanthropy does not attract him. Respecting the claims conferred by priority, he remembers that he was born first and baptized afterwards, and so metes out his allegiance between his country and his creed.

Such a sentiment, at once conservative, patriotic, and militant, has been evidenced all through the history of France, but never in a relief so salient as against the stormy background of the three Republics. The political Catholicism of modern France has had its periods of ebb and flow, its transmutations of colour and shade, its exaltations and its lapses. It has been royalist and absolutist with De Maistre and De Bonald, democratic with Lamennais, nationalist with Barrès. It has risen to the heights of *Les Paroles d'un Croyant* and sunk to the depths of the tirades of La Croix during the *Affaire*. But in general it has managed to combine with the fevers of combative emotion, engendered by the controversies of the hour, some of those gentler graces of mysticism and piety which properly belong to the religious temperament.

The future historian of the great war will take account of this element in the public consciousness of France. Modern war, as distinguished from the military amusements of the past, is a malady which can only thrive at a certain temperature. It may be plotted by Governments, promoted by armament firms, precipitated by the machinations of military cliques; but under whatever form or through whatever agency it may come, modern war always implies a general inflammation of the public mind. Nobody who studies the history of Europe during the last decade can fail to note a steady and alarming rise in the political temperature. It was most dangerous in Germany, because it was in Germany that it could be most easily used as the lever of grandiose and world-shattering ambitions. But it was not confined to Germany. The temperature was blazing in the Balkans. It was high in the British aristocracy, fast mounting in the British colonies, and had several times risen to the point of fever in the Catholic and nationalist circles of France.

The peculiar condition of the public consciousness in Europe, which alone made the war possible, was the product of forces and agencies too numerous and diverse to recount, but converging one upon another with accumulating momentum to increase the friction and mutual jealousies of the rival powers and peoples. Of these perturbing forces one of the most vivid and arresting was French nationalism. Other movements exercised a more direct influence upon the development of events, were more closely associated with the crucial turns of public policy, bear a larger measure of responsibility for the tragedy which ensued. The nationalist movement in France was not decisive in the sense in which the term may be applied to the stirrings of the Pan-Germanic idea or to the restless aspirations of the Southern Slavs. It never obtained entire control of the French Government; it was never a triumphant and overwhelming power in the sphere of opinion. Its central core of doctrine was associated not by inner necessity but through the tissue of historic circumstances with suspect causes, royalism on the one hand, ultramontanism on the other—and this in a country where Pacificism was vigorously preached and the old humanitarian gospel of the Revolution still exercised a wide and seductive appeal. Twice within a decade French nationalism had associated itself with an ill-judged enterprise and experienced a resounding defeat, and to onlookers on this side of the Channel a cause which was connected first with Boulanger and then with the accusers of Dreyfus seemed to be bankrupt of future and definitely overthrown.

But there is a certain type of minority opinion which can never be safely disregarded, and to this type French nationalism belonged. A minority opinion may be the craze of eccentrics, the plot of a sinister group, the airy fabric of prophetic minds dreaming of worlds to come—in all of which cases it is negligible; or it may be a creed, comprising, amid some unpopular or disputable articles, certain deep and widely shared instincts of the race—and that was the case with French nationalism. Its errors were the result not of corruption but of impatience. It caught at straws. It was anxious to be doing. It was full of inexperience, ardour, and desperate irritation. But it was a vital force in France because it represented an instinct, a tradition, and a dream; and being vital and vigorous there, it could not fail to radiate some part of its heat through the whole body of Europe.

The founder of the movement was a soldier-poet who, having fought the campaign of 1870 as quite a young man, dedicated the remainder of his long and stirring life to the idea of national revenge. Déroulède was totally lacking in balance, sagacity, and statesmanship. He was a wild, reckless, passionate figure, exercising by reason of his elemental force and sincerity an influence to which prudence can never attain. During the war his course had been marked by romantic vicissitudes. He had been wounded at Sédan, he had escaped from a German prison at Breslau, had stolen into Paris during the siege in the disguise of a cattle-drover, and had been shot in the arm fighting against the Commune. His great stature and martial bearing, his flashing eyes, with their stern glint of fanaticism, his gift of direct and vehement eloquence and rare capacity for throwing his whole nature into all that he did and said, would have won for him a hearing in any assemblage of his countrymen. But he was not merely a vigorous platform speaker. His little books of songs for soldiers hit the taste of the barrack-room between wind and water. Edition followed edition. Before the war his *Chants de Soldat* (published in 1872) had gone through a hundred and fifty-eight editions, his *Nouveaux Chants de Soldat* (published in 1875) had gone through a hundred and thirty editions, his *Marches et Sonneries* (published in 1881) through fifty editions. Of such work we do not ask whether it is literature, but whether it accomplishes the purpose for which it is designed. It is sufficient to say that

Déroulède achieved an extraordinary success. Having been a private in the Zouaves, and being a man of plain, wholesome, vigorous appetite, he knew exactly how to speak to the rank and file of the French army. His ballads and songs have no sense of strain or condescension about them. He does not fall into the fatal weakness of parading a familiarity with the technicalities of the military art or the curiosities of barrack-room slang. His metres are simple, rude, sufficiently intolerable to the cultivated ear, but well adapted to a marching tune or a rousing chorus:

> Dans la France que tout divise,
> Quel Français a pris pour devise :
> Chacun pour tous, tous pour l'État ? —
> > Le soldat.
>
> Qui fait le guet quand tout sommeille?
> Quand tout est en péril, qui veille?
> Qui souffre, qui meurt, qui combat ? —
> > Le soldat.

This is not a high order of art, and Déroulède, who came of a cultured family and was the nephew of that accomplished artificer in language, Émile Augier, could do a good deal better when he pleased. But in general it did not please him to do better, and he managed to discover just that subtle mixture of high spirit, sentiment, and moral platitude which seems to be demanded of the author of popular airs.

In an autobiographical fragment of characteristic sincerity Déroulède records how the shock of the Franco-Prussian War produced in him an abrupt and entire reversal of judgements, opinions, and sympathies.

'I was anything', he writes, speaking of the days before the Franco-Prussian War, 'but a patriot. There was a long period of my youth during which the glory of arms did not count for me compared with the glory of the arts. I had no comprehension of the grandeur of military service vaunted by Vigny, and I took pride in the fact that I loved Frenchmen no better than foreigners. This malady of cosmopolitanism, this coldness for France, this aversion to the army, had got hold of my brain during the last year of the *lycée*. My professor of philosophy had sown the first germs, which rapidly developed when I passed to the Law School. Every Sunday I read the *Rue* of Jules Valles, and, as Édouard Détaille recently recalled to me, there was hardly a student meeting in which I did not bawl out the old refrain:

> Les peuples sont pour moi des frères,
> Et les tyrans les ennemis.'

It was, however, one of those conversions which have more show than substance. Déroulède had always been a violent, combative young man, with a genuine love for the soil and scenery of France. Hitherto his enemy had been the tyrant Napoleon : henceforward it was the Prussian. If he was a professed cosmopolitan as a youth, it was because it was fashionable among the clever young men of the Latin Quarter to oppose the revolutionary catechism to the maxims of a decadent and unpopular Empire, not because he was in nature and temperament a pacificist, as he professes to have been. His conversion, in fact, like so many conversions, was a discovery rather than a change. He had hitherto not attended to Prussia, had not connected the great developments of European affairs with the future of his country, and had failed to realize the perils with which France was environed. The war taught him a new scale of values and made him known to his real self : and if his new philosophy was not the highest, it was now based on serious experience and was an integral part of a real and spontaneous man.

The most distinguished of Déroulède's disciples tells a story of an interview, which must have taken place some time in the early eighties, between the prophet of nationalism and Ernest Renan. Déroulède had come to the Collège de France to importune the great theologian to join his Ligue des Patriotes, a newly founded association devised to sustain the martial spirit of France and to promote the war of revenge against the German Empire. ' Jeune homme,' replied the sage, with the suave melancholy of resignation, ' la France se meurt, ne troublez pas son agonie,' words calculated to dash the bravest spirit, and to the philosophic student of comparative birth-rates not without a sinister background of plausibility.

But the strength of nationalism lay in its sanguine defiance of the oracles of prudence and the counsels of resignation. The air was full of self-questioning, of delicate cynicism, of exact, intelligent, but essentially despondent labour. One man wrote a book to explain the secret of Anglo-Saxon superiority. Others invited their countrymen to study and admire the Germans. The best minds took refuge in an atmosphere of intellectual criticism, disillusioned with each one of the political ideals which France had in turn tried and discarded with such bewildering rapidity. But the nationalist refused to be drawn off the scent. He despised the great Paris exhibitions, deeply distrusted colonial enterprises as likely to divert the nation from its proper work of recovering Alsace-Lorraine, and poured scorn upon the whole tribe of politicians as upon a gang of jobbers. Among a population deeply desirous of peace and rapidly outgrowing the crude ambitions of Continental militarism, Déroulède's men were a disturbing and upon the whole an unacceptable element. Why should France be required to brace herself up to an effort which upon every sane calculation of military probabilities must end in crushing disaster? Surely the wise course was to accept the inevitable, to find some means of living upon reasonable terms with the Germans, and to seek compensations for the lost provinces beyond the seas! So thought Hanotaux, the historian Foreign Secretary, and Caillaux, the coolest and best financial head in France.

Besides, there was something light-headed and preposterous about Déroulède's whole conduct of the affair. In England, where the sense of humour is comparatively strong and the dramatic instinct comparatively weak, movements are more easily killed by ridicule than they are in France. But even in France the Boulanger movement, though at one time decidedly formidable, suffered in esteem through the exuberant antics of its supporters. The enthusiasm lavished on the General, the crowds who escorted him to the station, the devotees who laid their bodies upon the railway line in order to prevent his departure from Paris—all this frothy ebullition of loyalty to a half-hearted, ineffectual soldier who, if he had been honest with himself, would have bartered all the dictatorships in Europe for a quiet life with his mistress, seemed to sober politicians little better than a fool's phantasmagoria. Visitors to Paris in the eighties will remember the smile which used to come to the lips of wise men when the name of Déroulède was mentioned. He was regarded as an attractive but rather dangerous madcap, picturesque as an incident in the landscape of politics, but of too fantastic a vehemence to give stable direction to any considerable mass of public opinion.

But the movement to which his energy had supplied an originating impulse gathered strength as it proceeded. When the Ligue des Patriotes was founded in 1881, the intellectual atmosphere of Paris was saturated with philosophic rationalism. The writings of Herbert Spencer, a thinker rarely mentioned without contumely in the lecture-rooms of Oxford and Cambridge, were accepted as the last judgement in the Latin Quarter not only by students but also by their most influential instructors. Scientific co-operation with Germany had been renewed, and the brilliant Curtius was elected a corresponding member of the French Institute. The giants in the world of letters were Taine and Renan, the one a strict determinist in philosophy, the other a sceptical historian of rare genius and learning, and both as far removed as possible from the temper which promotes or enjoys the animosities of nations. Cultivated ladies and gentlemen were beginning to taste the first fresh sallies of one of the most delicious inheritors of the spirit of Voltaire, and while the wits saluted the earliest romance of Anatole France, the vulgar devoured the laborious materialism of Zola.

Twenty years later the intellectual atmosphere of Paris was strangely transformed. The great captains of rationalism had disappeared. The old idols were deposed, and, while an anticlerical campaign was waged as briskly as ever in the sphere of politics, some of the most attractive of the novelists and critics were numbered among the orthodox fold. At the Sorbonne the idealism of Boutroux had prepared the way for a philosophy which exalted vital impulse at the expense of the reasoning faculty, now declared to be but a fractional and delusive element in the apprehension and evolution of reality. It was no longer an unfashionable heresy to allude to the soul, or to believe in its endurance after death. A philosopher of genius, with the pen of an artist and shining with an incomparable lucidity and grace as a lecturer, would throw a spell over a crowded and fashionable audience with a metaphysic which was surmised to give support to the supreme hope of religion.

In this cultured and more congenial atmosphere nationalism received from its Catholic and literary exponents all the illustration and support which deep feeling and penetrating imagination could bestow. During the rushing hours of his tempestuous life, Déroulède had recked little of the rites and observances of the Church, nor was it until his last illness, as we learn from the charming pages of a reverent disciple, that he was brought to accept the consolations of religion. But though the nationalist movement, as its name implied, was designed to include, and succeeded in including, men of the most various convictions and antecedents, its prophetic literature was in fact Catholic, if not in profession, at least in sentiment, drawing its strength from the older traditions and memories of France, and reacting powerfully against the cosmopolitan hospitality which had given to Jews and aliens so large a part in the economy of the State.

There was nothing distinctively Christian about the doctrine. ' Nos gentes, nationesque distinguimus. Deo una domus est mundus hic totus. . . . Igitur qui innocentiam colit, Deo supplicat, qui iustitiam Deo libat ; qui fraudibus abstinet propitiat Deum ; qui hominem periculo subripet optimam victimam caedit. Haec nostra sacrificia, haec Dei sacra sunt ; sic apud nos religiosior est ille qui iustior.' This was the primitive Christian spirit, the soul infusing that beautiful dialogue from the pen of Minucius Felix which is one of the few lovely things in early apologetic Christian literature. But it was not the spirit of French nationalism, even when expounded by the most devout and tender of its prophets, for the essence of nationalism was the hatred of Germany and the will to a war of revenge.

Hatred and revenge are not Christian sentiments, but imperfect human nature is so compounded that there is no easier way to produce cohesion among men than to show them an enemy whom they can agree to detest. It is a tenable hypothesis that the nationalist leaven in French thought tended upon the whole to sweeten the body politic and to rid it of some of its more rancorous humours. It is true that it administered in a very deplorable degree to foment anti-Semite prejudice; but if this aspect of its influence be deducted, the general trend of its operation was to infuse a wider and more generous tone into politics, to inculate a spirit of comradeship, a higher sense of devotion to the large interests of the State, combined with a greater feeling for the historic glories of France and for that invisible and imperious bond which binds the living to the dead in a spiritual and efficacious communion. This was the valuable side of nationalism, viewed as an ethical agent. It was estimable not because it preached the hatred of Germany but because it preached the love of France, not by reason of its antagonisms but in virtue of its generous affinities, not because it worked for a foreign war but because it endeavoured to compose a domestic peace. Its strength lay in the fact that it did succeed in restoring to the national consciousness a vivid sense of some precious things which had been overlooked, forgotten, or trampled underfoot. The admirable speeches delivered by M. Maurice Barrès in the Chamber in 1911, in defence of the small parish churches in France, at a time when the reckless iconoclasm of the Government was placing them in grave peril of destruction, not only exhibited in a true light the minor glories of French ecclesiastical architecture, but brought out in a very striking and eloquent way the value of the parish church to a village as a centre of age-long associations and a symbol of social unity and peace. And in general the nationalists rendered excellent service by their exaltation of all the natural forms of local and provincial piety which had been so greatly overshadowed by the centralizing policy of the revolutionary State, so that, in reading the literature of the party, one is conscious of a pervading tone of affectionate warmth about everything in France which might contribute to build up the patriotic purpose and character.

The weakness of the party, if party it can be called, was on the side of practical and constructive statesmanship. It represented emotion rather than a plan. 'Je croyais qu'on obtiendrait la Revanche avec quelque heureuse fièvre française,' says the most conspicuous of its later leaders. And again: 'Nous n'avons pas cessé de proclamer, je voudrais dire de chanter obscurément, obstinément, glorieusement, la nécessité de protéger notre sang et notre société, de nous méfier de nos envahisseurs pacifiques, de vérifier les intrus, de leur fermer notre maison et notre génie.'[1] But the 'happy French fever' was no scheme of national regeneration, and the doctrine of strict racial purity could never be applied in a country so full of miscellaneous elements and world-wide connexions. Indeed, it is one of the little ironies of life that it fell to Maurice Barrès to devote his *discours de réception* at the Academy to the praise of Hérédia the Cuban, and that Naquet, the political agent of the Boulanger party, was by origin a Jew.

Still, there are moments in history when it is more important to work for a general change of mind than for any defined scheme of practical reform. The nationalists in truth were not agreed upon the polity for France. Some worked for a restored and modernized monarchy ; others were suckled in the Imperial tradition ; but upon the whole they contrived to swing themselves free of the old dynastic anchorages, and were content to wait upon the tide. The one thing which mattered to them all was the ignominy of belonging to a vanquished and acquiescent nation. 'The important thing', says a character in *L'Ennemi des Lois*, 'is not the formulas by which one expresses one's emotion, but to be a little heated with life.' That was the position of the nationalists. They wished to spread a passionate, full-blooded way of feeling about the national problem.

In this they were greatly assisted by the fact that the memories of the Franco-Prussian War were still living and poignant among men who reached the summit of their literary power in the closing decade of the last century.

'La trouée de Charmes, le passage de la Moselle sur Mirecourt et Neufchâteau, voilà des pays nobles, des pays de

[1] M. Barrès, *La Croix de Guerre*, pp. 162-3.

grande histoire et qui furent, en tous siècles, la route des invasions. Quand j'avais huit ans, j'ai vu la retraite de MacMahon et du général de Failly après la bataille de Froeschwiller et tout derrière eux l'arrivée odieuse des Prussiens.'[1]

Barrès had seen with the impressionable eyes of a child enough of the tragedy of defeat and the insolence of conquest to furnish the basis for a life of political action. He remembered the weary and haggard Turcos streaming back in dejection from the field of Froeschwiller, the first Uhlans, revolver in hand, crossing the bridge at Charmes in the dusk of evening, the candles which by command of the conquerors were lit in every window of the village, the seizure of his father and grandfather as hostages to safeguard the trains, the murder of the chemist Marotte in the village street. On a sensitive artist-nature such experiences make an impression which colours every activity of the mind; an impression the more formidable seeing that it is of a kind eminently communicable to beings of the most ordinary clay.

These memories combined themselves with a vague and undefined aspiration towards a state of society governed more nearly as to its aims by the large popular instincts and traditions of the race, but in which military and clerical discipline should exercise a commanding influence upon character. The movement was not antagonistic to democracy, though its leaders rejected the particular form which democratic government had in fact taken in France. In all forms of Caesarism there has been a popular element, an appeal, as it were, from the refined philosophy of the Whigs to the elemental loyalties of the unlettered multitude, 'to the sumptuous treasure of the popular soul'. It was so with Napoleon; it was so with Disraeli; it has been so with the Catholic nationalists in France. They believed in the existence of a Tory democracy, and thought with our own Jew Prime Minister that an aristocracy could be so transformed as to undertake the neglected work of social reform, while giving effect to the full range of national ambition.

[1] M. Barrè, L'Union sacrée, p. 347.

The importance of such ideas to France cannot be gauged by the standards of a country in which the aristocracy has always borne its full share of the responsibilties and charges of public life. In England, it is so much a part of the established order of things that the upper class should devote itself to politics and render social service of one kind and another, that there was nothing specially startling or original in the notion that the aristocratic party might become the organ through which wide-reaching social changes were to be effected in the interests of the poor. But in France the doctrine pointed to a state of society and to modes of social action in the sharpest contrast to the known and established conventions of ostracism and *Fronde*. There was accordingly something startling in the suggestion that the legitimist aristocracy, so long dwelling in proud and embittered isolation, should once more plunge into the warm and genial currents of national life—something original in a programme which did not repose on dynastic principles and was not worked in the interests of a dynastic party. Frenchmen have always felt an air of unreality about our English party divisions. Our opposing politicians meet one another at dinner and at country-house parties, do not fight duels, very rarely bring charges affecting personal honour. While the amenities of life are allowed to be so little affected by the asperities of debate, may it not be inferred that there is either agreement upon fundamentals or a singular lack of interest in questions of principle? But in France it was just the fundamentals which were in dispute. The Chamber, and the country behind the Chamber, were always skirting fundamentals, touching the raw nerve of civil-war matters, such as the ultimate form of constitution, the dynastic claims, the issue between Christianity and secularism; so that the realization of national unity in France demanded a greater effort, implied a more violent change, and could indeed only be accomplished, even temporarily, by an immense displacement of interest and alteration of values.

Meanwhile, on the side of emotion and sentiment, the higher type of nationalist literature contributed in a marked degree to deepen the channels of patriotic feeling and to rekindle a spirit of hope in the destinies of France. One of its most distinguished features has been the attention which many of its writers have devoted to local history and to that resisting fabric of dialect, tradition, and belief which in many a province of France still retains something of its old richness of colour and pattern. This is specially apparent in the writing of M. Maurice Barrès, who has made it a large part of his political mission to spread through France a knowledge of his own native province of Lorraine and a sympathy with her political misfortune. M. Barrès is not, like Mistral, the epic recreator of a literary language ; but a tender vein of elegiac poetry runs through his musical and accomplished prose, and he is never seen to better advantage than when he suns himself in the sweet valley of the Moselle, meditating on its gentle beauties and the tragic vicissitudes of its fate. Here, for instance, is a charming description of the little military towns on the eastern border of France in the days before the war :

'Il est fâcheux que les romantiques qui nous disent avec des expressions saisissantes le grand secret de mélancolie des bois, de la mer et des prairies du centre, aient ignoré les petites villes militaires de l'Est et leur atmosphère propre à former les âmes : le son du clairon, tout le jour, le drapeau, le général, les promenades sur le rempart, et chaque soir soudain le fracas militaire de la retraite éclatant en apothéose. Ah ! les magnifiques tambours se déchaînant à huit heures sur un geste bref de la grande canne et s'engouffrant dans les rues avec toute la population derrière ! Cette discipline théâtrale et monotone pénétrait, pour en faire des héros et des amateurs de mort glorieuse les jeunes garçons des places à la Vauban. Il y a là un état d'âme français qui disparaît sans avoir reçu son expression littéraire.'[1]

Another prominent feature in the nationalist creed was a revolt against the domination of the 'intellectuals', and in particular against the cast-iron system of efficient but monotonous education which is part of France's heritage from the first Napoleon. So far as impatience with intellectualism went, the movement was only better than most young men's revolts against the existing order and its defenders by reason of its

[1] M. Barrès, *L'Appel au Soldat*, p. 340.

attachment to a fashionable but highly intellectual philosophy which tended to exalt instinct at the expense of analysis. But there is a good deal of pith and marrow in the bitter attack upon the *lycée* which so often recurs in the writings of M. Barrès—the *lycée* with its gloomy barrack, its rigorous and often unintelligent discipline, its neglect of individual aptitudes and susceptibilities, its hieratic type of instruction framed without reference to the spirit of the homes from which the boys were drawn, and imposed, often with considerable force of intellect and conviction, upon minds and characters for whom most of it could never be made real or organic.

' Une de mes thèses favorites est de réclamer que l'éducation ne soit pas départie aux enfants sans égard pour leur individualité propre. Je voudrais qu'on respectât leur préparation familiale et terrienne. J'ai dénoncé l'esprit de conquérant et de millénaire d'un Bouteiller qui tombe sur les populations indigènes comme un administrateur despotique doublé d'un apôtre fanatique ; j'ai marqué pourquoi le Kantisme qui est la religion officielle de l'Université déracine les esprits.'

Such criticism, though perhaps overdrawn and liable to correction in the light of the experience of the present war, contained the germ of some wholesome developments. The French schools of the Third Republic are certainly much better than the French schools of the Empire, more efficiently staffed, more enlightened in their methods, superior in the design of their studies and the quality of their text-books. It is only the exceptional boy who would gain by an exchange of the *lycée* for a scheme of private tuition assisted by a personally conducted tour to Rheims, Domrémy, and Lourdes. But the system of State teaching in France has its defects as well as its merits, and one notable defect, pointed out by M. Barrès, is that it tends to uproot provincial loyalty and to starve that aptitude for admiration and reverence which is engendered in the wondering mind of the small child and fostered by all the sweetest and most enduring influences of family life.

What then is patriotism as it is understood by the nationalist in France, whose creed and influence we have been attempting to describe? The love of country, for M. Barrès and his friends, is not, according to Renan's famous definition, the love of a soul, of a spiritual principle. It is nothing so ethereal. Rather it is first and foremost the love of a material thing, of an extended space upon the globe, of a land of plough and corn and meadow, shaded with trees, watered with streams, flowery with blossom, here offering some fat reposeful pasture to the sun, elsewhere broken into dark ravines and glistening crags, and bearing upon its surface the multiplied and appealing tokens of the long and diligent labour of man. And secondly it is an understanding 'with those who have engendered us according to the flesh'; and by an understanding we mean no conscious or reasoned pact, but a willing compliance with those mysterious and potent instincts which, being handed down from man to man through natural inheritance—'a secret effort of the Unconscious, a tiny shock propelled from the infinite past to the infinite future'—vanquish all reactions of the cold, discursive intellect, and so form the main tissue of human history upon this planet.

The Value of Small States[1]

UPON the old controversy between Brutus and Caesar the last two generations in Germany have had no difficulty in coming to a decision. The republic is decidedly out of fashion, and with it the whole fabric of idealism upon which in 1848 republican conclusions were wont to be erected. The modern German is all for Caesarism, for a big state, a big army, a big navy, and for a long course of progressive national expansion under the dazzling guidance of the Hohenzollern house. Of the old gentle cosmopolitan feeling, which suffused the literature of the classical period, there is now not a trace surviving. *Weltbürgertum* has given place to the *Nationalstaat*, just as the delicate melodies of Mozart have been succeeded by the obstreperous and clashing brilliance of Strauss. The

[1] Written and published in 1915.

2302 L

eloquence of Schiller is still popular, but the sentiment which inspired such a piece as the ' History of the Revolt of the United Netherlands ' is as dead in Germany as Kant's famous dream of Universal Peace. Realism is the fetish of the hour. Politics must be real or they are despised as shadows; and when a German speaks of *Realpolitik* he means a policy based on material interests, supported by brute force and liberated from the trammels of the moral conscience.

It is not surprising that the triumphs of German Caesarism in the world of fact and idea have led to a very general disparagement of the value and utility of small states. The argument may be gathered from the pages of Treitschke or indeed from any of the numerous journalists who have drawn their political sustenance from that bitter and uncompromising apostle of imperial methods. It runs very much as follows. In a small state civic life must necessarily be petty, humble, unambitious. The game of politics must centre round small issues, and thus circumscribed in scope, loses the ethical value of scale. Great affairs envisaged on a large horizon have a power of stirring the passionate and imaginative elements in man, which are apt, save in the rarer cases, to respond to stimuli in proportion to their magnitude. Existence in a small state may be elegant, charming, idyllic, compatible with the production of literature and art, but it can never be swept by the great passions which move the world. A small state may create among its members a mild humdrum kind of affection for its history and institutions, but can never be a source of that triumphant pride and hope which lifts citizenship up to the plane of heroism. In a sense it may be said that the history of small states is wound up. They may linger on, preserved by the mutual jealousies of rival Powers or because it is worth nobody's while to attack them, but their bodies will be starved and anaemic and their souls mere echoes of the great move-ments of mind and emotion which are liberated, almost automatically, by the diurnal movement in great and power-ful nations of the social and political machine. Sooner or later the small states will go. They will be absorbed in larger political aggregates. They will follow the line of historical development which has created the large modern states of Europe out of a mosaic of tiny and warring fiefs. And nobody will regret their demise, least of all the citizens themselves.

Indeed, from the point of view of peoples like the Belgians or the Dutch, the moment of inevitable absorption cannot be too rapidly hastened. Only then will they be compelled to discard trifles and to 'think imperially' of serious things. Their geography, political and intellectual, will be enlarged. The art of war will be earnestly practised. The spectator will suddenly become an actor. Great tides of national passion and aspiration will sweep into the tiny state, chasing away impurities, like the majestic ocean suddenly admitted in overwhelming might into a network of landlocked and stagnant pools.

The disciples of Caesarism will even proceed to contend that patriotism in its fullest sense is only possible to large nations. Great states march on, little states mark time. The movement of the great state is continuous and imposing, and, as in the case of other orderly developments, its future can be forecast with a certain degree of exactitude. Guided by the hand of God, the mighty organs which are the chosen vessels of the highest culture upon earth take up, one after another in due sequence, each item of their sacred and providential programme. Thus we have a long historic process ending in the formation of the Prussian kingdom, succeeded by another process leading to the establishment of the German Empire, and to be followed by a third process in the course of which the German Empire will become a world-power, not only supreme on the continent of Europe but exercising a predominant political influence over the whole surface of the globe. Great states have a destiny of which their citizens are conscious. *Et quasi cursores vitai lampada tradunt.* Men come and go, the seasons wax and wane, but each generation in its own brief allotment of life is sustained by the consciousness that it works on a providential plan, fulfilling one of the grand and mysterious processes of God for the improvement of the world by the spread of German culture. So did the divines of the Dark Ages applaud the forced conversions of Charlemagne.

Even in matters of technical equipment Destiny is said to have decided in favour of the big battalions. It is freely argued in Germany that a perfect organization of educational machinery is only possible to the opulence and minute articulation of a great nation, for the more powerful the state, the richer will be the fund available for museums, art galleries, and libraries, and the larger the class capable of enjoying them. Great states in fact resemble great businesses which on a given expenditure of capital realize a higher rate of profit than their smaller rivals, command wider markets, and exercise a stronger power in barter and sale.

It is easy to understand how the Germans have arrived at this confident and unqualified conclusion as to the worthlessness of small states, seeing that their own late arrival into the circle of the Great Powers was due to the long continuance of that *Kleinstaaterei*, that small-state system, which attracts so much hostile fire from the ranks of the Prussian historians. The humiliations suffered by Germany at the hands of Napoleon, the glory of the War of Liberation, which may be called the first common act of the German people, the fatal relapse into the old system of loose impotent federation, and finally the foundation of the German Empire under Prussian hegemony—these sharply contrasted periods of national history all point to the same lesson, the paralysis bred of disunion and the power generated by unity.

Even now the disciplinarian conscience of Prussia judges that the unity of Germany is all too imperfectly achieved. There are the separate states, there are the suppressed nationalities, there are the active and contentious political parties whose struggles impair the majesty of the Reichstag, and whose criticism weakens and perplexes the direction of imperial policy. When the Social Democrats, or the Poles, or the Catholics of the Centre embarrass the Government, good German imperialists look with envy at the social and religious cohesion of Great Britain. There is then no ground for wonder if, to the patriotic German of modern times, a contracted spirit of localism, only to be eradicated by a strenuous effort of the national will, seems to be the principal flaw in the political character of the

German race, as it has undoubtedly been the chief source of German political impotence in the past. And we can easily see how Germans, realizing the evils of past disunion, and exercising that tendency to generalize which is inveterate in the Teutonic intelligence, come to the conclusion that the happiness and advance of mankind are bound up in the expansion of great states and in the disappearance of small ones.

It must be confessed that this general attitude is affected by considerations of a different order. Outside the limits of the German Empire lies a *Germania irredenta*, a line of small states inhabited in whole or part by men of German stock and once included in the imperial orbit.

'Of the territory', writes Dr. Rohrbach, 'which belonged to the German Empire five hundred years ago and was inhabited by men of German stock, more than a third has been abstracted from modern Germany—the German lands of Austria, the Netherlands, Belgium and Switzerland. If you add in the Livonian territories from the Memel to the Gulf of Finland, where it is true the mass of the peasantry was not German, but where the townsfolk and the knights were German and the princes and nobility members of the Holy Roman Empire, then modern Germany is only half the size of Germany at the end of the Middle Ages. We leave out of our consideration those territories which at the end of the fourteenth and the beginning of the fifteenth century were only bound to the Empire by a loose connexion and belonged naturally to France and Italy, like the Free County of Burgundy, the duchies of Savoy, Milan, Mantua, Verona, and confine ourselves in the first place to territories inhabited by ancient German settlements, and secondly to the Slavonic lands of the East which were comprised in the German colonizing movement. To these Bohemia at that time belonged, for its penetration by German influence was only checked by the Counter-Reformation. It was not till about 1400 that the Kingdom of Poland pushed the German frontier further west. Posen and a piece of West Prussia and Schleswig, though not entirely inhabited by Germans, constitute the only territorial gain which the modern German Empire has to show in comparison with the old Empire. But what are these gains in comparison with the losses! The ring of territories encircling modern Germany, inhabited by more than 20,000,000, men of German stock, politically and even in national sentiment estranged from German thought.'

To a person imbued with a belief in the historical mission of Germany this contraction of the imperial orbit, so accurately described by Dr. Rohrbach, is one of those disagreeable facts only to be fitted into a rational scheme of the Universe if they are destined to be speedily reversed. Sooner or later Providence must intend that the broken unity of the mediaeval German Empire should be reunited to the parent stock. And so the argument descends from the high plateau of general ideas to the low ground of political appetite which is watered by the streams of national memory.

In view of this interpretation it is pertinent to ask what the world has gained from small states in the past, how far they justify their existence in the present, and whether they are likely to perform any valuable function in the economy of the future.

Almost everything which is most precious in our civilization has come from small states—the Old Testament, the Homeric poems, the Attic and the Elizabethan drama, the art of the Italian Renaissance, the common law of England. Nobody needs to be told what humanity owes to Athens, Florence, Geneva, or Weimar. The world's debt to any one of these small states far exceeds all that has issued from the militant monarchies of Louis XIV, of Napoleon, of the late Emperor of Germany. It may, perhaps, be objected that the apparition of artistic, literary, or scientific genius is an incalculable matter of hazard unaffected by the size of the political community in which the great man happens to be born, and that we are only entitled to infer from these examples that a small state may provide an atmosphere in which genius may thrive. It is, however, a relevant answer to much of the criticism now levelled in Germany against small states, to remind ourselves that in the particular points of heroic and martial patriotism, civic pride and political prudence, they have often reached the highest levels to which it is possible for humanity to attain, and that from Thucydides, Plato, and Aristotle, as well as from the illustrious school of Florentine historians and publicists, the world has learnt nine-tenths of its best political wisdom. America has particular reasons for gratefully recognizing one of the smallest and most illustrious of the city states of Europe. The seed of modern democratic theory was sown in Geneva, and being scattered on the hither shore of the North American continent by small communities, organized on the model of Calvin, burgeoned into the great Republic of the West.

Nor is it fanciful, in estimating the causes which contributed to the peculiar brilliance first of the Greek and then of the Italian city state, to attribute some weight to the question of size. Indeed, if we do this, we shall only be echoing the voice of antiquity itself. In the famous passage in which he depicts the lineaments of the ideal state, Aristotle gives the opinion that a city so large that its citizens are unable to hear the voice of a single town-crier has passed the limits of wholesome growth. This conclusion was based on the view that every citizen must take a direct part in the political deliberations of the state to which he belongs. Indeed, had the states of antiquity exceeded the limits compatible with direct government, the world would have lost a good part of its political education. As it was, the contracted span of these communities carried with it three conspicuous benefits. The city state served as a school of patriot virtue, not in the main of the blustering and thrasonical type, but refined and sublimated by every grace of instinct and reason. It further enabled the experiment of a free direct democratic government to be made, with incalculable consequences for the political thinking of the world. Finally, it threw into a forced and fruitful communion minds of the most different temper, giving to them an elasticity and many-sidedness which might otherwise have been wanting or less conspicuous, and stimulating, through the close mutual competition which it engendered, an intensity of intellectual and artistic passion which has been the wonder of all succeeding generations and such as can never be reached in great states organized for the vulgarity of aggressive war.

So much at least will be generally conceded. The question for us, however, is not to assess our debt to the city states of the past, but to consider what arguments may be found for safeguarding the existence of the smaller nation states of the modern world. And first of all it is relevant to ask whether there may not be some advantage to humanity at large arising from the fact that certain communities are withdrawn by reason of the scale from the competition of armaments. To certain military minds in Germany it seems to be a lamentable thing that any community of human beings should be organized on a basis of peace, or that the policy of any Government should be steadily directed towards the preservation of its subjects from the horrors of war. Let us assume for a moment that this extravagant proposition is true, and that the Swiss, the Danes, the Dutch, and the Belgians would be greatly improved in their general morality if they were thrown into some big military empire with an aggressive world-policy and a Providential destiny to impose its culture on the world, and all the other familiar paraphernalia of the Potsdam philosophy. We have still to ask ourselves the question whether, even from the selfish point of view of the Great Powers who are blessed with the moral luxury of a conscript army, there may not be some convenience attaching to the continued existence of small oases of peace in a world nervously equipping itself for Armageddon? Has Italy no cause to be grateful to the Swiss Confederation? Would the Scandinavian kingdoms preserve their unruffled neutrality if the Danish peninsula were swallowed up by Germany? And has the disappearance of Poland really benefited the two greatest partitioning Powers whose past appetites have brought them the heritage of restless anxiety which belongs to the vigil of coterminous states? Indeed it is not easy to measure the injurious consequences which have grown from the disappearance of that middle kingdom of Lotharingia which once served as a buffer between France and Germany, or from the extinction of the Polish nation at the close of the eighteenth century. By common confession European diplomacy suffers from nerves; and the nervous tension is necessarily increased with every addition to the ranks of the rivals. The entanglements likely to give rise to conflict are proportionate to the number and weight of the Powers which stand inside the ring.

Every ally who joins one or other of the coalitions brings with him a whole cluster of new interests which the coalition is bound to defend, and thereby increases the chance of war. Every Power which stands aside lessens the general strain and contracts the area of inflammable controversy.

But the advantages to be derived from the existence of small buffer states are subject to the clear condition that their independence and neutrality are respected. Let us consider for a moment what the world would have gained if the German Emperor and his advisers had all along regarded the violation of Belgian neutrality as an unthinkable crime. Not only would Great Britain be now at peace, but no general European war would have taken place at all. The challenge to Russia was thrown down by Germany because it was calculated in Berlin that by marching through Belgium the Germans could easily crush France before the Russian peril became insistent. It is absurd to speak of the violation of Belgian neutrality as a 'bitter necessity' forced upon a reluctant country in an unforeseen emergency. It was, on the contrary, the deliberate groundwork for a careful edifice of aggressive diplomacy. The entire plan of the campaign against France was framed on the supposition that the Germans would march through Belgium. The whole scheme of operations against Russia was based on the belief that the total weight of the German military power could be thrown on the eastern frontier by reason of the rapid and crushing success which a German army, advancing through the Belgian gateway, would be able to achieve in France. And upon these two military calculations the ambitious edifice of German world-policy was built. All the plans of the General Staff were secretly framed on the supposition that Belgium would be treated as part of the German Empire in the event of war. It was with this prospect in view that Germany thought it safe to defy Russia in 1909 and to repeat the defiance in 1914. And though it would be difficult to set bounds to the military presumption of Germany, it may be safely assumed that if the Belgian doorway had been patently barred, the diplomacy of the German Empire would have been tuned to a more modest key. The moral of all this is clear enough. The small states should not be abolished : on the contrary, their neutrality should be supported by a guarantee so formidable that the strongest Power would never be tempted in future to infringe it.

We may test the value of these communities by another criterion. The Hague Tribunal has been the object of much silly depreciation, and the military parties in the world are never tired of giving voice to the contempt in which they involve the whole principle of arbitration. It is true that the belief in the value of pacific solutions chiefly flourishes in small unmilitary states like Holland or in that large and imposing aggregate of small civilian states which goes by the name of the United States of America. And it is equally true that no nation has yet consented or, in the present state of public ethics, is likely to consent to refer matters affecting its ' vital interests, independence, or honour ' to an International Tribunal. Nevertheless a considerable number of arbitration treaties have been concluded agreeing to refer differences to the Hague Tribunal ; and in the course of the North Sea incident of 1904 the strained relations between England and Russia were greatly eased by the fact that the Hague Conference had already provided a method of procedure by which the dispute might be adjusted without loss of dignity to either side. Arbitration cannot banish war, but it can diminish the accumulation of minor grievances which, if untended, are apt to create that inflamed state of public opinion out of which wars easily arise ; and in the case of larger disputes recourse to arbitration has at least the advantage of gaining time. Now the condition of mind which supports the principle of arbitration, and which provides facilities for recourse to it, is only made possible by the existence of communities organized for peace, and standing outside the armed and vigilant rivalries of the great continental Powers.

It is symptomatic of the Prussian spirit to disparage any manifestation of natural feeling which runs counter to the assumed necessities of a militant Empire ; and so in books written even by such eminent and moderate men as Prince von Bülow, the late Chancellor of Germany, we find a fixed

intention to suppress, so far as may be, the national characteristics of the Poles, Danes, and men of Latin race who have
been incorporated in the Empire. We in England, who have
some experience of minor nationalities, cannot read of the
recent developments of Prussian policy in Poland without
feeling how unintelligent and oppressive it is, and how much
better it would be in the interests of internal peace and
consolidation, if Germany would throw her mind into a generous
and liberal attitude towards the men of alien type whom she
has absorbed by conquest. But it is part of the Prussian
genius—if a drillmaster can have genius—to regard all variety,
not only as troublesome, which it often may be, but as
injurious, which it very seldom is. Indeed, one of the principal
arguments in favour of the preservation of the small states of
Europe (and the same argument applies to the preservation
of the state system in America) lies in the fact that these
small communities do vary from the set type which is
imprinted by steady and powerful governments upon the life
and behaviour of the larger Powers. The mere fact of this
variety is an enrichment of human experience and a stimulus
to self-criticism and improvement. Indeed, the existence of
small states operates in the large and imperfect economy
of the European system very much in the same way as the
principle of individual liberty operates in any given state,
preventing the formation of those massive and deadening
weights of conventional opinion which impair the free play
of individuality, and affording a corrective to the vulgar idea
that the brute force of organized numbers is the only thing
which really matters in the world.

The critic of small states may also fairly be asked what he
means by the word ' civilization '. If civilization is a phrase
denoting the sum of those forces which help to bind men
together in civil association, if it means benevolence, dutifulness,
self-sacrifice, a lively interest in the things of the mind, and a
discerning taste in the things of the sense, then there is no
reason to think that these qualities are the special prerogative
of great states. Indeed, there is a certain type of harsh and
stoical patriotism which, by reason of its austere and arrogant

exclusiveness, is inimical to the growth of civilized feeling. It is not confined to big states, for it was present in ancient Sparta ; nor is it the necessary accompaniment even of huge military monarchies. But it is the spirit of modern Prussia, a spirit consistent indeed with the heroic qualities of the barbarous ages, but lacking the sane and temperate outlook of civilized life. All through history the great enemy of human reason has been fanaticism. And there is no reason to believe that the fanaticism of a military state, served by the most destructive artillery in the world, is any bit less injurious to mankind than the spirit which for many centuries of history condemned the religious heretic to the torments of the stake.

It is difficult rightly to assess the contributions which the smaller states of Europe have made during the past century to the sum of human culture. Nor would a mere list of eminent men such as Ibsen and Maeterlinck, of whom every cultivated person has heard, or Gramme, the Belgian inventor of the dynamo, or Van 't Hoff, the famous Dutch chemist, prove more than the indisputable fact that intellectual life of the highest quality may be carried on in such communities. It is of course possible that, if Holland were forced into the German Confederation, Dutch painting, which has now reached a level far higher than any attained in recent years in Germany, would suffer no eclipse, and that the Dutch universities would persevere in their work of scholarly theological exegesis. It is possible that, under the same conditions, the wonderful perfection to which the little kingdom of Denmark has brought the arts of dairy-farming and agriculture would still be main-tained. But it would depend entirely upon the degree of liberty and autonomy which a German emperor might be willing to concede, whether this would be so or not, whether the natural currents of hopeful energy would continue to flow or whether they would be effectually sealed up by the ungenial fiat of an alien taskmaster. Upon this it is unnecessary to speculate. But it is strictly pertinent to the argument to remember that the three small states, whose existence is closely and specially threatened by the expansion of Germany, have each developed not only a peculiar and strongly marked economy, but certain special excellences and qualities such as are most likely to be developed in an atmosphere of comparative tranquillity. Thus, apart from the school of landscape painting, the Dutch have set a model to the world in all that pertains to the scientific classification and management of archives, vanquishing in this particular even the French, whose organization of historical learning is so justly famed. Denmark, too, has its own speciality in a very perfect organism for co-operative production in agriculture.

Indeed, one of the advantages flowing from the existence of smaller states consists in the fact that they serve as convenient laboratories for social experiment—a point likely to be appreciated in America, in view of the great mass of material for the comparative study of social and industrial expedients which is provided by the enterprise of the American State legislatures. Such experiments as women's suffrage, or as the State prohibition of the public sale of alcoholic drink, or as a thoroughgoing application of the Reformatory theory of punishment, would never be seriously discussed in large, old, and settled communities, were it not for the fact that they have been tried upon a smaller scale by the more adventurous legislatures of the New World. Man is an imitative animal, and a study of such an organ as the *Journal of Comparative Legislation* exhibits the increasing uniformity of the problems which confront the legislator, and the increasing monotony of the solutions which he finds to meet them. All over the world industrial, educational, penal legislation tends to conform to type. And within limits the tendency is the necessary and wholesome consequence of the unifying influence of modern industrial conditions. But our enlarged facilities for imitation present obvious dangers, and among them the fatal temptation to borrow a ready-made uniform which does not fit. Small states may fall into this pitfall as well as big ones, but at least their continued existence presents some guarantee for diversity of life and intellectual adventure in a world steadily becoming more monotonously drab in its outer garment of economic circumstance.

No historical state can be driven out of its identity without suffering a moral impoverishment in the process. The evil is not only apparent in the embitterment and lowering of the citizens of the conquered community, whether they are compelled to the agonies of a Polish dispersion, or linger on nursing their rights and wounded pride in the scene of their former independence, but it creates a problem for the conqueror which may very well harden and brutalize his whole outlook on policy. It is never good for a nation to be driven to the employment of harsh measures against any portion of its subjects.

Upon whatever plausible grounds of immediate expediency such measures may be justified, they invariably harden the tone of political opinion, and create an atmosphere of insensibility which spreads far beyond the sphere of the special case and occasion. The acquisition of Alsace-Lorraine by Germany is a case in point. The result of the forcible incorporation of these provinces in the German Empire has been bad for the governed and equally bad for the governors. Coercion is a virus which cannot be introduced into any part of the body politic without risk of a general diffusion of the poison.

It is no idle fancy to suppose that the kind of policy which the Prussian Government has thought fit to adopt towards the alien nationalities of the German Empire has reacted upon its treatment of those German parties whose views do not accord with the strict official convention. No Conservative English statesman would ever dream of denouncing English socialists as Prince von Bülow denounces the Social Democrats of Germany. But then no English statesmen, Liberal or Conservative, would dream of treating any portion of the British Empire as Prince von Bülow treated the German Poles.

It is impossible accurately to assess the value to a nation of the self-esteem which is the legacy of its history. People who weigh everything in material scales may find nothing worth preserving in the historical consciousness of the small nations of Europe. They will argue that the Dutch, the Belgians, the Danes, the Swiss, might be incorporated in the German Empire not only without pain but with a positive accession of material comfort and wealth, and a larger political outlook in the future.

They will even deny that there need be any moral impoverishment in an exchange of historical memories, under which the incorporated Dutchman would hook himself on to a German pedigree and count Bismarck and Moltke among his deities, while the Dutch sea-dogs of the heroic age would give their names to the cruisers and submarines of the incorporating Empire. In all such reasoning there is very little allowance for the facts of human nature or for the working of the moral principle in man. As no individual can break violently with his past without a moral lesion, so too the rupture of the historical continuity of a state carries with it an inevitable weakening and abasement of public ideals, which may continue for several generations. We need not labour to establish a principle which is grounded on such obvious facts of individual consciousness. But one historical instance may be adduced in support. When in 1580 Portugal was annexed to Spain, then reputed to be the most formidable empire in the world, she suffered a moral as well as a political eclipse from which she has never since recovered. Her nerve seemed to go and by swift stages she sank into listlessness and decay.

Nowhere is the shaping power of this historical consciousness more evident than in the peasant nations of the Balkan Peninsula. These rude and valiant democracies live upon the memories of the past to an extent of which sophisticated peoples have little notion. The great ballad which commemorates the battle of Kossovo, fought against the Turks more than five hundred years ago, is still one of the most important political influences among the southern Slavs. Nor has the memory of the empire of Stephen Dushan, under whom Serbia was the leading Power in the Balkans, ever been allowed to fade among the Serbs, despite tragedies sufficient to break the spirit of a less stalwart race. To rob the Serbs of their political independence according to the present plan of the German Powers would be a measure difficult to surpass for cruel and purposeless futility. A race which had succeeded in preserving its historical consciousness through centuries of grinding Turkish tyranny would not be likely to renounce its past or its future under the guns of Austria. And even if the improbable came to pass, and a conquered Serbia were to become an obedient and contented fraction of the Austrian Empire, forgetful of heroic ballads and of a long tradition of hardiness and valour, would there be no loss of moral power in the process ? To those who measure all virtues by the standard of civic virtue, by intensity of emotional and practical patriotism, the loss would be beyond dispute. A great incentive to the performance of unselfish action would be destroyed, a source of heroic and congenial activity would disappear never to be replaced. Under the hypothesis the Serbs would sink below the level of their blood kinsmen the Slovaks, who, despite the manifold oppressions of their Hungarian masters, still nurture a flame of protesting nationalism. From such political apostasy no nation could ever expect to make a complete moral recovery.

It may be objected that the whole process of European history is summed up by the absorption of the smaller in the larger states ; and that if Hanover is reconciled to absorption there is no reason why Holland, Denmark, and Belgium should lodge a protest in advance against their impending fate. To this contention there is a simple answer. These outlying nations can only be brought into the German fold under compulsion. Their frame of mind is not German, their habits are not German, their history for the last four centuries has served to multiply points of difference from Germany. They have no desire to submit themselves either to the military or to the financial system of the German Empire. They are not ashamed of their present condition, and are singular enough to hold that human happiness and goodness do not depend upon the size of an army or navy or a budget. It is enough that the citizen of each of these states can call his country his own. Patriotism has nothing whatever to do with spatial extent nor are emotions to be measured by square miles. Great empires are generally full of the variances of unassimilated and discontented men ; and though a country may be weak and small, it may yet be capable of inspiring among its inhabitants the noblest and purest forms of affectionate devotion.

Indeed, the supreme touchstone of efficiency in imperial government lies in its capacity to preserve the small state in the great union. If the British Empire has succeeded in retaining the affections of its scattered members, the result has been due to the wise and easy tolerance which has permitted almost every form of religious, political, and social practice to continue unchecked, however greatly they may vary from the established traditions of the English race. Thus in the Province of Quebec we suffer the existence of a French ultramontane state based on the philosophy of St. Thomas Aquinas, and preserving even to this day many of the social features of a French colony in the age of Louis XIV, a community more extreme in its ecclesiastical rigour than any Roman Catholic state in Europe, and in language, religion, and social habits presenting the sharpest contrast to the English provinces of the Dominion of Canada. The same careful deference to the pre-existing conditions is shown in every part of our Indian administration, which carries tenderness to the religious scruples of the Mohammedans and Hindoos to a point of delicate solicitude, which no Government in the world has ever before attempted, and only the most practised experience can supply. These, however, are not the methods of the German Empire, nor can they be the methods of any empire which practises a uniform and universal system of military conscription. As soon as the words State and Army become coterminous, a philosophy of violent unification is set up within the body politic, which sooner or later carries everything before it, save the spiritual forces which cannot be broken by any machinery, however despotic and powerful. The Germans have not succeeded in winning either the Poles or the Danes or the Alsatians to their rule, because they have repeated the mistake which England made in Ireland in the sixteenth and seventeenth centuries, and which England has never since ceased to lament. They have attempted to manufacture German citizens by violence; and the history of Alsace-Lorraine under imperial rule has shown how little the policy of violence, however carefully it may be masked by specious political concessions, is availing to change the spiritual allegiance of a people. Indeed the case of Alsace-Lorraine supplies a fair indication of the misfortunes which would ensue upon the compulsory annexation of any one of the small states of Europe by a big military Power. It is not to be imagined that the forced union of these two provinces with Germany has been productive of material injury. On the contrary, they have shared in the expanding industry and commerce of the Empire, and any loss in population due to the emigration of the French has been more than compensated by an influx of Germans. Nevertheless, they have been and continue to be unhappy under the Prussian yoke, Alsace more unhappy than Lorraine, but both sensible of the fact that while material interest binds them to Prussia, the voice of spiritual affinity unites them with the French Republic.

Statistics indeed prove that, even allowing for immigration, the Germans are still in a minority in the two provinces; but this fact in itself is not sufficient to account for the continuing attraction of the French Republic, despite the strong material inducements offered from the other side. The phenomenon indeed is worthy of attention. Here are two provinces which have never enjoyed political independence or the sense of cohesion which such independence confers. For the greater part of their history they have counted as members of the German Confederation; for Alsace only became part of France in 1648, and Lorraine was not effectively incorporated in the French monarchy till 1764. And yet, though they have been replaced in their original German connexion, the natives remain French at heart. The explanation is simple. The French Revolution initiated these two provinces into the democratic ideals of the modern world, which the majority of the inhabitants still continue to prefer to the Prussian doctrine of blood and iron and to the methods of the Prussian garrison at Zabern.

The truth is that the quantitative estimate of human values, which plays so large a part in modern political history, is radically false and tends to give a vulgar instead of a liberal and elevated turn to public ambitions. There is no virtue, public or private, which cannot be practised as fully in a small and weak state as under the sceptre of the most formidable tyrant who ever drove fifty army corps of conscripts to the slaughter. There is no grace of soul, no disinterested endeavour of mind, no pitch of unobtrusive self-sacrifice of which the members of small and pacific communities have not repeatedly shown themselves to be capable. These virtues indeed may be imperilled by lethargy, but they are threatened even more gravely by that absorbing preoccupation with the facts of material power in which the citizens of great empires are inevitably involved.

The great danger of Continental Europe is not revolution but servitude. This war could never have been possible if the intellect of Germany had been really free, if a servile Press supported by a system of State universities had not instilled into the vast mass of the German people ruthless maxims of Caesarism, for the most part repugnant to their real temperament and nature. There are other military autocracies besides Germany, and other countries in which political thought is fettered by the Government. But whatever may be their several shortcomings, the smaller states of Europe are not among the despots. Here at least men may think what they please, and write what they think. Whenever the small states may come up for judgement the advocate of human freedom will plead on their behalf.

The Resurgence of Prussia

IT has been said of Napoleon that, though he accomplished several vast changes in the world, they were commonly unforeseen and unintended. Very much the same thing may be predicated of every leading actor on the stage of history. Even in quiet times the strongest gifts of foresight and circumspection are unequal to the task of assessing all the consequences of political action; and the difficulty is vastly increased in periods of crowded and excited action. We speak indeed of a science and of an art of politics as if the matter admitted of rigorous certainty and delicate polish, whereas a moment's serious inquiry shows that politics, if an art, is of all arts the roughest, and if a science, is of all sciences the least exact. A clerk in an office may be able approximately to forecast the immediate result of his humdrum operations. Not so the statesman whose action affects whole societies of men. The larger his canvas, the bolder and more original his conception, the less likelihood of a picture conformable to the original design.

At the beginning of the nineteenth century Prussia was still in essentials a mediaeval state. Its vaunted army and its vaunted administration, the products of enlightened despotism, coexisted with a system of rigorous social caste which it was the object of the monarchy not to break down but to maintain. The greatest of the Prussian kings had given his sanction to the theory that there must be three orders in the State, nobles, citizens, and peasants, and that it was the business of law to keep distinct the interval between one order and the other. As the army was to be officered only by nobles, so commerce and industry were to be the exclusive monoply of the middle class. The noble might not embark in trade or make a lawful marriage with the daughter of a trader or a peasant. The peasant might not marry or regulate the future of his children, still less quit his holding, without the consent of the lord. Certain properties were regarded as noble, for ever to be held by nobles, and not to be alienated to commoners without the special consent of the Crown. Other properties belonged to the peasantry, a class the maintenance of whose numbers was held to be a prime object of State policy. In other words, the enlightened monarchy of Prussia was not occupied during the eighteenth century in the task of paving the way for modern equality and individual liberty. Its object was precisely the opposite. In M. Cavaignac's apt words it appears as 'the vigilant guardian of the most rigorous classification'.[1] It kept class distinct from class, town distinct from country. 'Only the most indispensablè trades were tolerated in the country—tailors, blacksmiths, carpenters, wheelwrights, thatchers, and weavers. Even so their number was limited and they could only reside on bits of land specially set apart for small traders. If a peasant or even a lord wished to replace a piece of glass, or to buy a table or a chest of drawers, or to repair a wall, or to procure a cask or a pot for his kitchen, to get a pair of shoes, or to eat a piece of meat which had not been killed in his courtyard, he had to go to the town, often many miles distant.' Such was the spirit which informed the Government of Prussia in the concluding decades of the eighteenth century.

It is hardly necessary to point out that the political doctrines of the French Revolution were essentially opposed to the fundamental axioms of Prussian policy. We do not mean to imply that the Prussian monarchy was dead to humanitarian impulses. On the contrary, ever since the death of Frederick II it had been considering, for the most part ineffectually, various plans for ameliorating the lot of the poorer members of society, and in 1799 actually carried out the very important reform of permitting the peasantry upon the royal domains to commute their services in kind and labour. But every effort of reform was necessarily circumscribed within iron limits. No Prussian king wished to diminish the feudal power of the noble on his own estate. Social experiments might be tried on the royal domain ; general political powers might be and had been absorbed by the central government. It was part of the natural conception of public discipline that while the County Council (Landrat) acted for the State in the districts and the Financial Council

---

[1] Cavaignac, *La Formation de la Prusse contemporaine.* Paris, 1891.

(Steuerrat) in the towns, the lord should exercise judicial, administrative, and police functions on his own lands. A Prussian historian has spoken of the 'tribunician powers of the monarchy' during this epoch. The Prussian kings were no tribunes of the people, but the lot of the poor would have been worse without them.

It should always be remembered that in the age of Napoleon Prussia was one of the poorer states of Europe. In 1808 there were in the whole Electorate of Brandenburg only four towns with a population of more than ten thousand inhabitants. The whole economic output of the country was about equal to that of the Lyons silk industry in the time of Colbert. Berlin was a town smaller than Salisbury; Frankfort and Potsdam, the next biggest cities, were only twice the size of Abingdon. The whole population of the Prussian monarchy could have been comfortably housed in modern London without the building of an additional tenement. There was nothing to be ashamed of in this: but it explains two facts which might otherwise arouse inquiry. The first is, there was not in Prussia, as in France, a large educated middle class, accessible to new ideas and capable of formulating the social grievances of the class beneath them, and the second is correlative to the first. Prussian reform came from above not from below. It was the work of the monarchy and its civil servants, not of the people.

It has been a point of honour with a certain school of Prussian historians to deny to the French Revolution any share either in provoking or in shaping that great series of reforms which brought about the remarkable recovery of Prussia after the catastrophe of Jena. They do not like to be told that Prussia borrowed from her enemy or that there is anything here but a natural development, some what accelerated indeed by the pressure of calamity, but still an organic growth, a Prussian flower springing from a Prussian root. '*Aus dem ureigenen deutschen Geiste ist die Steinische Reform hervorgegangen.* The reforms of Stein are the product of the original and peculiar spirit of Germany.' And with great emphasis they repeat that whatever might have been its influence in other quarters, the French Revolution was quite powerless in Prussia, and that the initiation of a series of far-reaching and comprehensive reforms was due not to the attractiveness of French ideas, but to a military calamity which braced the Prussian Government so to adapt its ancient institutions and traditions to new needs that, without any breach of historical continuity or servile acceptance of alien remedies, it became once more a great Power on the Continent.

Even on this showing the impulse comes from Napoleon. Without Jena no decisive reforms. The unmistakable completeness of the calamity, the loss of men, of treasure, of provinces, of prestige, the crushing war indemnity, the continued military occupation, must have convinced the blindest optimist that the Prussian State needed reformation from basement to rafter. It is all very well to say with von Meier that the catastrophe indicated nothing deeper than a diplomatic and military blunder.[1] That was not the view held by the most enlightened Prussian contemporaries of the event. They asked themselves, not unnaturally, the question why the verdict of Rossbach had been reversed, why the Prussian army long vaunted as the finest in the world had been cut into ribbons by the Frenchmen, and what was the secret of that sudden and wonderful military supremacy of the French nation which had placed central Europe under Napoleon's heel. A distinguished and thoughtful officer in the Prussian service put his finger upon the real point.

' One cause ', wrote Gneisenau in July 1807, ' has contributed to raise France to this degree of power.

' The Revolution has aroused all the social forces and secured to each an appropriate circle of action. What a treasure of latent unutilized force lies in the bosom of nations ! In the soul of thousands and thousands of men there dwells a genius, the spring of which is depressed and stopped by external circumstances. The Revolution has put into action the entire national force of the French people, and if the European states wish to restore the old relations of nations and the old balance of power, they must draw from the same sources. If they appropriate the results of the Revolution, they will have the double advantage of opposing their national force in all its

[1] *Französische Einflüsse auf die Staats- und Rechtsentwicklung Preussens im xix. Jahrhundert.*

power to the enemy and of avoiding the perils of an internal revolution.'

It is hardly likely that the perception of this important truth was confined to Gneisenau. We may feel pretty certain that his views were shared by more than one member of the intelligent and industrious civil service of Prussia.

It may, however, be at once conceded that the initiator of the Prussian reformation was both by temperament and conviction violently opposed to all the distinctive principles of the French Revolution. Baron von Stein was German to the backbone. The inventions of other countries did not appeal to him ; the tides of intellectual fashion washed round him without leaving a dent upon the solid granite of his strong, pious, and conservative nature. Philosophy was quite alien to the temper of his mind, literature hardly less congenial, but he found in historical study the nutriment which his nature required. He had read Adam Smith but continued to support frontier tariffs and usury laws, and if he had dived into history he none the less remained an anti-Semite. Nobody was less of a doctrinaire than this strong rugged Franconian noble, whose achievement is regarded by patriotic Prussians with feelings analogous to those evoked among us by the combined names of William Pitt and Sir Robert Peel. And nobody was less willing to take a lesson from France. Stein hated the French and all their ways, from the bottom of his heart.

In a history of the revolutionary period written for the instruction of his daughter, he argues that the French Revolution can find no apology in social grievances and no explanation save in the spirit of the times—an ugly compound of wickedness and folly. He will not admit that any part of the revolutionary cause was grounded on social justice or substantial reason. He condemns the doubling of the Third Estate, applauds the ancient distribution of the States General into three orders, and consequently denounces the establishment of a legislature founded upon the principle of social equality. The House of Bourbon claims throughout his loyal allegiance. He deplored its fall in 1792, he advocated with all the energy of his passionate nature its restoration in 1814, and when sixteen years later the folly of Charles X brought about the exile of the elder line, Stein lamented their fate as a blow at once tragic and undeserved.

Such was the man whose name is specially associated with the destruction of the caste system in Prussia : and arguing from what is otherwise known of his character and temperament, historians have urged that all Stein's remedial measures must have been woven of good Prussian homespun. The truth is that the most important reform of his ministry, the emancipating edict of October 9, 1807, which gave the villein liberty to quit his holding, introduced free trade in land, and abolished the mediaeval system of caste, was not in any special sense his work. The business was prepared and the measure was already drafted before Stein came into office, and received his signature five days later. Stein has the credit of deciding that the edict should extend to the whole kingdom, a point upon which the commission had been unable to reach a unanimous conclusion ; and to his power of action we must attribute its prompt passage into law ; but for the substance of the edict we must look elsewhere, partly to the general spirit of the age and partly to the special pressure brought upon Prussia by recent developments of French policy.

It is natural that Prussian historians should be anxious to deny that the vitality of their country is in any way proportioned to the degree to which she adopted the principles of her enemy ; but nobody surveying the general course of the great reforms undertaken by Stein and Hardenberg in Prussia can fail to see that in effect, if not in intention, they represent a remarkable resemblance to the changes which were wrought in France by the French Revolution. The French abolished serfdom and struck at the territorial privileges of the nobility, so did the Prussians. The French proclaimed the principle of industrial freedom, and the Prussians, after some partial and temporizing measures, destroyed the monopoly of their industrial guilds. The French submitted the nobles to their proper share of fiscal burdens ; the Prussians swept away privileged exemptions from the land-tax. In both countries the military system was transformed and on identical lines ; the nation became the army.

In both countries the civil administration was consciously fortified by centralizing measures and by a clearer partition of departmental functions. In both countries there was a perception of the necessity of separating judicial from administrative activity.

It would be a poor compliment to Stein and his coadjutors to suppose that they deliberately closed their eyes to the grand lesson of the French Revolution, that they failed to see the truth which the eagles of Napoleon had carried far and wide through Europe, that a polity framed on principles of social equality and enlisting the co-operation of a whole people is necessarily stronger than one which acts upon a caste-ridden and divided population by the dreary method of mechanical pressure. In saying this, however, we do not mean to imply that the first Prussian reformers thought only of France, or were so shallow as to believe that a wholesale importation of French models would save the State. English self-government numbered its admirers in Berlin, and the economic teaching of Adam Smith had found in Theodor von Schön at least one devoted disciple in the committee which drafted the emancipating edict. It is never the part of wisdom to exclude a ray of light, and least of all in an hour of black calamity do prudent men reject wholesome remedies because they have proved their worth in other places.

We may take it then that the Napoleonic conquest not only stimulated a root and branch reform of the Prussian state, but that it contributed to drive home to intelligent Prussian minds, as nothing short of so complete a disaster could, the strength which France had obtained by her adoption of certain social and political principles, and the weakness under which Prussia suffered from the fact that she had not yet incorporated those principles into her polity. And there was a further consequence of a more direct, palpable, and pressing character. Under the territorial arrangements sanctioned at Tilsit, Prussia was stripped both of her Polish and of her Westphalian provinces. The Polish provinces were handed over to the King of Saxony and formed into the Grand Duchy of Warsaw, while at the same time the western possessions of Prussia were thrown into the new Westphalian kingdom governed by Napoleon's youngest brother Jerome ; and as each of these new states was to be ruled upon French principles, an active laboratory of revolutionary legislation was established on either flank of the diminished Prussian monarchy. Now both the Polish and Westphalian constitutions decreed in clear and peremptory terms the abolition of serfage and noble privilege. The Constitution of the Grand Duchy of Warsaw appeared in the *Moniteur* on August 2, the Westphalian Constitution on November 15, Stein's emancipating edict between the two, on October 9. Is it likely that Stein's action, inconsistent as we know it to be with the colour and bent of his temperament, was quite independent of these transactions? There is conclusive proof to the contrary. The drafting committee in Berlin expressly refers to the Warsaw precedent as one of the grounds of their recommendation ; and a Cabinet order of September 3, 1807, states that the abolition of serfdom had become a pressing necessity through the step which had been taken by a neighbouring Government. Indeed, no fine gift of discernment was necessary to perceive that if freedom were proclaimed in the Polish provinces, the Prussian peasant would not long be chained to his ragged and miserable life of servile drudgery. There would be an exodus of the rural population from the land of crushing tributes and forced road-making and compulsory menial service to the free country across the border where there was equality for all. With every absconding Prussian serf the rank and file of the Prussian army would be diminished by one and the prospects of a military recovery proportionately lowered.[1]

Here, then, we find one cogent argument for hurrying on the emancipation of the Prussian peasantry. If the thing were not done quickly, the yokels, who bear the brunt of the Prussian wars, would stream away into Poland, and swell the forces of the arch-enemy. But apart from the contagion of the new revolutionary state there were pressing reasons for a revolution.

---

[1] Meier, *Französische Einflüsse auf die Staats- und Rechtsentwicklung Preussens im xix. Jahrhundert*, ii. 289; Knapp, *Die Bauern-Befreiung . . . in den älteren Theilen Preussens*, ii. 152, 155, 161.

in the land-system of Prussia. The country had been bled white by Napoleon and was in an unexampled state of destitution. The army, which provided a profession for the nobility, had been temporarily ruined, and the ports being blocked against oversea trade, there was a shrinkage in the profits and consequently in the purchasing power of the mercantile class, the effects of which were soon felt in every nook and cranny of the economic structure. In this state of economic dissolution the maintenance of caste would have been a disaster. Was a ruined nobleman to be still debarred from entering a house of business or from selling a portion of his noble land to a tradesman or a peasant? It was to the interest of all classes that land should be bought and sold in an open market, and that every citizen of the State should be at liberty to choose his calling in accordance with his natural affinity. The famous ordinance of October 9, 1807, provided all this. It abolished serfdom, inasmuch as it permitted the peasant proprietor freely to quit his tenement and released him and his children from the obligation of forced menial service. It introduced free trade in land. It allowed nobles and peasants to embark in trade and commerce, and conversely permitted traders to acquire the lands which had formerly been reserved for the nobility or their serfs. These were striking changes of principle, though it is likely enough that the immediate economic effects were slight. Under Stein's ordinance the lord still retained his jurisdiction intact, and the peasant, though nominally free, still bore his crushing load of services, and since the one was too dejected to throw up his holding, the other too poor to buy him out, a traveller journeying through the country a few months after 'the Magna Carta of Prussian liberty' would have found little or nothing in the outward surface of affairs to remind him that a great change had been accomplished in the legal and economic status of the country folk—no migration and interfusion, no crowded auctions of land and stock, nor any of that active bustle and movement which accompanies the opening of fresh markets and the promise of fresh careers.

Shrewd conservative critics read in the new free trade the inevitable doom of the old rural order. Manorial jurisdiction would go, church patronage would go, feudal rights of police and general administration would go, now that it was open to every upstart with a long purse to purchase the land in respect of which these rights and powers had been exercised. Marwitz, the clarion of the old Tories, protested that Stein was a revolutionary, pitting indigence against property, industry against agriculture, the present against the past, and the individual against the family; and there is a kernel of truth in the humorous exaggeration. 'Better three Auerstädts than this edict' was a sentence overheard in the Berlin casino. A revolution was sheathed in an agrarian settlement which seemed at first to effect no change, and was issued under the signature of a conservative statesman.

In the second great measure which characterizes his ministry Stein has been held up to admiration as a wise and courageous architect of popular liberty. Sir John Seeley, following Maurer, reminds us that the municipal ordinance of 1808, so far from being a copy from French models, was founded upon opposite and independent principles. The French drew no distinction between town and country, giving to urban and rural communes the same non-popular framework of government, a nominated mayor for executive functions and a nominated council with limited powers of advice. Such was the type of local government introduced into the Grand Duchy of Berg and the kingdom of Westphalia and faithfully copied in many other client states of the Rhenish Confederation. Now Stein's municipal ordinance has nothing whatever to do with the country districts. It prescribes for the Prussian towns and for these alone, and it further differs from the French plan in providing the towns with a really liberal and democratic scheme of self-government. Nevertheless even here, where contrariety is patent, it would be unwise to disparage the influence of French example. The idea of superseding, by a uniform and simple plan of administration, that curious miscellany of vested interests which passed for the government of a mediaeval town sprang up first in France, and was spread by the Napoleonic conquests through Germany. And while the government of every town in the French occupation was being transformed upon a frame designed to increase the control of the French Empire in Germany, the Prussians were clearly prudent to parry the blow with a scheme of urban reform no less radical and effective. That the Prussian plan differed from the French is due to the fact that, whereas France had to reckon with local disunion and hostility, the problem for Prussia was to coerce into a spirit of active co-operation a fund of unanimous but slothful support. That here again the ultimate impetus came from Napoleon, is suggested by the fact that three not unimportant clauses in Stein's famous measures are almost verbally copied from the French.

Long before his programme of reform had been exhausted, Stein was driven from office by the fiat of Napoleon. There ensued upon his fall a brief period of ministerial paralysis followed by one of the most fruitful administrations of modern history. It is somewhat the fashion to disparage Baron von Hardenberg, who from July 4, 1810, till his death at the close of 1822 was virtually Prime Minister of Prussia. In greatness of heart, in purity of morals, in depth and dignity of character, in intensity of political conviction, in all the gifts which inflame the imagination or exalt the passions of men, Hardenberg stands far below Stein. He was no hero, martyr, or prophet. He was merely an alert, intelligent, charming man of the world, unencumbered by a heritage of romantic instinct or class prejudice, hospitable to new ideas and soaked through and through with the spirit of political compliance. In sweetness of temper, in refreshing immunity from spite and mistrust, as well as in his blithe untroubled gaiety, he reminds us of Lord Melbourne. A finished aristocrat of the old school and yet always on the side of intelligent solutions, he attended only to the sunny and wholesome parts of his associates, and was inclined to think the better, not the worse, of an idea if it bore the familiar hall-mark of the French genius. Of his own frailties he was duly conscious and would at times affect to regret them. Really he regarded his lapses from virtue as inseparable from those winning ways which made him the idol of women and an incomparable manager of men. That he was a complete and rounded statesman would not be claimed for him even by his most sincere admirers, for his gifts lay chiefly in diplomacy, and he had neither the patience, the knowledge, nor the industry which are essential to great administration. He was the parent of some still-born measures, but rebuffs neither disturbed his judgement nor lowered his self-esteem. He went on none the less in his quick-witted, indolent, courageous way, charming the Court with his nice blue eyes and pleasant smile and braving the wrath of the bitter and stupid Junkers, until his purpose was substantially accomplished. He was called Jacobin and leveller. In truth he was the most distinguished Prussian disciple of the Napoleonic state, as Bismarck recognized in 1851, when he wrote to General von Gerlach that the Hardenberg legislation was all taken from the Westphalian *Moniteur*.

The achievement of Hardenberg consists of four groups of legislation, each more or less directly inspired by precedents set in the French Empire. First, there was a complete recasting of Prussian finance, prompted by the instant necessity for finding fresh sources of supply, and based upon the true principle that financial elasticity implies industrial freedom and fiscal equality. Secondly, there was the establishment of that free peasant proprietary which is still a valued feature of the economy of Prussia. Thirdly came the edict emancipating the Jews, and fourthly a very radical reconstruction of the organs of central and local government upon a bureaucratic plan analogous to the French.

The valuable part of the new finance consisted less in the taxes themselves, which were borrowed from the kingdom of Westphalia (where the portfolio of finance was for some time in the hands of Count von Bülow, the Prussian Chancellor's nephew), as in the fact that they were levied upon a uniform and equal plan without respect to provincial privilege or social caste. It is true that Hardenberg was compelled to withdraw that portion of his scheme which promised a complete system of land-valuation and the disappearance of exemptions from and abatements of the land-tax. So far the aristocracy scored a triumph. On the other hand, he succeeded in introducing a general scheme of indirect taxation, a general tax upon industry, and finally a steeply progressive income-tax. The effect of a new tax is never limited to the resources which it brings to the Treasury ; and over and over again in European history far-reaching political and economic consequences are found to flow from a sudden and steep increase in financial burdens. So it was with Prussia in the Napoleonic age. The competition with France raised the scale of public expenditure all over Europe. The old domestic notion of state-finance, that the King could and should live of his own, finally disappeared, and the notion of elastic taxation based upon popular consent began to take its place. In a memorandum drafted at Riga immediately after the shock of Jena, Hardenberg pronounced that 'democratic institutions in a monarchical government seemed to be the formula for the future', and upon his assumption of office in 1810 he promised to give to Prussia a central representative assembly. Riper experience showed him that in such a body he would find nothing but aristocratic pride and the jealous clash of provincial interests, and the Liberal in him rapidly gave way to the Napoleonic bureaucrat. Still it was under his administration that for the first time in Prussian history a body of representatives from the whole monarchy was summoned to give advice to the King's ministers. The assemblies of February 23, 1811, and April 10, 1812, were not parliaments elected on a popular suffrage, but small nominated bodies representing the four classes in the kingdom, officials, nobles, citizens, and peasantry. The experiment was widely denounced by the feudal caste, who considered that a monarch who summoned peasants to his council might as well be capering round a tree of liberty with a red cap upon his head : nor did it procure for Hardenberg the support which he expected. Still, precedents once created are never forgotten ; and it was an important landmark in Prussian history when for the first time a minister sought to secure for large schemes of social and financial reform some general expression of national assent.

The original idea at the basis of Hardenberg's agrarian reform was that every tenant, whatever the size and quality of his tenure, should become the absolute owner of his holding ;

and that the tenant's labour-services and dues should be written off against the charges which the lord was compelled to sustain in respect of restoration and repairs. Such a scheme, framed for the benefit of 350,000 peasant families, was far too radical for the Prussian nobility, and the strongest class in a feudal state succeeded in abridging its munificence in three important particulars. The landowners of Prussia claimed and secured a third of the peasants' holding as part payment for the loss of corvées and services, acquired the right to buy up peasant holdings, and succeeded in limiting the operation of the reform to the wealthier peasant proprietors. Even in this mutilated form the measure of September 1811, if executed with force and fidelity, would have liberated about a million acres and seventy² thousand proprietors; but the stubborn soil of Prussia opposed innumerable obstacles to the ploughshare of reform; the harvest ripened slowly; and by the end of 1820 the edict of September had only created 18,236 peasant proprietors.

The same liberal impulse which aimed at the conversion of serfs into freemen was employed in the manufacture of citizens out of Jews. Here, too, the example of the Westphalian kingdom, where legislation was exceptionally generous to the Hebrew community, weighed with the Prussian Chancellor. The decree of March 3, 1812, is the charter of Jewish emancipation in Prussia, providing as it does that Jews settled in the old provinces should be admitted to civic rights if they would take family names, sign in the German or Latin script, and use German or some other living language of the West in their commercial transactions. By this one act Hardenberg accomplished more for the cause of religious toleration than Frederick the Great for all his boasted enlightenment had been able to achieve; but the pictures of Napoleon which used to hang in the drawing-rooms of Jewish houses in Berlin testify to the general belief that the original power working for Jewish liberty in Europe was not so much the Prussian Chancellor as the Emperor of the French.

It is curious to observe how under the shock of the Napoleonic wars a double tendency was set up in Prussia, partly in the direction of evoking spontaneous national effort and partly in the direction of tightening the reins of national discipline. Stein's municipal reform was an example of the first tendency; so too was his contemplated reform of provincial government in something of the English fashion, with Justices of the Peace and Quarter Sessions; but Hardenberg, although far more radical than Stein in his social and industrial legislation—indeed for the reason that he was more radical and probably also more impatient—was all for centralization and bureaucracy. If he could have had his way he would have made an end of the old historical provinces of the Prussian kingdom, with their separate charters and rights and customs, and have substituted for them a set of entirely artificial and convenient administrative districts. As it was he brought forward a scheme upon the French model designed to transfer the judicial and police powers hitherto employed by the nobility to a State official, the *Kreisdirector* (director of a district), served by a *gendarmerie* and assisted by a small nominated council. So bold an invasion of feudal privilege was bound to fail in a country where the city population was hardly less conservative than the nobles themselves. Protestations rained in from every quarter, from patriots who descried the French prefect in the Prussian *Kreisdirector*, from publicists who believed in local freedom, and from nobles who practised local tyranny. If a handful of peasant representatives in the so-called national assembly of 1812 spoke up for the edict, that was about the full measure of its acceptance. The pliant chancellor shrugged his shoulders and beat a retreat. Even when it flew the flag of peasant emancipation his light bark had never run into such ugly weather.

In his classical treatise on the Art of War, Clausewitz makes the just observation that the prodigious effects of the French Revolution abroad were brought about not so much by changes in the military art as by transformations in statecraft and civil administration. It is to the eternal honour of the Prussian reformers that they grasped this important truth from the very beginning. They saw that the revolution militant could only be effectually combated by a radical and comprehensive reform of Prussian society and Prussian government. They did not confine their criticism to questions of military policy and organization. They allowed their minds to travel over the whole surface of public affairs from the ordering of armies and the assessment of taxes to the traditional style of official documents. From the first they grasped the great truth that the secret of military power is political and social unity, that a national aim implies not a state but a nation. They accomplished only part of that wide programme of innovation which Hardenberg had sketched out at Riga in September 1807. They began, but were unable to complete, the destruction of the territorial power of the nobility. They were forced to abandon as hopeless a scheme designed to make the civil service of Prussia as powerful as the bureaucracy of France. Complete and scientific unification on the French plan, even had it been desirable, could never have been carried out in face of the tenacious provincial and aristocratic opposition. Nevertheless in the sphere of public administration the long rule of Hardenberg left a durable mark on Prussian history, for just as the office of Prime Minister in England may be said to have grown up during the twenty years of Walpole's power, so Hardenberg created the office of State Chancellor in Prussia. In 1807 he had urged that a Prime Minister or State Chancellor was a necessity, and it was vouchsafed to him, through his twelve years of Dictatorship, to make title and office familiar and acceptable. To him, too, Prussia owes the constitution of that Council of State, with its three categories of members, princes of the blood, ministers of the Crown, and members specially summoned by the King, which persisted until the fall of the Hohenzollern dynasty. Thus even though he was unable to introduce prefects and departments and the French system of bureaucratic centralization, Hardenberg left Prussia less obstinately various and provincial, and more easily reducible to the direction of a central mind than she had been in the years of irresolution, chaos, and incompetence which preceded the salutary shock of Jena.

In the great fields of scientific knowledge and material

power the Napoleonic conquest, acting on minds rendered plastic by defeat, produced two lasting and fruitful results, the University of Berlin and 'the Prussian army, the first the creation of William von Humboldt, the second the work of a man as academic as Stonewall Jackson himself, General Scharnhorst, the modest and learned Hanoverian artillerist. Universities have played a large part in German life, and during the whole course of the nineteenth century have exercised a special influence over political thought and action in Germany. The University of Berlin, which owes its foundation to the incorporation of Halle, formerly the academic seminary for the Prussian civil service in the upstart kingdom of Westphalia, has now conquered for itself an unchallenged supremacy among the homes of German learning and has helped to obliterate the older reputation of Prussia as a rough, ignorant, and unlettered country. It has also performed something of the service which Napoleon expected of the University of France. Created and fostered by the Government, this pliant and powerful corporation has readily placed its vast sources of moral influence and intellectual strength at the disposal of the State, preaching the gospel of Prussian patriotism, resisting the insidious advance of disintegrating theory, and framing elaborate and learned apologies for violations of public law and economic fairness. It has defended the seizure of Silesia, the partitions of Poland, the treaty of Basle, the annexation of the Danish duchies, and the violation of Belgian neutrality. It has invented the doctrine of 'a Prussian mission', discoursed eloquently and learnedly on the untenable thesis that Prussia had always maintained, as Austria has continually abandoned, the true interests of Germany, and in a word has given far more support to the Hohenzollern policy than the University of France ever brought to the House of Napoleon. As it has never been degraded by the servility of a Fontanes, so it has never gained lustre from the brilliant defiance of a Renan or a Michelet.

Universities had long been an honourable and prominent feature in German life, and there was nothing either in the constitution or in the early character of the University of Berlin which marked it as distinct from, or in any way superior to, such older seats of learning as Göttingen or Heidelberg. But the Prussian army of 1814 was a new apparition in German history. It was the nation in arms. Conscription there had been in the days of Frederick the Great, but so lamed by the system of privileged exemption that the total weight of military service fell upon the servile peasantry. Armies so levied might by a rare effort of genius be kindled to a certain professional zeal, but could never, even under the most splendid leadership, rise to the height of patriotic devotion. The new conscription admitted of no privileges, no exemptions, no degrading punishments. It viewed service in the ranks not as a special trade connoting a low and degraded social position, but as a common and honourable duty to the State, a school of patriotic virtue. No purely administrative or legal reform has imprinted so deep an impression upon the life of Prussia as this compulsion placed upon the whole population to undergo a training in arms. It has unified Prussia more speedily and effectively than any arrangement of prefects and departments could have done, and given a military direction to the thoughts, feelings, and aspirations of a vigorous people. The reforms of Scharnhorst conferred some immediate benefits upon the Prussian state. They helped to procure the downfall of Napoleon and the liberation of the Prussian territory from an intolerable yoke. They restored to its ancient self-respect a proud and strenuous nation. They made Prussia once more the leading figure in Germany, and the army so created in the stress of a great national calamity has been ever since the principal bulwark of Prussian strength. For good or evil the Prussian army helped to maintain through all the enthusiastic surges of liberal and democratic opinion which agitated central Europe in the nineteenth century the strict autocracy of the Hohenzollern crown and, through its tendency to promote and sustain a military temper in the country, preserved for the territorial class a greater degree of authority than the landlord has enjoyed in any other country of equal intelligence. Whether this has been an advantage or the reverse to the world has been declared by the outbreak and the issue of a war more calamitous than any recorded in the history of man upon this planet.

Thoughts on the Influence of Napoleon

IT will probably be admitted, even by the most strenuous opponent of French imperialism, that with two exceptions Napoleon has exercised a greater influence upon the political and social state of Europe than any other single man. Nothing in the achievements of the Consulate and the Empire was fraught with such tremendous consequence for the future of European civilization as the conquest of Gaul by Julius Caesar or the assumption of the imperial crown by Charlemagne; but then we must remember that Caesar and Charlemagne were operating upon political conditions which were still comparatively simple and susceptible of receiving a deep and durable impress from a powerful will, while Napoleon, living many centuries afterwards, suffered the penalty of time. He was brought up against complex masses of tradition, political, social; and ecclesiastical, which had been hardened by ages of settled European life and were protected by the great vested interests of an old community. He affronted many things which Europeans were wont to consider respectable and even holy, monarchical sentiment, aristocratic caste, the Catholic Church, the sentiment of nationality. Much of his work was immediately undone upon his fall. All of it was compressed within a period of twenty years. But when all deductions have been made for ill-calculated plans, transitional expedients, and policies triumphantly cancelled by his opponents, there remains a residuum of durable political influences so great as immeasurably to overshadow any which can be ascribed to any other modern ruler of a European state.

In saying this we do not mean to imply that there have not been minds in Europe of finer, higher, and more original quality. The most durable and successful features of Napoleon's statesmanship are not those parts which one might be tempted to call extravagantly Napoleonic, but those which seem to satisfy deep-seated needs and to crown long processes of historical development. Again, there have been many influences in Europe, on the religious and moral side, which have made more difference to the lives of ordinary men and women than the career of Napoleon. What creative ideas can we ascribe to him comparable to those which were put into circulation by Aquinas, Calvin, or Rousseau, or even by his own contemporaries Goethe and De Maistre? The *Idées Napoléoniennes*, even if we accept them at the nephew's valuation, are still borrowed ideas, long familiar in Europe, some of them first practised in the Revolution, others derived from the traditions of the *Ancien Régime*. The system of Napoleon did not start full-fledged from his brain, and was indeed not so much a system as a series of brilliant improvisations made in reponse to the stress of fortune. With that wonderful tact for circumstance which Madame de Staël notices as his principal characteristic, he adapted the ideas of his age to the needs of the situation.

This really comes to saying that Napoleon was a statesman. It is not the business of a statesman to be original. It is his business to measure the human forces about him, to take stock of the conflicting traditions, the complex interests, the hidden currents and open water-ways of thought and feeling, and so to contrive his political and constitutional formulae as to rally for their support the best and highest energies of his people. Exactly in proportion as he is successful in doing this, his work will stand the test and strain of time.

The great transfiguring ideas in politics, even where they originate with men of action, can seldom be safely used until they have survived some controversy and become the familiar property of political thought. It is therefore no more a condemnation of Napoleon's genius to observe that he merely worked with the ideas of the French Revolution than to say that he breathed the air and trod the earth. The supreme proof of his genius lies, on the contrary, in the fact that he harnessed the wild living spirit of the Revolution to his own career.

These observations will prepare us to consider the general question of Napoleon's legacy to Europe. We should naturally expect to find that those parts of his work would be most permanent which are founded upon common sense, and might therefore have occurred to any man of ordinary high abilities on a survey of the political situation, and that those parts are least permanent which could only have come from Napoleon and are stamped by the peculiar idiosyncrasy of his temperament. This is in the main true. The civil work of the Consulate, the Codes, the Concordat, the Prefects, the Legion of Honour, together with the Imperial University and the Lycées —this is the work for which the previous history of France was fitting prolusion, so that being adjusted to the needs of the country it was able to endure through a century of factious strife and revolutionary upheaval. The Grand Empire on the other hand perished, for it belonged to the peculiar temperament of Napoleon to imagine a monster which almost everything in its previous history had prepared Europe to reject.

The true greatness of Napoleon as a civil ruler lies in the fact, firstly that he saved for France the most valuable conquests of the French Revolution, social equality and industrial freedom, secondly that he brought to a conclusion the difficult operation of securing for the remodelled state the sanction and support of the Church, and thirdly that he gave to France a code of laws and a system of administration which remain substantially unchanged to-day. He saved equality which was a fierce national passion, and sacrificed liberty which had become a disease. The Code Napoléon, which he regarded as his main title to glory, is, so to speak, the last testament of the French Revolution. In a small portable volume which may be read in a railway carriage or by the fireside you may find the image of a society where all creeds are tolerated and all men are equal before the law, where private property is respected and the rules of inheritance are based on the principle of equality, where the wife is subject to the husband, and the children to the parents, where the power of the churches is sharply curtailed by civil marriage and divorce, and where no corporations, religious, legal, or industrial, are suffered to abridge the liberty of the individual or to intercept the power of the State. Such a polity, democratic, centralized, and saturated with the lay spirit, was the inevitable result of the French Revolution.

Modern France is still very much as the Consulate left it.

Parliamentary government has taken root, the Concordat has been denounced after an uneasy life of a hundred years, and some measure of decentralization has been effectually introduced into local government and the fabric of the University. The ideal of the lay state has become more widely held with the lapse of time, and is embodied in the scheme of compulsory secular education which the Third Republic owes to the oratory of Gambetta and the strenuous powers of Ferry. These changes, however, important though they be, have neither transformed the political spirit of France nor swept away the main blocks of Napoleonic granite, the Prefects, the Codes, the Legion of Honour, the *Lycée*. The most serious innovation is the Parliamentary system, introduced during the Hundred Days in deference to the public opinion of Paris and without faith in its merits by Napoleon himself, and accepted as the unpleasant necessity of vulgar times by the restored Bourbons. But though we cannot easily overrate the negative influence of French parliamentary life as a guarantee against madcap policies and domestic oppression, we may be tempted with British examples before us to form too high a notion of its action upon French society and upon the normal work of government. Ministers may rise and fall, but clerks sit steadily scribbling on their office stools. Laws may be issued by the Chambers, but it is customary to draft them in the most general terms so that the details are filled in by the administration. However mutable may be the balances of parliamentary power, the tradition of a cogent civil service, an inquisitorial police, and a special body of administrative law has been handed down from the days of Napoleon.

One change, not of institutions but of political spirit, is certainly notable. France is no longer the firebrand of Europe. For fifty good years after the battle of Waterloo she continued to be tormented by the shade of Napoleon summoning her to redeem the frontier of the Rhine and to reverse the work of the Congress of Vienna. It may be open to question how far this survival of the Bonapartist spirit was a wholesome element in European political life, how far a virulent poison. A spirit of empty, vainglorious, military imperialism, chafing under the lassitude of enforced peace and the ignominy of frontiers restricted in the general interests of Europe, does not command much natural sympathy. But it was part of the singular history of the Napoleonic memory that it became associated with liberal ideas in France and with national hopes in Italy and Poland. When Europe was given over to the autocrats, the faults of Napoleon were forgotten and his merits called to mind. Over and against the petty conventions of court and caste he stood out as the supreme type of unaided human energy mounting to the highest pinacle of fortune, and moulding the destiny of the world. It was forgotten that he had tried to manufacture a new nobility, that he had introduced privileged entails, that he had married an Austrian Archduchess, and copied the stiff ceremonials of Spain in Italy and of the *Ancien Régime* in France. In the sentiment of the common people he remained the Little Corporal sprung from nowhere, of the same humble clay as themselves, an everlasting proof that for the highest tasks of war and government it is not blue blood that is wanted, but the brain, heart, and nerve of the heroic man. So conceived the Napoleonic memory was at once a valuable safeguard against a possible reaction to the *Ancien Régime* and an important auxiliary to liberal ideas. The mischief was that this democratic and wholesome sentiment did not exhaust the content of the Imperial tradition, but was allied in it with the evil precedents of domestic tyranny and military expansion. The Second Empire was a testimony both to the living power of Napoleon's name and to the vitality of the ideas which were assumed to be associated with his system': and perhaps it is true to say that no catastrophe less complete than the Prussian War of 1870 would have been availing to exorcise the passion and lust of conquest which, having been aroused by the triumphs of the Revolution and the Empire, could not at once, as Alfred de Vigny shows us, be sent to sleep, but continued for half a century to vex and inflame the political conscience of France.

Outside the frontiers of France the system of Napoleon seemed to be most firmly secured in the Piedmontese, Rhenish, and Belgian departments of the Grand Empire. Of these territories, the first became, after the cataclysm, the scene of a reaction so stupid and violent that all the good results of the French period were swept away, so that the work of liberalization had to be done over again almost from the beginning by D'Azeglio, Siccardi, and Cavour. In the Rhenish departments the seeds sown by the French Revolution were not so easily uprooted, and a numerous and prosperous peasant proprietary continued to testify to the enduring benefits conferred by twenty years of government under the French law. The third case is even more important.

Among the conquests of the French Revolution there was one so well grounded upon conditions of natural affinity and convenience as to hold out a reasonable expectation of permanence. The annexation of Belgium had been the earliest and most precious triumph of revolutionary arms, and if England could only have been deleted from the map of Europe no acquisition could have been more easily made secure. The Flemings, it is true, are of Teutonic lineage and speech, but the peasantry and factory hands of the Walloon provinces speak a Romance dialect, while for many generations every educated Belgian had been accustomed to use French as a medium of education, culture, and social intercourse. A people without a national history, in one century the subjects of a Spaniard in Madrid, and in the next offering a scarcely less docile submission to an Austrian in Vienna, might naturally be expected, if not to welcome, at least to accept with complaisance a union with a neighbour, so wealthy, so powerful, and connected by so many ties of common civilization with themselves. France indeed had little to give the Belgians in the way of political liberty which they did not already enjoy under chartered rights ; but for many years before 1789 a party in Belgium had been driving hard for an extreme democratic revolution, and a course of wise government might have converted the creed of a Vonckist or Gallophil minority into the common possession of the Belgian people.

Never was a great political opportunity so shamelessly squandered. The rule of the French Republic in Belgium opened with an orgy of plunder and tyranny and closed with a persecution of the priesthood and a revolt of the peasantry. Compared with these seven miserable and distracted years the Consulate of Napoleon shone out as an epoch of signal content and prosperity. The breach with the Church was healed by the Concordat, and Belgium at last began to enjoy some of the fruits of its incorporation in a well-governed, powerful, and enterprising state. But as the continental war developed, the country began to experience the methods of a new barbarism comparable to the horrors which it had suffered at the hands of the revolutionary commissioners. The hunt for conscripts, pursued with activity all over Napoleon's dominions, was marked with peculiar activity and accompanied by exceptional rigours in a country unused to the tradition of arms and consequently swarming with deserters and refractories. At the same time the Emperor's quarrel with the Pope, reopening as it did the deep wound which had been temporarily closed by the Concordat, led to a recrudescence of bitter feeling among the ultramontane clergy of Belgium. Sixty of the professors and pupils of the Seminary of Ghent were committed to prison for refusing to submit to a schismatic bishop; of these sixty, forty-eight died in confinement. Meanwhile trade was perishing under the restrictions of the continental blockade and the ceaseless requirements of the tax-collector. The most stable houses were forced into liquidations: and Antwerp, which in the imperial scheme was designed to be the great arsenal of the north, witnessed a shrinkage in its population variously estimated at twenty or twenty-five per cent.

Despite these oppressions and calamities it is probable that many Belgians would, upon the fall of Napoleon, have welcomed the rule of Louis XVIII as preferable to the government of Holland which was ultimately imposed upon them by the diplomacy of the Powers. Language, law, religion, trade advantages, all the principal constituents of Belgian civilization drew them towards France. Indeed, after the storm and stress of a hundred years the inscription of the Revolution and the Empire is still clearly legible on the face of Belgian society and government.

The two outstanding facts in the modern economic condition of Belgium are firstly a numerous peasant proprietary and secondly a great mass of low-paid and ill-organized labour in the towns. For each of these circumstances an explanation may probably be found in the history of those twenty years during which Belgium was an integral part of France.

Mr. Seebohm Rowntree, who has made a scientific inquiry into the economic conditions of the country,[1] reports that the establishment of the Belgian peasant proprietary is due primarily to the extensive sales of the State Forests and of the common lands which were carried out between 1815 and 1850, but in a secondary degree to the laws of succession which prevail in Belgium. Those laws date from the French Revolution and were codified by Napoleon, and with some emendations and additions govern the Belgian kingdom to-day. The consequences are clearly inscribed in the agrarian map of the country. For instance, one of the special features brought out by Mr. Rowntree's inquiry is the large proportion of land, approximately one-tenth of the whole country, held jointly by two or more owners, a feature which is due to the laws of succession which 'oblige a landowner to divide his property equally, with the exception of one share which, though legally at his disposal, in practice is almost invariably divided with the rest'. The effect of these laws of succession, combined with economic causes, is that 47 per cent. of the soil is owned by persons whose holdings do not exceed a hundred acres, that the average size of a farm is $14\frac{1}{2}$ acres in Belgium as against 60 in Great Britain, and that the agricultural population per square mile of the cultivated area is three times that of Great Britain. It is interesting that though a law was passed on May 16, 1900, to prevent excessive subdivision, there has never been any tendency to revert to primogeniture, entails, or family settlements. The Code Civil, which has received from the University of Louvain a long line of illustrious commentators, has been amended in certain particulars, but not in any point affecting the cardinal principle of equality.

The other noteworthy feature in the present economic

---

[1] B. Seebohm Rowntree, *Land and Labour Lessons from Belgium.* Macmillan & Co., 1910.

condition of Belgium may likewise receive a partial explanation from revolutionary theory and Napoleonic law. The French violently broke up the trade guilds and corporations which were the glory of Belgium, substituting for these close and privileged groups the reign of unfettered individual competition. To the Napoleonic Code a private corporation or association was a thing regarded as inconsistent alike with state-power and individual freedom ; and the jealousy of collective action thus exhibited in the legal system of the country has been one, though certainly not the sole and perhaps not the principal, cause of the tardy development of trade unions and of the very unsatisfactory condition of the Belgian industrial population.

It is usual to attach great importance to the encouragement which Napoleon gave to the idea of Polish nationality, and to find in this phase of imperial policy the secret not only of the close sympathy between France and Poland which subsisted until the fall of the Second Empire, but also of some influences working in the Polish revolutions of the nineteenth century. We have no wish to underrate the spell which Napoleon cast upon Poland, or the reality of the hopes excited by the creation of the short-lived Grand Duchy of Warsaw ; but the case must not be overstated. The alliance between France and Poland was a diplomatic tradition of the *Ancien Régime* and, had Napoleon never been born, a Frenchman would still have been more acceptable to a Pole than a Prussian, a Russian, or an Austrian. By force of circumstances revolutionary France, attacked by the autocratic powers of the East, was the natural ally of revolutionary Poland, and the Polish regiments in the French armies of the Directory were serving their own national cause in helping to procure the military and political abasement of Austria. Every blow struck for the French Revolution was a blow struck for Polish liberty. What Napoleon did then was not to create a new sentiment of friendship, but to give to this inherent connexion of interest a certain amount of additional and palpable support by the creation of the Grand Duchy of Warsaw, to indoctrinate the Poles with the notion of a civilized state by the abolition of serfdom, by the introduction of the Civil Code, and by the grant of a parliamentary constitution, and finally to commend to the supporters of his dynasty the cause of Poland as a debt of honour and an article of faith. More than a century has passed since the hopes of a free Polish state were shattered on the field of Leipzig ; and the Civil Code, which still forms the legal basis of what was known until 1918 as Russian Poland, is now almost the only memorial of the Napoleonic rule at Warsaw. Yet the scheme of the Grand Empire for a free Polish state to be created as a foil to Prussian aggression has recently been renewed, so persistent is the trend of French diplomacy, so indestructible the spirit of the Polish people.

With the southern Slavs the influence of the Emperor has been still more decisive. Napoleon was never in Croatia, but with the possible exception of Belgium there is no outlying part of the Grand Empire which has felt in a more effective and enduring way the power of his person and his policy. ' In Croatia ', writes Dr. Seton-Watson,[1] than whom there can be no higher authority, ' the real awakening of national sentiment dates from the Napoleonic era. Dalmatia, which on the fall of the Venetian Republic (1797) had for the first time become an Austrian possession, was ceded to the French after the defeat of Austerlitz ; and the genius of Napoleon revived the name, and with it perhaps something of the spirit, of ancient Illyria. The new state thus suddenly created comprised the provinces of Carinthia, Carniola, Görz, and Istria, the sea-coast of Croatia, Dalmatia with its islands, and from 1808 onwards the republic of Ragusa. In Napoleon's own words : ' Illyria is the guard set before the gates of Vienna.' Under the enlightened, if despotic, rule of Marshal Marmont the long stagnation of the Middle Ages was replaced by feverish activity in every branch of life. Administration and justice were reorganized, the Code Napoléon superseding the effete mediaeval codes ; schools, primary, secondary, commercial, and industrial, sprang up in every direction : the first Croat and Slovene newspapers appeared : the old guild-system was reformed and commercial restrictions removed ; peasant proprietary was introduced,

---

[1] *The Southern Slav Question,* p. 26.

reafforestation was begun, and the splendid roads were constructed which are still the admiration of every tourist. Official business was conducted in French and Croatian, with the addition of Italian along the coasts. A well-known story relates how the Emperor Francis, during his visit to Dalmatia in 1818, plied his suite with questions as to the origin of the various public works which struck his eye, and met with the invariable answer, 'The. French, your Majesty'. 'Wirklich schad, dass s' nit länger'bliebe 1 sein ' (It is a real pity that they didn't stop longer), exclaimed the astonished Emperor in his favourite Viennese dialect, and there the matter rested for eighty years !

The Empire then was most permanently effective where it co-operated with national sentiment or was brought into contact with rude peoples still in that tribal stage of civilization which made the barbaric world so pliant to the impress of Imperial Rome. One of the most curious revenges of history is the fact that the revolutionary movement in Russia took its origin from the victorious entrance of the Russian troops into Paris in 1814. Here in the capital of Napoleon these half-barbarian visitors from the far East of Europe beheld for the first time the spectacle of a progressive state, a well-appointed government, and a liberal civilization. The ferment did its work and the Decembrist revolution of 1825 was the result. From this curious military disturbance, which had for one of its incidental effects the development of the Siberian prison system, we may date that active and continuous working of Western political ideas in the Muscovite world which has emancipated the serfs, established county councils, and given to Russia the unreal phantom of a Parliamentary government.[1]

It is only natural to expect that the Napoleonic influence would be specially strong in the Latin countries. The union of Italy was the product of many forces, among which an Englishman is not likely to undervalue the influence of English liberal ideas upon the mind, the character, and the career of Cavour. Indeed the unity of Italy is the most

[1] It is hardly necessary to add that the prophet of the Bolshevik Revolution is neither Rousseau nor Napoleon, but Karl Marx.

signal triumph of English liberalism upon the continent of Europe, as the success of Bismarck has been its most important defeat. Yet as all histories of modern Russia should begin with Peter the Great, so the epic of the *Risorgimento* opens with Napoleon. He made the Revolution a vital thing in Italy, and without a revolutionary party Italian unity would never have been achieved. For a brief period all Italy was gathered under his sway, administered on French principles and ruled by French law. It was he who revived the military spirit of the Italian race, gave them a new hope, a new energy, a fresh standard of what a government might do and be. Many of his closest relations, including his mother and Lucien, the most talented of his brothers, made Italy their home after the catastrophe of the Empire and earned the admiration and respect of their neighbours. It became a tradition of the House of Bonaparte to be on the liberal side of Italian politics and to forward the political emancipation of Italy, an end believed to have been among the cherished projects of the great Emperor. Jules Favre, defending Orsini in 1858, argued that the Italian patriot had spent his life in efforts to achieve the grand purpose which had inspired Napoleon I, and which Napoleon III himself had pursued in his own generous and enthusiastic youth: and thenceforward the Emperor became like a man seeking to lay the unquiet ghost of an ancestor.

The new kingdom of Italy owes much of the spirit and form of its local administration to Napoleonic models. Italy has the commune, enjoying, like its French prototype, functions and powers unrelated to differences of size and importance. The syndic of the Italian commune corresponds to the French mayor, and was also until recent times the nominee of the national Government. Fifty-nine provinces, artificial and unhistorical as the French departments, are ruled by prefects, assisted by small provincial councils or juntas of six; and the prefect, who is appointed by the Government, is, as in France, both an administrative officer and an instrument for the execution of political pressure. This system, borrowed from the French in the first difficulties of national fusion, was intended to check the recrudescence of that provincial spirit which was properly regarded as the greatest obstacle to Italian unity. Perhaps it was necessary to have the prefect, but it was certainly a grave mistake to draw no administrative distinction between a great town like Milan and a small sub-alpine village, and to subject the proceedings of influential town councils to the control and sometimes to the caprice of a single official. The administrative condition of Italy is an exact image of that uneasy dualism which underlies the whole surface of Italian political life. On the one hand there are the communes, full of local patriotism, nourished by historic memories, instinct with vigour and activity, and endowed with spacious powers. On the other hand there is the prefect, a French import, representing the new monarchy which was helped into existence by French bayonets and driven to resort to French models for the necessary but alien system of a centralized government.

A very fair test may be proposed to determine whether or no a Roman Catholic state has come under the dominion of Napoleonic ideas. Does it or does it not admit the principle of Civil Marriage? If it does, then the civil power stands outside the churches as in the concordat. If it does not, then instead of the Church being within the State, the State is within the Church. Judged by this criterion, Spain, which only accepted Civil Marriage in 1877, cannot be ranked among the nations which inherited from Napoleon. And yet the Napoleonic invasion of Spain does in a very real sense mark an epoch in the history of the Iberian people. The Peninsular War created Spanish liberalism and was the means of disseminating, especially in the more forward maritime provinces, the doctrines of progress, equality, and popular sovereignty. By a curious paradox the cause of Ferdinand VII, himself the embodiment of unintelligent autocracy, was defended by a nationalist coalition, part of which was largely affected by the spirit of the French Revolution. In those years of bloodshed and distraction, when the lawful king was in exile at Valençay, and the nation was thrown upon its own resources, Spaniards, and more particularly Spanish soldiers, learned to like the trade of politics, so that what with soldiers fancying themselves statesmen, and civilians playing at soldiers, the history of Spain was marked by a succession of military *pronunciamientos* and radical revolts. In all this, however, there was nothing of Bonapartism. The two forces arrayed against each other were the autocratic and Catholic monarchy of old Spain and the spirit of progress in all its shades and colours, moderate, radical, republican. The method of Napoleonic bureaucracy, despite the division of the country into forty-nine artificial governments in 1834, has never been able to conquer the powerful and ancient traditions of local autonomy which have been handed down in an unbroken chain from the Middle Ages. Despite the new-fangled *Gobierno Civil*, the Alcalde is still the real governor of the Spanish town, and the strength of the feudal movement of the seventies is sufficient to show how vivacious is the spirit of Spanish separatism and how faint the influence of Madrid on the political currents of Spanish life.

The place of the Teutonic race in Europe and therefore in the whole world has been decisively altered by the career and policy of Napoleon. It is among the least of the effects of his action in this quarter that his Code survived in Holland till 1838 and in the Rhine provinces till 1900. The larger consequences of his masterful intervention in German affairs were the disappearance of the Holy Roman Empire coupled with an immense simplification in the political geography of that composite and cumbrous state; and when these changes are coupled with the great series of reforms accomplished in Prussia under the stress of the Jena disaster and with the general spread of pan-German feeling in the War of Liberation, it becomes clear that Napoleon must rank as one of the makers of modern Germany.

It is needless to say that nothing was further from Napoleon's intention than to go down to history in such a rôle. His intention was precisely the opposite—to denationalize the Germans, to fix upon them French laws and institutions, and to harness them to the ambitions of the French Empire. Nor was it his purpose to sow the seeds of political liberty among his Teuton subjects. The princes of the Rhenish Confederation were on the contrary encouraged to govern in an arbitrary fashion, that they might supply their contingents to the imperial army with the least possible degree of friction. And this being so, the really astonishing thing in the history of Napoleon's dealings with Germany is not the reaction which he provoked but the support that he received. Princes and prelates overwhelmed him with servile flattery. Philosophers and poets united to acclaim him as the hero destined by Providence to show mankind the way to higher levels of combined action. That he should have been regarded with peculiar veneration by the German Jews is not unnatural, seeing that everywhere he removed their political and social disabilities, but it is singular proof of his magnetism and power that in the kingdom of Westphalia, a country as alien as any part of Europe to French modes of life and thought, many of the prefects were drawn from the noblest families in the land, and that in none of the French states founded upon German soil was there any noticeable reluctance to accept or even to forward the work of an alien government.

We have spoken of Napoleon as one of the makers of Germany : and to some extent the achievement of Bismarck was the easier for his work. On the other hand the Napoleonic intervention left a legacy of bitter memories behind it. For how could Prussia lightly forgive the crowned members of Napoleon's Confederation of the Rhine who had profited by her downfall, or how could Bavaria, Saxony, or Wurtemberg pretend to share the glow and exultation of the War of Freedom ? The gulf between the North and South, always a factor to be reckoned with in German politics, was deepened by the events of the Napoleonic age. The Prussian despised the South-German and the South-German repaid him in a thorough heartiness of dislike. When von Reumont went as a Prussian delegate to the Parliament of Frankfort in 1848 the contrariety of temperament and feeling between North and South was one of the facts most painfully impressed upon his mind. To have taken opposite sides in one of the grand issues of political history is a dividing memory which only joint action in issues equally grand can certainly efface.

To curious persons asking his opinion of Napoleon the Duke of Wellington was wont to observe that he was 'no gentleman', and it would be easy from a thousand instances to corroborate the truth of this excellent and most English observation. Turn over the old files of *The Times* and you will find the greatest conqueror and State-builder of the world treated as a mere mountebank, a vulgar charlatan aping the costume and manners of his betters. There was indeed a more balanced view held by some English contemporaries, as the memoirs of Lord Holland and the letters of John Cam Hobhouse may remind us, but it was not widely spread, and an impartial estimate of so dangerous an antagonist could hardly be expected until the end of the war. The history of the British view of Napoleon offers a large and interesting field of inquiry. There have been fluctuations, there have been gusts of sympathy shading into hero-worship, but upon the whole the admirers are still regarded by the mass of their fellow-countrymen as a handful of eccentrics engaged upon a forlorn errand. In Central Europe the Napoleonic fashion spread with the development of domineering ambitions. The more recent Prussian commentators, swayed by the rising tide of their imperial appetites, have been unreserved in applause, and among the intellectual currents in the Pan-German movement no historian will neglect to note the spread of Napoleonic idolatry in Germany or the acceptance which, during the years preceding the Great War, was so widely pronounced for the political and military ethics of a conqueror without scruple and without fear.

F I N I S